AT ZERO POINT

AT
ZERO
POINT

DISCOURSE, CULTURE, AND SATIRE IN RESTORATION ENGLAND

ROSE A. ZIMBARDO

THE UNIVERSITY PRESS OF KENTUCKY

Publication of this volume was made possible in part
by a grant from the National Endowment for the Humanities.

Scholarly publisher for the Commonwealth,
serving Bellarmine College, Berea College, Centre
College of Kentucky, Eastern Kentucky University,
The Filson Club Historical Society, Georgetown College,
Kentucky Historical Society, Kentucky State University,
Morehead State University, Murray State University,
Northern Kentucky University, Transylvania University,
University of Kentucky, University of Louisville,
and Western Kentucky University.

Editorial and Sales Offices: The University Press of Kentucky
663 South Limestone Street, Lexington, Kentucky 40508-4008

98 99 00 01 02   5 4 3 2 1

Library of Congress Cataloging-in-Publication Data

Zimbardo, Rose A.
    At zero point : discourse, culture, and satire in Restoration
England / Rose A. Zimbardo
        p.   cm.
    Includes bibliographical references and index
    ISBN 0-8131-2039-X (cloth : alk. paper)
    1. Satire, English —History and criticism. 2. English literature—
17th century—History and criticism. 3. Language and culture—
England—History—17th century. 4. Great Britain—History—
Restoration, 1660–1688. 5. Discourse analysis, Literary. 6. Semiotics
and literature. I. Title
PR934.Z56   1998
827'.409—dc21   97-40936

This book is printed on acid-free recycled paper meeting
the requirements of the American National Standard
for Permanence of Paper for Printed Library Materials.

Manufactured in the United States of America

This book is for my husband, Martin Stevens,
and my son, Adam Zimbardo.
It is also in loving memory of my mother and father,
Angeline Abd El Nour and Albert Abd El Nour,
and my aunt, Margaret Alleva.

These five taught me
all that a human being needs to know
about love.

CONTENTS

ACKNOWLEDGMENTS

One of the few—perhaps the only—advantage of being old is that it gives one a clearer perspective upon one's own life. I have discovered that a human life really is "a dance to the music of time," and that the music is a madrigal. One returns again and again to a theme, improvising and embroidering upon it in every round. Therefore, this book, like every other piece of work I have done, was born at Yale in the glorious days when I was a graduate student there. The problems I have addressed here are the same problems that confronted me in 1960. Of course, the theoretical instruments I use in approaching them are different from those I used then. The older I grow, however, the more certain I am that the gift of scholarship was given to me by the extraordinary people with whom I studied: Eugene M. Waith, William K. Wimstatt, Maynard Mack, and Marie Boroff. They gave me all that I needed to conduct what has been a very satisfying career.

More immediately, I must thank Dr. Robert C. Ritchie, the director of Research at the Huntington Library, for the Mellon Fellowship that enabled me to complete the book. My debt to Huntington is very deep. Not only has every bit of scholarship that supports my hypothesis in this book been done in summers of work at the Huntington, but my dear friends there—James and Betty Thorpe, Elizabeth and Dan Donno, John Steadman —and the host of excited and exciting young scholars I have met there in recent years have inspired me.

I can never sufficiently thank my wonderful Dean of Humanities and Fine Arts at Stony Brook, Richard Kramer. Because he himself is so sterling a scholar, he values the scholarship of others. I thank him for the research leave he granted me that enabled me to write this book, and I also thank him for his unfailing kindness and support in a very dark time.

I thank my son, Adam Zimbardo, and my best friend, his father, Philip Zimbardo, for their constant help and support. I thank my friend and research assistant extraordinaire, Deanna Weber, who is not just a keen critic of literature but the computer wizard who got my ungainly text onto a disk. I thank Dr. Richard Kroll, who was a reader for the Press and who gave my work the best and most intelligent reading I have ever received.

Finally, I thank with my whole heart my dear husband, Martin Stevens. It has been a Herculean feat for him to come through hell alive for my sake. I thank him too for being the one person in the world who loves me, warts and all, just as I am.

INTRODUCTION

Until the resurgence of interest in Restoration studies that has taken place in the last fifteen or so years we understood the Restoration period and its literature in one of two ways. On the one hand, we have seen the period in terms of some notion of historic or literary evolution, as a prelude or preamble to the crowning achievements of the eighteenth century. So, for example, we have thought of Behn's *Oroonoko* as an Ur-novel foreshadowing the "true" novels of Richardson and of *MacFlecknoe* as a not yet perfect *Dunciad*. We consider the roughness of Oldham's satire "retrograde," and think of Wycherley's verse, which the young Pope tried in vain to "regularize," as the product of a decayed mind. On the other hand, we were trained by generations of Whiggish historians to see the period as a morally, politically, and intellectually degenerate time, a pit from which English civilization and "democracy" were rescued by the "Glorious Revolution." But whether positively, as the soil from which eighteenth-century masterworks in time sprouted, or negatively, as the purgatory through which English culture passed to emerge as pure Augustan gold, we have understood the period only in relation to, and continuous with, the eighteenth century. Indeed, we name courses and sections of the *Norton Anthology* "Restoration and Eighteenth-Century Literature"; we use the blanket term "the Augustan Age" to cover the years 1660 to 1750 or "the long eighteenth century" for 1680 to 1832. That is in large part because until recently we have thought of history as a transparent record of documented knowledge rather than as a narrative—or severally competing narratives—constructed by historical agents. We have failed to take into account that historians and critics of the period held conceptions of knowledge that were determined by the epistemological constructs of the age about which they wrote, the eighteenth century. And because scholars were so conditioned, their investigations rested on the assumption that discourse is mimetic, that writing, transparent in itself, merely describes a first-order realm of things and circumstances "as they really were." So deep-seated and unconsciously held was this conviction that it kept us from recognizing that mimetic discourse itself has a history, that it was invented at a particular time (the late seventeenth century) to meet the demands of a particular culture. We have, indeed, assumed the transparency of language and history because we ourselves are products of eighteenth-century, early modern culture.

In discussing ways in which a historian of discourse might escape the constraints imposed upon him by the epistemological limits of his own time, J.G.A. Pocock says, "Faced with problems such as how far he may use twentieth-century categories to explain categories used in the seventeenth century, he may impose on himself the discipline of explaining how changes in seventeenth-century language indicated changes in the historical context, what changes were indicated, and what changes occurred in the ways of indicating them."[1]

In conducting this study I have attempted to impose such a discipline upon myself, to engage not in current scholarly and theoretical debate but rather to converse with the past—and, in so far as it is possible, to enter into the conversations of the past. Starting with the assumption of Dominick La Capra, that historical narratives "may be opened to some extent by the attempt to explore alternative possibilities in the past that are themselves suggested by the retrospective or deferred effects of later knowledge,"[2] I compare two dominant competing discourses and the satire they produced at a period of radical epistemological break, which I have named "Restoration Zero Point." This is a period which, by the simultaneous operation of its *constructive* and *deconstructive* thrusts, can be understood epistemologically as two periods—one looking backward to Renaissance models, the other looking forward to eighteenth-century Enlightenment models.

The Restoration period in England is an epistemological break of the kind that the philosopher Hans Blumenberg calls a "zero point:" "The zero point of dissolution of order and the point of departure of the construction of order are identical; the minimum of ontological predisposition is at the same time the maximum of constructive potentiality."[3] Blumenberg argues that, philosophically considered, each age is in conversation with the age that precedes it in that its epistemology is a response to the crisis brought about when the epistemology that preceded it collapses under the weight of questions it has itself raised. The Restoration period in England is a zero point in that, on the one hand, it responds to the abyss that is left when the idea of *essential* eternity embodied in medieval and Renaissance cultural forms is no longer tenable; on the other hand, however, it is also the point of maximum constructive power in that it is the time when the basic constructs of "modernity" were forged: "modernity had need of a radical anthropology to meet the crisis brought about by claims in behalf of a transcendent absolute."[4]

The zero point dissolution of order gives rise in the English Restoration to a deconstructive discourse designed to dismantle medieval/Renaissance codes in order to reveal their artifactuality and the underlying emptiness they are no longer adequate to conceal. The zero point constructive impulse, on the other hand, produces a constructive discourse, the mimetic analytico-referential "discourse of modernism," which Timothy J. Reiss has so well described.[5] These simultaneously operant discourses are so antithetically different as to be understandable in Foucaultian terms as existing under the governance of two different *epistemes.*

My approach is not, however, entirely Foucaultian. I follow Foucault's reasoning only in so far as, like him, I believe: 1) that "each age . . . has an episteme that determines and limits its ability to conceive and represent reality"; 2) that "the transition from one episteme to another is abrupt"; 3) that "when an epistemological break occurs it changes the basic configuration through which knowledge is legitimate"; and, finally, 4) that "two periods separated by a break become comparable in terms of the cognitive processes that adopt different strategies but serve the same purpose for each age."[6] I am, of course, concerned with a single historical "period," the moment of breakage, but I believe that the two epistemological systems—the collapsing medieval/Renaissance system and the new system of modernism—fall on either side of the epistemological divide and are therefore comparable in the Foucaultian sense.

I depart from Foucault in three fundamental ways. First, I do not believe that an epistemological break is entirely "unexplainable." Second, and more importantly, I do not consider the *episteme* that governs a particular age to be as contained, as static, or as orderly as Foucault's examination of the French Enlightenment *episteme* in *The Order of Things* suggests. Finally, I believe that an epistemological break can sometimes be understood in connection with historical and political events. For instance, the Revolution of 1689, because it marks the placement of a new power structure, may also mark the dominance of a new "writing" and a new "reading" of reality. That is not to say that the revolution *caused* the change, but rather that the revolution, the political and sociological changes to which it gave rise, and the discourses concomitant upon those new politico-sociological constructs must be understood equally as "texts," so to speak, within an epistemological context.

In this study I take the position of the "mirror-watcher" that Pocock advises a historian of discourse to be:

Instead of supposing a single mirror reflecting happenings in the world at the moment of their occurrence, it would be better to suppose a system of mirrors facing inward and outward at different angles, so that they reflect occurrences in the mirrored world through the diverse ways in which they reflect one another. Discussion among mirror-watchers therefore has to do with how the mirrors reflect one another, even before it focuses on the possibility that there is something new in the field of vision. It would be better still to suppose that the mirrors are arranged diachronously as well as synchronously, so that while some of them share the same moment in time, others are located in its past and future.... the historical animal deals with experience by discussing old ways of perceiving it, as a necessary preliminary to erecting new ways, which then serve as means of perceiving both the new experience and old modes of perception.[7]

It is not possible to conceive "reality" (especially not a reality four hundred years past) nor to experience anything except through the mediation of language. As La Capra puts it, "language prefigures and informs the historical field."[8] Moreover, "[l]anguage . . . talks largely about itself; the response to new experience takes the form of discovering and discussing new difficulties in language."[9] I would go farther and argue that all cognition is in language. There is no experience knowable to us that is not filtered through language. Language "interacts with experience; it supplies the categories, grammar, and mentality through which experience has to be recognized and articulated."[10] To cite an example, in 1722 Daniel Defoe looked upon London, and he saw a city on a river that had never been seen before the end of the seventeenth century. Moreover, he quite deliberately chose a new discourse to describe his vision:

> I shall sing you no Songs here of the River in the first Person of a Water Nymph, a Goddess (and I know not what) according to the Humour of the ancient Poets. I shall talk nothing of the Marriage of old *Isis,* the Male River, with the beautiful *Thame,* the Female River, a Whimsey as simple as the Subject was empty, but I shall speak of the River . . . as it really is made glorious by the Splendour of its Shores, gilded with noble Palaces, strong Fortifications, . . . and publick Buildings; with the greatest Bridge and the greatest City in the World, made famous by the Opulence of its Merchants, the Encrease and Extensiveness of its Commerce, by its invincible Navies and by the innumerable Fleets of Ships, sailing upon it from all Parts of the World. . . . I shall speak of [the river inland] as it is a Chanel for conveying an infinite Quantity of Provisions from the remote Counties to *London,* and enriching all the Counties again by the return of Wealth and Trade to and from the City; and in describing these Things I expect to inform and divert my Readers and speak, in a more Masculine Manner more to the dignity of the Subject . . . than I could any other way.[11]

This passage is illuminating in a number of ways. It not only very obviously reveals a new eighteenth-century mercantile, capitalistic redefinition of public space and values, but, perhaps less obviously, it reveals and promotes a new discourse, a gendered and mimetic discourse that inscribes "reality" in a new way. Pointedly anti-metaphoric, the new discourse of modernism conceives of writing as a second-order construct, referring to, and entirely dependent upon, a first-order empirical realm of *things as they are*—and by implication as they have always been and will always be: stable, unchanging, unchangeable. The old medieval/Renaissance "discourse of patterning,"[12] wherein terrestrial signs (things as well as words) exist by analogy to celestial Ideas and all signs refer always and inevitably to other signs, revealing by their very nature "that which is forever absent,"[13] has disappeared. The old metaphor that figured "reality" as ideally a microcosmic *harmonia* reflecting back to heaven its own face, is, in C.S. Lewis's words, "a discarded image": "a Whimsey as simple as the Subject was empty." Instead the world is described in terms of material things and delineated in terms of trade routes. "A Merchant in his Counting House," Defoe had written in 1697, "converses with all Parts of the known World."[14] His discourse is buttressed with the heavy weight of "Noble Palaces, strong Fortifications . . . [and] publick Buildings."

Consider for comparison a late sixteenth-century discourse upon the same prospect. In 1578 the anonymous writer of "A Discourse upon London" sees London as "the City"—that is, as subsumed under the *Idea* of city—and understands it by analogy to a multilayered abstract idea, moral and metaphysical, terrestrial and celestial, historical and typological. The sign "London" participates in that complex abstraction; the entity "London" can be understood only in terms of it:

> At once the Propagation of Religion, the Execution of good Policy, the Exercise of Charity, and the Defence of the Country, is best performed by Towns and Cities [n.b., *all* cities, not just London]. And thus Civil Life approacheth nearest the Shape of that mystical Body whereof Christ is the Head, and Men be the Members. Whereupon both at the first that Man of God, *Moses* in the Commonwealth of the *Israelites* and the Governers of all Countries in all Ages sithence, have continually maintained the same. And to change it, were nothing else but to metamorphose the World, and to make wild Beasts of reasonable Men. [See Ebstorf world map.] [15]

The sixteenth-century writer's "discourse of patterning" is a calligraphy of emblems, a concatenation of analogies that points toward but cannot describe a "reality" which is not, and can never be, available to sense. The eighteenth-century writer's analytico-referential "discourse of modernism" mimetically (re)presents an empirically observable "reality" which is

Die Ebstorfer Weltkarte im Auftrage des Historischen Vereins für Niedersachen (1891).
Courtesy of the Harvard Map Collection.

seen through the lens of a new conceptual/perceptual construct. The cultural inscriptions that by 1722 are etched on the eyeballs of Defoe, through which he sees, understands, and mimetically reproduces (in that order) London, were forged in the Restoration period. They are products of zero point's new constructive discourse of modernism and reflections of the new epistemology born in that period. By the beginning of the eighteenth century those cultural inscriptions were fully embedded in—indeed, may be said to have shaped the contours of—the conceptual unconscious consciousness of Englishmen.

I have elsewhere discussed the discursive conflict in Restoration culture in terms of the controversy between the wits and the latitudinarians, with Rochester and Stillingfleet as their respective spokesmen.[16] And it is true that that particular war of words does rather neatly emblematize the discursive collision that so radical an epistemological break engendered. However, no particular conflict between individuals, causes, or points of view is adequate to encompass the magnitude of the historical and epistemological change at work in Restoration England.

Jonathan Dollimore has said, "The author is never the autonomous source of meaning, but the articulation of historical process which may be present in the author's text might well be intentional. . . . On the other hand, aspects of the historical process may be unconsciously pulled into focus because, irrespective of intention, it is already there in the language, forms, conventions, genres being used."[17] For that reason my study focuses upon a variety of "languages, forms, conventions," and texts, some of which, like Rochester's satires or *A Tale of a Tub, intentionally* use language to undermine language itself and thereby deconstruct the epistemological system it generates; others of which, like Wilkins's *Toward a Real Character and a Philosophical Language, intentionally* attempt to design a new discourse of modernism exactly consonant with the material and mechanistic "reality" it imitates; and still others of which, like *The Way of the World, The Original and Progress of Satire,* or *Don Sebastian, unintentionally* pull into focus aspects of the historical process of deconstruction/construction at work during the time that they were written.

My study does not hew to the line of a single theoretical approach but rather picks out from among a variety of approaches—from Eco to Said— the particular theoretical tool required at the moment to pry open a problem or a text under investigation. Similarly, I have been influenced by some contemporary literary criticism and history that I do not cite in the text (Steven Zwicker's work on Dryden's political discourse and Margaret Jacobs's work in the history of science, for instance), and I take stands that would seem to be in opposition to others (for example, Richard Kroll's conception of "the material word" or Deborah Payne's contention that satire is not possible in the dramatic mode). And while I agree with Dustin Griffin that satire is more often the *sprezzatura* display of an author's style than a serious attempt to correct immoral or vicious behavior, I would take issue with his universal and transhistorical conception of the genre. Similarly, although I find Robert Markley's work on the "fallen languages" of Newtonian England extremely interesting, I would not *locate* the crisis in representation that he finds in the language of the seventeenth-century "new science" where he has done. I have deliberately chosen not to engage in discussion or debate with my contemporaries here; that is simply not the kind of work I want to do, and such discussion would not produce the kind of book I want to write. My conversation is with the past.

My attempt has been to focus upon not one but a number of aspects of the cultural milieu of the Restoration period—from the transformation that occurred in gender coding, for example, to the birth of "orientalism." My rationale for using such a format are two: 1) at the end of the seventeenth century disciplinary boundaries had not yet been established. For example, as Steven Shapin has demonstrated, the formulation of a code of "gentlemanly civility" and the scientific search for truth are not separate, compartmentalized behaviors in the seventeenth century, but, on the contrary, are intrinsically interrelated.[18] And, as my study reveals, homophobia, married love, and macroeconomics are similarly interconnected. 2) The chapters of this book and the problems upon which they concentrate are meant to be understood as avenues that converge upon a central issue under investigation: the discourses of zero point and the satire they produced.

The antithetical operation of the two "languages" competing for dominance in Restoration England can best be appreciated in a comparison between the discourse of "wit" and the discourse of "natural philosophy." Restoration wit, especially as the generic determinant of satire, is quintessentially the deconstructive discourse of zero point, when, as Sandra Luft, following Blumenberg, says, "Art becomes the only response to the realization that a knowledge 'adequate' to reality is impossible. . . . Awareness of the radical contingency of the world forces art to accept its own radical creativity: forces it to embrace the artifactuality of the 'real,' the fictiveness of truth, the finitude of the world it makes in the face of the abyss."[19]

In direct antithesis to the deconstructive discourse of wit was the new constructive discourse advocated by the Oxford group, the proponents of "natural philosophy" and advocates of "natural reason." John Wilkins, the teacher of Locke, may in some ways be considered the father of mimetic discourse. The declared purpose of Wilkins's treatise, *Toward a Real Character and a Philosophical Language* (1668), was to create a complete taxonomic system whereby perfect sign = thing equivalency could be effected: "If to every thing and notion there were assigned a distinct *Mark* . . . , this might suffice as to one great end of a *Real Character,* namely the expression of our Conceptions by *Marks,* which should signifie *things* and not *Words.* . . . and so likewise, if the *Names* of things could be so ordered, as to contain such a kind of *affinity* or *opposition* in their letters and sounds, as might be answerable to the nature of the things which they signified; This would be yet a farther advantage superadded."[20]

The main epistemological effect of the discourse advanced by Wilkins is the conception of language as a secondary construct. The "real" is empirically observable matter. God is no longer the mysterious, eternal center of a dance of cosmic essences; his presence may, and indeed must, be traced in the visible actual—as Samuel Parker attempted to demonstrate in *A Demonstration of the Divine Authority of the Law and Christian Religion*[21]—and in history, now conceived as a *transparent record* of observable and recordable experience—as Robert Boyle argues in *Some Considerations Touching the Style of the H. Scriptures.*[22]

The discursive centers around which the new constructive "language" revolved were trade, science, and empire—as well as the latitudinarian movement in the church, which was a powerful instrument in promoting those interests.[23] These centers were realized in: 1) the newly reconstituted Board of Trade of 1696 (the plan for which was designed by Locke) under the direction of such macroeconomists as Charles Davenant and Josiah Child; 2) the Royal Academy and the Oxford academicians who inspired its founding, like Robert Boyle, John Wilkins, and the naturalist John Ray; and 3) a new nationalism which envisioned not Christ but the English Nation as the natural "Head" of a new world order and English "natural reason" as the originary from which that order should be mapped.

Politically and sociologically the mimetic discourse of modernism fosters institutional stability, social cohesion and nationalism. The primary linguistic enemies in the eyes of the champions of mimetic discourse— natural philosophers like Boyle and Wilkins, men of business and the professions, like Defoe and Blackmore, and latitudinarian divines like Stillingfleet and Tillotson—were metaphor and wit. (John Ray banned all use of metaphor from the writing of naturalists.) That is because metaphor, the building block upon which the logic and rhetoric that shaped medieval/ Renaissance epistemology rests, and wit are persistently concerned with the "not that" and "not there" components inherent within any linguistic sign—a semiotic phenomenon that Saint Augustine discussed many centuries before Derrida.[24] Wit's deconstructive discourse discloses absence, the "great Negative," the abyss over which it plays and of which we get glimpses through wit's *craquelure* designs. Burnet tells us that Rochester "said the lies [in his writing] came often as Ornaments that could not be spared without spoiling the beauty of the Poem."[25]

The art of the Restoration wit satirist—Rochester, Oldham, Wycherley, Etherege, or the early Swift—is the art of designing zero, the art that Umberto Eco associates with the "open form" of Baroque:

> Here it is precisely the static and unquestionable definitiveness of the classical Renaissance form which is denied. . . . Baroque form is dynamic; it tends to an indeterminacy of effect (in its play of solid and void, light and darkness . . . its broken surfaces, its widely diversified angles of inclination). . . . Its search for kinetic excitement and illusory effect . . . never allows a privileged frontal view; rather it induces the spectator to shift his position continuously in order to see the work in constantly new aspects, as if it were in a state of perpetual

transformation. . . . here for the first time, man opts out of the canon of authorized responses, and finds that he is faced . . . by a world in fluid state which requires corresponding creativity on his part. The poetic treatises concerning 'maraviglia,' 'wit,' 'agudezas,' and so on, really . . . seek to establish the new man's inventive role.[26]

Because it challenges the validity and stability of all linguistic signs and conceptual constructs, wit was considered by the cultural allies whose discourse shaped the new epistemological order to be especially threatening to institutional cohesion: "Just as truth-telling was understood to be the cement of society, so untruthfulness was seen to be a potential social solvent."[27] "I am very much mistaken," wrote Bishop Tillotson, "if the State as well as the Church, the Civil Government as well as Religion, do not in short space find the intolerable inconvenience of this Humour."[28] There are powerful institutional forces at work in the assumption that language is mimetic; what the institution cannot tolerate, as Derrida has said, "is for anyone to tamper with language, meaning both the national language and, paradoxically, an ideal of translatability. Nationalism and universalism . . . [the institution] can bear more readily the most apparently revolutionary ideological sorts of 'content' if only the content does not touch the borders of language and of all the juridico-political contracts it guarantees."[29] In *Leviathan* Hobbes warns that instability in language can "Distract the people" and "cast . . . [the State] into the Fire of a Civill Warre."[30]

In addition to the political and sociological threat it poses, wit was supposed by the new thinkers of the Restoration period to be psychologically destructive—its products designed to unsettle and undermine the highest human faculty and the seat of truth, "natural reason." Stillingfleet argued that it is impossible for the champions of the cause of wit "to defend their extravagant courses by *Reason* [and therefore], the only way left for them is to make *Satyrical Invectives* against *Reason;* as though it were the most uncertain, foolish and (I had almost said *unreasonable*) thing in the World; and yet they pretend to shew it in arguing against it; but it is a pity such had not their wish, *to have been beasts rather than Men* (if any can make such a wish that have not it already) that they might have been less capable of doing mischief among mankind."[31] Sir Richard Blackmore, in his "Essay on Wit" (1699-1700), says "it is evident that Wit cannot essentially consist in the Justness and Propriety of the Thoughts, that is, the Conformity of our Conceptions to the Objects we conceive."[32] Blackmore's advocacy of a strictly mimetic language ("the Conformity of our *Concep-*

tions to the *Objects* we conceive," ital. mine) brings into focus the confluence of currents—from the newly empowered and categorized "professions," the new, capitalistic valuation of labor and productivity, and the new science—that were surging together to sweep the discourse and epistemology of modernism into dominance. Blackmore condemns wit as a threat to scientific discourse. "Ridicule and Satyr, that entertain Laughers," he says, "put solid Reason and useful Science out of Countenance."[33] "Natural philosophy," or the "new science," required an absolutely mimetic discourse because its aims "were no less than an accurate description of the universe and a rational explanation of its physical phenomena."[34] But Blackmore's primary objection to wit is that it is a danger to social cohesion, class hierarchy, and institutional stability.

We have never taken Blackmore sufficiently seriously because Pope numbered him among the dunces (largely because he had so thoroughly condemned *A Tale of a Tub* as an expression of "atheistic" wit). When scholars have referred to him at all it has been to provide evidence for the case that "sentimentalism" was responsible for the death of "Restoration comedy." However, Blackmore's "Essay on Wit" is a most valuable index of the new cultural climate emerging at zero point. For example, Blackmore's essay gives voice to new capitalistic assumptions about the value of poetic language and imagination in comparison with work and public wealth. Blackmore argues that "the Labour of the meanest Persons, that Conduce to the Welfare and Benefit of the Public, are more valuable, because more useful, than the Employments of those who apply themselves only, or principally to divert and entertain the Fancy."[35] If poetry, which in the old Renaissance epistemological conception lifts the human mind to an apprehension of the highest metaphysical truth, has any use at all in Blackmore's view, it is to provide entertainment for tired businessmen: "men of Business and studious Professions [medicine and law]" can be refreshed by brief exposures to poetry and wit from time to time, as it "gives them new Life and Spirit to resume the Labour of their respective Employments."[36] Materially enriching employment for professionals and productive labor for the "mean" are the cultural ideals that are being inscribed by the new epistemology and the new society emerging from it.

But, one might argue, Blackmore stars in *The Dunciad;* surely his views are not those of the important thinkers of the day. On the contrary, Blackmore's greatest admirers were the leading figures of his time—among them Defoe and Locke, the latter of whom wrote in a letter to Molyneux that not only must "everybody . . . allow [Blackmore] to have an extraordinary talent," but "the Preface to *King Arthur* shows as great a strength and penetration of judgment, as his poetry has shown flights of fancy."[37] Blackmore was best known as a successful and prosperous physician, a member of the increasingly powerful and valued "professional" class.

John Locke, "the Whig philosopher himself,"[38] whose theory of knowledge finally formalized the conception of "mind" that had been determined by the new epistemology, held views almost identical to Blackmore's. As a founding member and commissioner of the Board of Trade of 1696, Locke must have known Josiah Child and Charles Davenant. Peter Laslett tells us that he "had in his library some . . . of the relevant works of these writers and 127 titles in all which can be classed 'economic,' very many of them concerned with trade and currency."[39]

The newly reconstituted Board of Trade of 1696, "His Majesty's Commissioners for promoting the Trade of this Kingdom, and for inspecting and improving His Plantations in America and elsewhere," was, of course, the "architect and instrument of the old Colonial system":[40] the progenitor of British imperialism. It was also the forum for a "really weighty body of expert opinion on political and economic matters,"[41] and was, therefore, among the most powerful discursive centers in post-Revolutionary Restoration culture. Locke was not only one of the leading architects of this body, but was also a driving force behind its policy making. When we consider that Locke was so committed to the principle of mimetic discourse that he conceived of a dictionary that would make perfect word = thing equivalency ("Words standing for things, which are known and distinguished by their outward shapes [should] be expressed by little Draughts or Prints"),[42] and when we further consider that Locke was the intellectual "son" of the founders of "natural philosophy" at Oxford as well as the father of philosophical empiricism, we can appreciate the ways in which the discourses of trade, empire, and science converged to produce the discourse of modernism.

Nationalism and universalism, social cohesion and uniformity, changeless, empirically observable truth and "natural reason," its sole instrument: these are the constructs that comprise the *episteme* newly emerging out of the zero point epistemological break in the Restoration period. These are the "givens" that govern the consciousness of Locke, the student of Wilkins and Boyle, and therefore the inheritor of the principles that shaped the new conception of "mind" to which *An Essay Concerning Human Understanding* gave full voice and authority. "Truth is always and everywhere the same," Locke wrote, "time alters it not,"[43] and "Reason . . . [is] the common bond whereby humane kind is united into one fellowship and societie,"[44] they are the "social cement" of which Shapin speaks. However, if truth is always the same and reason is the common bond among human beings, whose "truth" and whose "reason" are the standards against which "truth" and "reason" are to be measured? In the judgment of John Locke, the "new" Restoration Englishman, his *own* mind, the *English* mind, is the exact equivalent and perfect mirror of absolute, *universal* human mind: "All I can say of my book [*An Essay Concerning Human Understanding*] is that it is a copy of my own mind, in its several ways of operation . . . [and] the intellectual faculties are made, and operate alike in most men."[45] From the merchant in his counting house to the Royal Society virtuoso to the farthest reaches of the known world *the English* mind has become the universal mind, and, correspondingly, any deviation from the norms dictated by English "reason" must be considered a deviation from humanity.

It is from these new conceptions of universalism and nationalism, uniformity and social cohesion, and in the conviction that literary discourse is mimetic, that we derive our binary model of satire: that is, that which posits a satiric "thesis" that ridicules foolish or vicious behavior as a deviation from the ideal moral "norm" which satiric "antithesis" upholds. The new satire, like Gould's or Young's, and its eighteenth-century heirs', like Pope's, or Gay's, *upholds* the institution, for however "apparently revolutionary . . . its 'content,' " it does not challenge "the borders of language and . . . all the juridico-political contracts it guarantees."[46] Rather, the satire which is produced by the *new* epistemology and the *new* mimetic discourse of the Restoration becomes more and more markedly Horatian, and, as Howard Weinbrot has said, "The Horatian satirist . . . lives in a world that includes discourse with the great. . . . His norms are not only his family's and his own best selves but the nation's watchful guardians."[47] The "antithesis," or moral standard, generally upheld in eighteenth-century satire can be summarized in an observation Shaftesbury makes in *Characteristics* (1711): "There is no love of virtue without knowledge of public good."[48] The conceptual constructs that make such a statement possible were forged in the constructive thrust of Restoration zero point.

It has been said that postmodern theory signals a turn in critical thinking from mimesis to semiosis—that is, from the unwritten assumption that language and literature imitate and reflect experience and material, empirically observable "reality" to the awareness that, as Pocock says, language "talks mostly about itself,"[49] that language is self-reflexive and that a literary text is a linguistically self-referential *process*. I believe that a reverse paradigm shift occurred at the end of the seventeenth century. With the collapse of medieval/Renaissance epistemology, which had envisioned truth and "reality" as a world of words, literary art became deliberately and ostentatiously self-referential and self-deconstructive. Many of the best poems, plays, and prose fictions of the Restoration are "explorations both of the power of language to create thought and of the limits of discourse."[50] And particularly does Restoration *satire* become a deconstructive enterprise. Whether verse, drama, or prose this satire is not concerned to "correct" behavior or to hold up models for emulation; it is, indeed, not concerned with external existents at all. "Awareness of the contingency of the world . . . forces . . . [this literary art] to embrace the artifactuality of the 'real,' the fictiveness of truth, the finitude of the world it makes in the face of the abyss."[51] This satire signals the collapse of all order; it erases all constructs; it exposes as illusory all that we perceive or conceive.

> Great Negative, how vainly would the wise
> Inquire, distinguish, teach, devise,
> Did'st thou not stand to point their blind Philosophies.[52]

So Rochester writes in "Upon Nothing." The deconstructive satire of the Restoration is the art of designing zero, of adumbrating the abyss. We may say of any of the best satires what Barbara Everett says of Rochester's "Artemisia to Chloe," that "it is a progressively more ruthless, more searching light turned toward the darkness that cannot be 'dissembled' or 'disowned.' And it is in that darkness, the lack of anything beyond the self-cancelling illusions of the poem that it rests; there is nothing else and nothing is what it is."[53]

For example, Oldham's "Aude aliquid. Ode" ("A Satyr Against Vertue") makes the libertine case for rejecting all cultural inscriptions and moral boundaries through its speaker, the fictional "Rochester." But it simultaneously cancels the case made, for its speaker is very obviously a fiction and a target of mockery. The poem's binary opposition is not between virtue and vice, but is a purposefully inconsistent, slippery opposition between discourse and genre, between libertine reasoning unreason and the heroic, Pindaric form that contains/does not contain it. The poem deliberately creates generic instability to reveal the fictiveness of its truth, the artifactuality of the "real." As Robinson says, "[Oldham] is not simply a satirist but a meta-satirist."[54]

There is no comforting, reassuring "I" at the heart of a Restoration deconstructive satire, no good man of common sense speaking to us and assuring us of our community in the empire of reason. Rather, the authorial "I," indispensable in the new, constructive discourse, is exploded in deconstructive satire—as in *A Tale of a Tub,* whose writer is not its author, Jonathan Swift, but is Swift's duplicitous sign of a writer who is also nowriter. The very idea of "self" is exposed as a counterfeit. Rochesterdisguised-as-Dr. Bendo says, "All I shall say for myself on this score is this: If I appear to any one like a Counterfeit, even for that chiefly, ought I to be considered a true Man. Who is the Counterfeit's example? his Original, and that on which he employs his Industry?"[55] "Self" is a series of performative gestures, a "show." Etherege's figures in *The Man of Mode,* for instance, are not "characters"; they are linguistic signs which are used to expose the contingency of sign itself and to exhibit "self" as sign. The dramatic satirist's method is what Keir Elam calls "the gesture of putting on show the very process of semiotization involved in performance."[56] For the deconstructive satirist of the Restoration, as for the deconstructionist of our own day, the counterfeit is "what makes truth possible, thereby destroying truth."[57]

The satiric discourse that aimed at dismantling the old Renaissance epistemology destroys the possibility of knowledge itself and exposes it as one more delusion of endlessly hallucinating man, who "climbs with pain / Mountains of Whimseys heap'd in his own Brain" (*A Satyr Against Reason and Mankind*). The "discourse of the great" like their laws and cultural inscriptions, are nonsense:

> Further to plague the world [man] must ingross
> Huge codes and bulky Pandects of the Laws,
> With Doctors glosses to perplex the Cause
> Where darken'd Equity is kept from light
> Under vast Reams of non-sence buried quite.
> [Oldham, "8th Satire of Boileau Imitated"]

Every "professor" of knowledge is a busy imposter, a

> stirrer up of doubt
> That frames deep mysteries, then finds 'em out,
> Filling with frantic crowds of thinking fools
> Those reverend Bedlams, colleges and schools.
> . . . modern cloister'd coxcombs who
> Retire and think cause they have nought to do.
> [*Satyr Against Reason and Mankind*]

Man is an empty "micro-coat," a bag of wind (*A Tale of a Tub*). The satirist himself is not a fearless crusader for truth, a lover of virtue and public good; he is a snarling misanthrope, an ineffectual crank: "You rail and nobody hangs himself, and thou hast nothing of satire but in thy face" (*The Plain Dealer*).

Raman Selden has said, "of Rochester's remarkable vigorous materialism there can be no doubt. As a court wit and as an amateur of poetry, he invariably failed to *think through* his philosophical ideas in a *consecutive and discursive* form. Yet embedded in his poems, there is a warmly realized materialism which is far removed from libertinism" (ital. mine).[58] Selden's opinion is the inevitable consequence of assuming that logic is linear and logical discourse is narrative and mimetic. That very idea is a *product* of the new conception of the relation of logic to language that was born out of the epistemological rupture at Restoration zero point. Rochester's discourse—as, indeed, the deconstructive discourse of zero point in general—is not mimetic. It rests on the assumption that what is "out there" is not material, empirically observable "reality," but NOTHING. This discourse principally exhibits its own self-reflexivity, "that taste for examination of language, for pursuing poetry into its own words."[59] Of all the various kinds of literary expression in the period Restoration deconstructive satires are the most linguistically self-referential in their operation. They are what Roland Barthes calls "texts of bliss": "the text that imposes a state of loss, the text that discomforts . . . unsettles the reader's historical, cultural, psychological assumptions, the consistency of his tastes, values, memories, [and] brings to a crisis his relation with language."[60]

The architects of the new order were quite right to fear the wits; they were acutely perceptive in recognizing that the writing of the deconstructive satirists is subversive of "the State as well as the Church, the Civil Government as well as Religion" because the function of this deconstructive discourse is to make its readers *participate* in the process of "undoing" in which it is engaged and which *constitutes* it. Those "texts that according to Barthes produce the 'jouissance' of the unexhausted virtuality of their expressive plane succeed in this effect just because they have been planned to invite their Model Readers to reproduce their own processes of deconstruction by a plurality of free interpretive choices."[61] One half of my task in this book will be to explore some of those processes of deconstruction; the other will be to examine the processes of the constructive discourse that triumphed over and succeeded upon the deconstructive discourse of zero point.

Chapter 1, "From *Words* to Experimental *Philosophy*," considers the ways in which so radical a paradigm shift changed conceptualization, reasoning, and, indeed, the very conception of the human mind and its functions. The zero point *deconstructive* impulse came to "comprehend" the medieval/Renaissance semiotic system, the relation of logic to language, "at the very moment [it was] calling that system into question and therefore destroying it."[62] Examining a wide variety of sixteenth-century treatises on logic and rhetoric—like Thomas Wilson's *Rule of Reason* and *The Art of Rhetorique*—this chapter demonstrates that Renaissance logic is entirely *in* language and *of* language. Knowledge is produced, tested, and transmitted solely by means of linguistic manipulation. However, this "old" medieval/ Renaissance epistemology raises the very questions that cause its collapse: for example, if word alone equals truth, what is the relation to truth of the products, movements, and manipulations of physical matter? Are the "works of Nature," existents external to the syllogistic system of logic extraneous to truth? In answering those questions "natural philosophy" was the bridge discipline that led—in the *constructive* movement of zero point—to the formulation of a new semiotic code, a new system of signification. This chapter goes on to examine the new conceptions of the relation of language to the mechanical operations of physical nature. The call for a transparent, mimetic discourse by new scientists like Boyle, language theorists like Wilkins, the Royal Academicians and their historian, Sprat, and, of course, Locke are examined here—as well as the new valuation of "self" and experience as the fundamental sources of "truth": "the new philosophers of nature and their cultural allies avowed the supremacy of direct individual experience or intuition over trusting the authority of previous writers."[63] The chapter ends by examining a double-edged prose satire, *The Whores Rhetoric,* which mocks both the old and the new language theories.

Chapter 2 concentrates on the semiotics of Restoration deconstructive satire. In this chapter I argue that the eighteenth-century binary model of satire, which determines that in order to *be* satire a text must direct its reader to a positive norm, or must, at least by implication, uphold a clear alternative to foolish and vicious behavior, a moral "satiric antithesis," is inappropriate to the kind of deconstructive satire written by Oldham, Rochester, Wycherley, the early Swift, and others. Restoration deconstructionist satires are texts that overrun all limits. They are *processes,* dubious systems of signs having relation without positive terms that can never arrive at closure. Theirs is a discourse that operates "to undermine everything that was set up in opposition to writing (speech, the world, the real, history . . .)."[64] They recognize no empirical "reality" but rather simultaneously inscribe and erase conceptual frames, which, because they too are linguistic, are inherently dubious. We associate deconstruction with post–modern theorists like Derrida and de Man; this chapter argues that as a semiotics deconstruction is rather related to *pre-modern* conceptions. The chapter demonstrates that the central premises of deconstructionism—the presence of absence in the sign and the essential indeterminacy of signs— are principles laid down by Saint Augustine. The chapter examines Augustinian semiotics and shows that, like any postmodern semiotician, Augustine allows for the *real presence* only of *language.* The immediacy of Augustinian thought for Restoration writers is demonstrated in a three-way "conversation" among Augustine, Hobbes, and Rochester on the Augustinian observation that "time *is* only because it inclines not to be."[65] The chapter concludes by analyzing the semiotic operation of two deconstructionist satires: Mel Brooks's *Blazing Saddles* and Rochester's "A Ramble in St. James's Park."

Chapter 3, "No 'I' and No 'Eye'," argues that there is neither a consistent central persona nor a consistent frontal perspective in Restoration deconstructive satire, and, indeed, that such elements would be antithetical to its generic intent. "Author," "character," and "speaker" are all purposefully destabilized and destabilizing tropes. The chapter begins with a thumbnail history of the satyr-satirist trope in the native English tradition, which was the Restoration's inheritance from its Renaissance predecessors. There follows an examination of the self-combative, deconstructive discourse of Juvenalian satire, the preferred model in satire for Renaissance satirists and for Restoration writers whose satire aimed at dismantling Renaissance epistemological codes. Chapter 3 then divides into three sections, each of which closely examines an exemplary Restoration deconstructive satire to demonstrate its purposeful destabilization of genre, "character," and language. Section I deals with Oldham's "Aude aliquid. Ode," (a.k.a., "A Satire Against Virtue"). Oldham's verse satire brilliantly employs a double reversal of the structure of Pindaric ode, at once maintaining the functional operation of ode to an antiheroic/ and also/ heroic end. The libertine "speaker" is a highly complex figure that uses the philosophy of libertinism to erase all moral, social, and cultural constructs and then to erase itself and its own inscriptions. Section II of the chapter uses Wycherley's *The Plain Dealer* to demonstrate the operations of deconstructive satiric discourse, its double function of exploding all cultural institutions and codes and, at the same time, challenging its own linguistic integrity. The section also treats of the nature of "character" as a bubble thrown to the surface to be instantly burst by boiling satiric discourse of this kind. Finally, Section III focuses on *A Tale of a Tub,* the most perfectly wrought of all deconstructive satires. *A Tale* has an "author" who is also no-author "writing" a text that comes into being in the process of undoing itself. It is a deconstructionist's dream, a text that "overruns all limits assigned to it," having three false beginnings and ending in a "pause." Section III fully displays the ways in which Restoration satire in this mode *is* in fact deconstruction.

Chapter 4 is concerned with gender coding and sexuality, centrally significant indexes of cultural change. At zero point Renaissance codes collapsed and a new modernist coding simultaneously came into being. The chapter is concerned to reveal the economic and nationalistic underpinnings of new attitudes toward homosexuality and libertinism, and the new "money and marriage" formulation that arose with the advent of modernism. Using the influential macroeconomist Charles Davenant's *An Essay Upon the Probable Methods of Making a People Gainers in the Ballance of Trade* (1699) as a primary source, the chapter discloses the inextricable connection between the discourse of early nationalistic capitalism and the discourse of sentimental marriage. The chapter goes on to disclose the presence of modernism's new constructions in *The Way of the World,* and then examines the deconstruction of Renaissance heroic "love and honor" coding in the mock-heroic satire *Sodom.*

Chapter 5, "The Discursively Central 'I' and the Telescope of Discourse," balances against chapter 3 in the structure of my format. According to Foucault, the central epistemological construct of the modern age is "Man." This chapter demonstrates that that construction grew out of a late seventeenth-century coding that reformulated the idea of "self," invented "interior space," and relocated "Truth" to that inner human arena. In the *constructive* thrust of Restoration zero point thought the locus and *font* of truth is the inner arena of the self, and the human mind is most worthily engaged when it contemplates its own operations. Boyle, for instance, says, "Amongst the great Variety of Employments which I have fancy'd to take up my thoughts with, I have scarce found any more noble nor more worthy of them than Contemplation of themselves."[66] Locke considers self-reflexive observation of our own internal mental operations the basis of all human understanding. Curiously enough, however, in the new model of mind the movement inward, once it has reached the locus of truth in the deepest self, *reverses direction.* The Self, or what I shall call the discursively central "I," the rational mind of the knowing subject, projects itself outward as a universal human standard, an ideal applicable to all humanity. "I" becomes the discursive center from which all order arises to be projected and imposed upon the external world. As Timothy J. Reiss describes the discourse of modernism, "Its exemplary statement is *cogito-ergo-sum* (reason-semiotic mediating system-world).... Its principal metaphors will be those of the telescope (eye-instrument-world) and the voyage of discovery (self-possessed port of departure-sea journey-country claimed as legitimate possession of the discoverer)."[67]

From that cohesive entity, the self, emerge increasingly expanded enlargements of the self: the nation, the empire, the world. At the very moment when the *deconstructive* thrust of zero point was erasing the "I" and shattering any possibility of a univalent perspective, the gaze of any single eye, the *constructive* new epistemology was reformulating the idea of self and making its core, "natural reason," the central switchboard of all social discourses. Radiating from that discursive center a vast network of ordered and ordering discourses were redesigning "reality" and reconstructing the human world.

Chapter 5 goes on to argue that when self becomes discursively central, satire becomes Horatian, mimetic, and binary, an instrument for ordering and amending human behavior. No longer an instrument for exploding all whimsies of order, erasing all concepts of subjectivity, exploring the limitations of language, and adumbrating the abyss, satire becomes a single voice, issuing from, and reinforcing the validity of, the deepest self. Satire becomes a careful delineator of boundaries, a nice weigher of moral judgments, and a sharp instrument for discriminating not just "right" from "wrong," but also "us" from "them" and "English" from "Other."

Like chapter 3, chapter 5 is divided into three sections. Section I begins by examining William Wollaston's influential critical preface to *The Design of Part of the Book of Ecclesiastes . . . Represented in an English Poem* (1691), which looks at Roman satire through the lens of the new modern paradigms. Wollaston prefers Horace above all satirists because Horace is rational, serious, and logically argumentative. The section centers upon a careful examination of Dryden's *Discourse Concerning the Original and Progress of Satire*. Ironically enough, though the *Discourse* is prefatory to a collection of translations of Juvenal's satires, it is quintessentially a new *modern* document, and it formulates a new *modern* (i.e., zero point *constructive* and therefore anti-Juvenalian) theory of satire which has influenced us to the present day.

Section III, "Satiric Discourse and the Sacred Nation," discusses the ways in which the new theory of satire is implemented in *Absalom and Achitophel* and demonstrates the relation between the new discourse of satire and the discourse of nationalism. The last section of chapter 5, and of the book, tests the validity of an argument offered by Edward Said: "the imaginative examination of things Oriental was based more or less exclusively upon sovereign Western consciousness out of whose unchallenged authority an Oriental world emerged."[68] I consider this idea in the light of the Restoration new model of English "mind," which Sprat declared was "sovereign in the empire of reason," and the new discursively central "I." The chapter compares the accounts and diaries of Englishmen travelling in the Orient at the end of the sixteenth century with those of Englishmen travelling at the end of the seventeenth century. I have discovered that the "discourse of Orientalism" *is* the new Restoration discourse of modernism. Chapter 5 demonstrates that a zero point change occurred in the representation of Orientals—from heroic (even when "evil") to grossly satiric—that corresponds exactly to the shift from the Renaissance meta-

phoric discourse of patterning to the new mimetic discourse of modernism. Restoration depictions of Orientals, which are invariably self-pro-
claimed as transparent, neutral accounts, like that of the "natural historian"
Leonhart Rauwolff, portray the Oriental "Other" as ignorant (because he
prefers poetry to "science"), as lecherous (because his sexual codes do not
correspond to the new English gender coding), and as cruel and irrational
(because he does not govern by "rational," ordering judgment). From the
discursively central English "I" whole orders of thought radiate outward
to design the world. The discourse of modernism becomes the discourse
of empire and the discourse of colonialism. English mind writes itself
upon the whole world, and, as it names it, takes possession of it.

ONE

"From *Words* to Experimental *Philosophy*": Language and Logic at Restoration Zero Point

semiotics . . . seeks to identify the conventions and operations by which any signifying practice . . . produces its observable effects of meaning.
—Jonathan Culler, *The Pursuit of Signs*

Following Blumenberg, I have named as "zero point" the moment in late seventeenth century English culture wherein medieval/Renaissance epistemology collapsed under the weight of questions it had itself raised and simultaneously the new epistemology of modernism was constructed. We have briefly considered some implications of the process in discussing the turn to mimetic discourse in the Introduction. To appreciate the full extent of the epistemological break, however, we must consider the ways in which so radical a paradigm shift changed conceptualization and reasoning itself. In his essay, "On the Possibility of Generating Aesthetic Messages in an Edenic Language," Umberto Eco outlines the process by which a semiotic shift of the kind we are considering occurs in the context of the Edenic myth. In Eco's examination the simple language system of prelapsarian Adam and Eve, based upon Adam's primary emotional response to Eden in his act of naming the animals, is fundamentally and forever undermined by God's prohibition of the forbidden fruit. According to Eco, God's pronouncement designates as "bad and inedible" something that Adam and Eve's language designates as "good and edible." The resulting contradiction allows Adam to perceive that "language is responsible for ambiguities and deceptions" and that signs are arbitrary.[1] These contradictions permit Adam to manipulate the linguistic system, an act that allows him to comprehend the "system at the very moment he is calling that system into question and therefore destroying it. Just as he comes to understand the rigid generative code which had governed him, so he realizes that there is technically nothing to stop him from proposing a new code."[2]

Eco's parable comes curiously close to describing the revolution that occurred in late seventeenth-century semiotics. The zero point deconstructive impulse came to "comprehend" the medieval/Renaissance semiotic system, the relation of logic to language, "at the very moment [it was] calling that system into question and therefore destroying it." The zero point constructive impulse, on the other hand, "just as [it came] to understand the rigid generative code that had governed [it] . . . realize[d] that there [was] technically nothing to stop [it] from proposing a new code."

Medieval/Renaissance logic is *in* language, is totally and entirely *of* language. Knowledge is both produced and transmitted by means of linguistic manipulation; "For," as Ralph Lever, the premier logician of his day, puts it, "how can a man eyther invent [i.e., uncover, or discover, truth] or teach any good reasons to prove matters that lye in doubt [i.e., conduct logical investigation and disquisition], the nature of sentences and wordes, being not first knowne . . . seeing eche question standeth of them and is not thoroughly knowne, afore the force of eche woord be deeply considered, with dire consideration had, how the wordes, agree or disagree in a perfect sentence."[3] For the sixteenth-century logician logic *is* language; reasoning *is* the manipulation of language; mind is the repository of preexistent Ideas and the storehouse of words. The sixteenth century, indeed, considered logic and rhetoric branches of the same art, which differed, it was thought, only in the degree to which they amplified the truth they conjointly discovered (i.e., "invented") in the process of disseminating it. Thomas Wilson, who wrote the first complete treatise on logic in English (1551), says, "Both these Artes [logic and rhetoric] are much alike saving that Logique is occupied about all matters and doth playnly and nakedly setfurthe with apt words the summe of thinges by way of Argumentation, Againe of the side Rethorique useth gay painctted Sentences and setteth furth those matters with fresh colours and goodly ornamentes, and that at large."[4]

What a deconstructionist might call the "navel of unravelling" this code of knowledge, that is to say, the key questions raised by Renaissance epistemology under the weight of which the whole epistemology collapsed, are these: If words are multivalent and ambiguous, as the copious systems of categories in highly esteemed rhetorics like Fraunce's and Wilson's testify[5]—for example, trope, metaphor, metonymy of the cause, metonymy of the subject, ironia, and so forth—is the relation of word to pure, immutable Idea not questionable? And, if word alone equals truth, what is the relation of knowledge of the products, movements, and manipulations of physical matter to truth? Are the "works of Nature," existents external to the syllogistic system of logic, extraneous to truth?

"Natural Philosophy," which "some over-zealous *Divines* do reprobate ... as a carnal knowledge, and a too much minding worldly things,"[6] was the bridge discipline which led to the formulation of a new semiotic code, a new system of signification. Once logicians were forced to acknowledge that "language is responsible for ambiguities and deceptions," thinking came to be permeated with, and then dominated by, the ontology and epistemology of physical science. Sprat deplores the language of traditional logic/rhetoric as "the devices of *Fancy,* or delightful deceit of Fables."[7] The greatest contribution to knowledge of the Royal Society, he thought, was to lead "from *Words* to *Experimental* Philosophy." He argued that the reason Oxford had been the stronghold against "enthusiasm" that it was during the Interregnum was the presence there of the founders of "Natural Philosophy"—Wilkins, Boyle, Wallis, and others—for "such *spiritual Frensies,* which did then bear Rule, can never stand long, before a cleer, and a *deep skill* in *Nature.* It is almost impossible that they, who converse much with the subtility of *things* should be deluded by such *thick deceits.*"[8] If language is capable of deceptions and ambiguities then it must follow that a logic that exists exclusively *within,* and *by means* of, language must be a false logic: "the *Society* has been most solicitous . . . [of] the manner of their *Discourse:* which, unless they had been very watchful to keep in due temper, the whole spirit and vigour of their Design, had been eaten out, by the luxury and redundancy of *speech.* The ill effects of this superfluity of talking, have already overwhelmed most other *Arts* and *Professions;* insomuch that . . . I can hardly forbear . . . concluding that *eloquence* ought to be banish'd out of all *civil Societies.*"[9]

Discourse must be mimetic, the new thinkers argued, for the only reliable relation of language to truth lies in its second-order descriptive function. Language must be a servant to matter, an instrument to record as accurately as possible "Histories of Nature," the mechanistic operation of material bodies, and actual human experience. In the view of the new thinkers, the seven liberal arts must be banished as useless extravagances of fancy and chimeras of imagination:

> The complaint [against the Ancients, and particularly against Aristotle as the formulator of traditional logic] ... will appear the Juster; if we consider that the first *learned Times* of the Antients, and all those that follow'd after them, down to this day, would have receiv'd no prejudice at all; if their Philosophers had chiefly bestow'd their pains, in making *Histories* of *Nature,* and not in the *forming* of *Sciences* [in the original sense of "ways of knowing"]. . . . We have reason enough to believe, that these later Ages would have honour'd *Plato, Aristotle,*

Zeno, and *Epicurus,* as much, if not more, than now they do; if they had only set things in a way of propagating Experiences down to us; and not impos'd their *imagination* on us, as the only *Truths.*[10]

Traditional thinkers in the old code—which I shall call the old logic— did, of course, have a place for the natural sciences, though they would not have called them "sciences," but that place was far subordinate to the seven liberal arts:

> But yet physyke can not be lyberall
> [as the seven, premier among them logic and rhetoric, are]
> As the vii science by good auctorite,
> Which ledeth the soule the way in specyall
> By good doctrine to dame Eternitie;
> Only of phisike is the properte
> To ayde the body in every sekenes,
> That is right frayle and full of bryttilnes[11]

On the other hand, rhetoric for the sixteenth century provides the very basis for conceptual reasoning; it is the "ryall arte for to perceyve in mynde."[12] To begin his treatise on logic, Wilson provides students with "A brief declaration in meter, of the vii liberal artes, wherein Logique is comprehended as one of theim,"

> Grammar doth teache to utter wordes.
> To speke both apt and playne,
> Logique by art settes furth the truth,
> And doth tel us what is vayne.
> Rethorique at large paintes wel the cause,
> And makes that seeme right gay
> Which Logique spake but at a worde,
> And taught as by the way.
> Musicke with tunes delites the eare
> And makes us thinke it heauen,
> Arithmatique by number can make
> Reconinges to be euen
> Geometry thinges thicke and brode
> Measures by Line and Square [i.e., makes abstract].
> Astronomie by sterres doth tel
> Of foule and else of fayre.[13]

What is most striking about the seven branches of learning, or knowledge, is that all reasoning—conceptualization, argumentation, and judgment— is 1) abstract, or meta-physical, and 2) can take place only within language, *within* the "rigid generative code" that governs all thinking (hence Grammar is the first of the sciences).

In the sixteenth and early seventeenth centuries the *word* is the beginning and end of all truth, and therefore of all thought.

> By worde the world was made orygynally,
> The hye Kynge sayde, it was made incontient;
> He dyd commaunde, al was made shortly,
> To the world the worde is sententious judgemente.[14]

Words are perfect and complete signs—"A Word is an absolute & perfect voice, whereby something is ment and signified"[15]—and are therefore perfect conduits for conveying pure Ideas from mind to mind, from the storehouse of received truth to mind, from the Idea of Truth itself to mind. "Words are voyces framed with hart and toung, uttering the thoughtes of the mynde," Ralph Lever tells us in *The Art of Reason*, "and wordes expresse the thoughtes of the minde without ioyning of thynges together at all."[16] Since the form of the word and the form of the thought are one and the same, mind can communicate directly with mind without hinderance from the fleshly instruments of tongue and ear. As Saint Augustine puts it, "In order that what we are thinking may reach the mind through the fleshly ears, that which we have in mind is expressed in words and is called speech. But our thought is not transformed into sounds; it remains entire in itself and assumes the form of words by means of which it may reach the ears without suffering any deterioration in itself."[17] We might, indeed, rightly say that pre-modern epistemology supposes *identity* between mind and language: "Look, as in Mind there is a certain *Character* or *Idea* of things; so likewise in oration or speech there is a *Character* or *Idea of the Mind*."[18] Truth exists within the mind and within language, for language does not signify anything other than itself, and words call to mind knowledge that is already *in* mind and in eternity.[19] For the Middle Ages and the Renaissance signs are "not merely . . . intramental entities but indices of realities existing outside of and prior to the knowing subject."[20] Nevertheless, because the speculative grammarians and nominalists of the fourteenth century had opened out the assumptions of an earlier sign theory that focused on a fixed, universal, prior object of knowledge in the direction of a logically based grammar, by the sixteenth century the semiotic code was "an energetic tool of analysis, constitutive as well as reflective of reality."[21] The sixteenth- and early seventeenth-century logician, then, uses the semiotic code as an instrument of analysis to uncover the signs of truths that exist prior to the knowing subject, but also—since language *constitutes* mind—within the mind of the knowing subject. As Peter Ramus puts it, although man may be ignorant of all things, this is not in any sense to declare that he should not seek or that he cannot invent [i.e., know, find, uncover] in view of the fact that he has naturally in himself the power to understand all things; and when he shall have before his eyes the art of invention by universal kinds, as a sort of mirror reflecting for him the universal images and generals of all things, it will be easier for him by means of these images to recognize each single species, and therefore to invent that which he is seeking; but it is necessary by very many examples, by great practice, by long use to burnish and polish this mirror before it render up these images.[22]

For the sixteenth and early seventeenth centuries, knowledge is the union of the mind with truth; logic, or the production of knowledge by reasoning, is the process of rightly locating and uncovering universal "characters," word-thought signs, within systems of discourse that *are* (*not* that [re]present) both metaphysical ideas and mental operations.

Robert Sanderson, the "chief English Systematic," or follower of Ramus, whose *Logicae Artis Compendium* (1615) was reissued eight times in the seventeenth century, defines logic as the method of discovering and presenting knowledge in discourse. The parts of logic, says Sanderson, are three, "by virtue of the mental operations directed by it. The *first* directs the first operation of the mind, that is *simple conceiving* and is *about simple terms* . . . the *second* part of logic directs the second operation of the mind, that is *connecting* and *dividing* and is about *propositions* . . . the *third* and final part directs the third and final operation of the mind, that is *discoursing.*"[23] Let us examine these parts of logic and their operation. A "simple term," as the logician Samuel Smith tells us in 1627, is "the sign of a thing and of a concept, written or spoken in a certain configuration of letters or syllables, according to an arrangement divine or human."[24] It is, in short, a *word.* The second operation, "connecting and dividing," is the arrangement of a proposition, which, again according to Smith, is "a certain fixed series of words expressing simple states." Once again, the process operates *by* language and *in* language. The third part of logic, "discoursing," was further divided into two parts: "invention" and "judgment." While for us in post-Enlightenment culture, "invention" means the production of a thing or idea that has never before existed, the term had the almost exact *opposite* meaning for pre-modern thinkers. In Scholastic and Ramist logic "invention" was construed not as a process of discovering or creating the *unknown,* but rather as a process of establishing connection with the *known,* "subjecting traditional truths to syllogistic examination, and accepting as new truth only what could be proved to be consistent with the old."[25]

Memory was considered to be the most crucial mental attribute of the logician because in the process of syllogistic examination his mind had to search all the "places" of known truth to test the validity of a proposition: "A Place is the restyng corner of an argument, or else a mark which giueth warnyng to our memory what we may speake probablie, either in one parte or, the other, upon all cases that fall in question. . . . So he that will take profite in this part of logique [i.e., invention] must be like a hunter and lerne by labour to know the boroughes [fox burrows]. For these places be nothyng els but couertes or boroughes, wherein if any one searche diligentely, he may fynde game at pleasure."[26]

As invention entails the discovery of truth by exploration of pre-existent linguistic constructs, so judgment, the second half of "discourse," tests the validity of any new proposition by determining its conformity to linguistically constructed, established truth. "Iudgement is the second part of Logicke, whereby every proposite or oration is iudged, and censured, whether it be according to Truth and sound Reason, or otherwise. It is the Consequent Effect, and End of Disposition."[27] Thomas Wilson gives an example of the process whereby the validity of a proposition—"It is lawful for priests to marry"—can be judged. We must examine the word "priest" and the word "wife" each in nineteen "places" (i.e., linguistic categories—of definition, of genus, of species, of property, of whole, of parts, etc.). We then compare the similarities and dissimilarities of the final tallies reached for each of the words in order to 1) find agreement between the words in all their associations, definitions, and connotations, and thereby 2) establish the truth of the proposition. As Howell says, for the sixteenth-century logician "the act of judging . . . [is] the act of evaluating a discourse already divided and arranged."[28] In seventeenth-century England, then, all logic takes place *within* language: conceiving is naming; formulating connection among thoughts is constructing arrangements of words; syllogistic reasoning is placing such arrangements into pre-existent linguistic categories. Reasoning upon evidence of the senses, which would be the cornerstone of the new logic proposed by "Natural Philosophy," was considered by the old logicians to be a subhuman activity: "let us remember that the syllogism is the law of reason . . . a law of reason proper to man, not being in any sense shared with other animals, as the preliminary judgment can be in some sense shared, but solely in things pertaining to sense and belonging to the body and physical life."[29]

In 1693 John Locke's friend William Molyneux urged him to write a logic, a textbook based on *An Essay Concerning Human Understanding*. Told that an "Abridgement" of *An Essay* was being made by "a judicious hand at *Oxford*" for use as such a textbook,[30] Molyneux expressed delight, "for," he said, " 'tis what I have always thought might be of good use in the universities, where we yet want another sort of language, than what has hitherto prevail'd there, to the great hindrance of science."[31] Molyneux was a scholarly generation behind the times. Although it is true that Locke's great contribution in the field of linguistic theory was expressly to connect his thoughts on language to a coherent, systematic theory of knowledge,[32] it was Locke's teachers, the experimental philosophers, scientists, and mathematicians of the Oxford group, the founding members of the Royal Society, who first questioned the validity of traditional logic on linguistic grounds and proposed a new relation of language to knowledge. Restoration "Experimental," or "natural philosophy" demanded not so much a new language, but a new semiotics, a new code of *what* and *how* signs signify. The linguistic enemy of the new philosophers was the trope (metaphor, metonymy, synecdoche, irony), which, as its name implies, brings instability and indeterminacy into the semiotic field: "Trope is a style by means of which the natural and proper meaning of a word is changed to another, as is indicated by the word trope, which in French means interchange."[33] The trope glaringly calls to attention the "other," the not-that not-there component necessary in signs. As early as 1661 Boyle, arguing that the didactic superiority of Holy Scripture to Ancient Greek and Latin texts lies in the simplicity and mimetic nature of its discourse, expresses the anxiety that the Oxford new scientists and philosophers felt once they came to question the semiotic code upon which the old logic, which had, after all, shaped them, rested: "the pretty Similies [i.e., metaphors], quaint Allegories and quick Sentences . . . [of the Ancient logicians and rhetoricians], I find all these Topicks I say, such two-edg'd Weapons, that they are as well applicable to the service of Falsehood, as of Truth, and may by Ready Wits be brought Equally to countenance Contrary Assertions. . . . each of these Popular Topicks [in logic] is such an Unsolid or uncertain Foundation, that one can build little on it, that an equally able Antagonist may not with as specious Probability Over-throw."[34] Natural philosophers saw Bacon as their forebear, a pioneer in the search for a new theory of knowledge, and they wrongly attributed to Bacon a distrust of metaphor. Abraham Cowley in "To the Royal Society," the prefatory poem to Sprat's *History,* for instance, praises Bacon for effecting the turn from metaphor to mimesis as a *mental operation.*

> From Words, which are but Pictures of the Thought
> (Though we our Thoughts from them perversely drew)
> To Things, the Minds right Object, he it brought.[35]

Thomas Sprat makes up an interesting fictional past for rhetoric. In a 180-degree reversal of Renaissance language theory, Sprat argues that language was *originally* mimetic, and that the devices of rhetoric were at first merely instruments to ground abstract concepts in sensory experience: "an admirable Instrument . . . when they were onely employ'd to describe *Goodness, Honesty, Obedience;* in larger, fairer, and more moving *Images;* to represent Truth [n.b. *not* invent or uncover, but (re)present], cloth'd with Bodies; and to bring *Knowledg* back again to our very senses, from whence it was first deriv'd to our understandings."[36] But, Sprat goes on to argue, language, which was originally the servant of matter and experience-grounded truth, has now become an obstacle to knowledge: "who can behold without indignation, how many mists and uncertainties, these specious *Tropes* and *Figures* have brought on our Knowledg?" Skill in dialectical reasoning—which for Renaissance thinkers was the sole medium of intellectual investigation and the only conduit for the transmission of knowledge among experts—is no more than tricky manipulation of empty words in the eyes of Sprat and the Society he celebrates. Rhetoric, now detached by them from logic and thought, is considered to be not only an obstacle to right reasoning, but a sort of pop art, an "easy A" course of study: "of all the Studies of men, nothing may be sooner obtain'd than this vicious abundance of Phrase, this trick of *Metaphor,* this volubility . . . , which makes so great a noise in the World."[37]

The premier study for the new thinkers is history—not just natural history, but cultural history as well—because history is conceived by them to be a transparent record of things, of ordinary events, and of mechanical operations. John Ray and Francis Willoughby, the first English naturalists, reject and outlaw from use in their field of study all but the most strictly mimetic language.[38] In 1673 Ray excludes from the language he believes to be proper to the study of natural history all "hieroglyphics, emblems, morals, fables, presages, or aught else appertaining to divinity, ethics, grammar"; he sharply restricts the function of language to the strict mimetic representation of "only what properly relates to natural history."[39]

The aim of the Royal Society was "to regard the *least* and *plainest* things . . . as well as the greatest Curiosities," for the express purpose of creating a transparent mimetic language and structuring the design of learned inquiry as a linear, open-ended *process.* In this endeavor, once again, they envisioned as an obstacle to their project the tropic, self-reflexive language of the old logic: "The *Histories* of *Pliny, Aristotle, Solinus, Aelian* abounding more with Pretty Tales and fine monstrous Stories; than sober and fruitful Relations. . . . It stops the severe progress of *Inquiry:* Infecting the mind, and making it averse from the true *Natural Philosophy;* It is like *Romances,* in respect of *True History.*"[40]

As was the case for natural history, so was it for cultural history. For the

new thinkers of the Restoration all knowledge is experientially and materially based and therefore all understanding is historically determined. The
meaning of the Scriptures themselves was not considered to be transhistorical. Indeed, the value of the Scriptures was thought by Boyle to be
precisely that they were transparent historical records, not that they were
the invisible Word of God. Where the Scriptures are considered to be
wanting is where they are incomplete records, obscured by the changes of
time. "How much the want of other Historians contemporary with the
Pen-men of the Old Testament may make things seem obscure that might
by such stories be easily cleared up, we may observe from diverse Passages
of the New Testament, which can scarce be well understood without an
account of *Herod's* family, and the changes that happened about our saviour's
time in *Judea*."[41]

Boyle everywhere historicizes the Scriptures, "excellently suited [to]
the Genius of Those Times its Several Books were written in; and have
been very Proper for those People it was Primarily design'd to Work
upon."[42] History—that is, the record of *what actually happened*—is no longer,
as it was for medieval and Renaissance thinkers, a dark veil of "appearances" obscuring Truth. On the contrary, it is the only possible way to
apprehend Truth: "It is not to be expected that out of those Books [of the
Old Testament] we should be able to collect and comprehend either complete *Idaeas* of the *Israelitish* Government Civil and Ecclesiastical, or of the
true State of their several . . . Opinions and affaires in matters of Religion;
and yet without the Knowledge of those it cannot be but that many Texts
will seem Obscure to us."[43] The Word of God, like the language to which
the Royal Society aspired, must consist in "positive expressions; clear senses;
a native easiness; bringing all things as near the Mathematical plaines, as
they can."[44]

As we can see, the new semiotic code is radically antithetical to the old.
In the old system truth is metaphysical, ideational, and prior to the knowing subject, though the "character" of truth exists mentally within, as well
as prior to, the knowing subject. In the new code matter and experience
are prior to the knowing subject and are pre-existents to knowledge. Truth
is deferred, subordinate to the mental operations necessary to its discovery,
and methods of arriving at truth are themselves mutable and open-ended.
Knowledge and language both are second-order constructs entirely dependent upon the first-order operations of material nature. Sprat prefigures Locke in proposing a new conception of the relation of mind to sense
in the acquisition of knowledge, which, in the new code, lies always in the
realm of the not yet known: "All *Knowledg* is to be got the same way that
a Language is, by *Industry, Use,* and *Observation*. It must be receiv'd before it

can be drawn forth. 'Tis true the mind of Man is a Glass, which is able to *represent to it self* [ital. mine], all the Works of *Nature;* But it can onely shew those Figures, which have been brought before it."[45] When we compare this with Ramus's conception of the mind as a glass, quoted above, we discover that the new theory of knowledge and mental process is the exact obverse of the old.

In like manner the Renaissance equivalency between "character in the mind" and "character in language" has been fundamentally and forever broken. The cornerstone of Locke's theory of knowledge is his rejection of the idea that the human mind is the repository of innate ideas and a storehouse of pre-existent "characters": "I know it is a received Doctrine, that Men have native Ideas and original Characters stamped upon their Minds in their very first Being. This Opinion I have at large examined . . . and . . . what I have said . . . will be much more easily admitted, when I have shown, whence the Understanding may get all the *Ideas* it has, and by what ways and degrees they may come into the Mind; for which I shall appeal to every one's own Observation and Experience."[46] He can appeal to everyone's and anyone's experience and observation to verify his claim because, for Locke, all knowledge *is* experience, and truth can be validated only by reference to, and reflection upon experience: "In [experience] all our Knowledge is founded; and from that ultimately derives itself. Our Observation employ'd either about *external, sensible Objects; or about the internal Operations of our Minds, perceived and reflected on by our selves, is that which supplies our Understandings with all the Materials of thinking.*"[47]

When we recall that, as Culler says, "semiotics . . . seeks to identify the conventions and operations by which any signifying practice produces its observable effects of meaning,"[48] we can appreciate the Restoration zero point epistemological break as a jump from the track of one semiotic coding to another. In the old code a word is the exact equivalent of an Idea inherent in the mind, which can move from mind to mind without the aid of, or distortion by, sense. There is exact equivalence between the character in the mind and the character in language. In the new code the word is the arbitrary sign of ideas derived wholly from sense, and all knowledge is finally traceable to its origins in sensible Ideas:

> It may . . . lead us a little towards the Original of all our Notions and Knowledge, if we remark, how great a dependence our *Words* have on common sensible *Ideas;* and how those, which are made use of to stand for Actions and Notions quite removed from sense, *have their rise from thence, and from obvious sensible* Ideas *are transferred to more abstruse significations,* and are made to stand for *Ideas* that come not under the cognizance of our senses. . . . And I doubt not, but if we could trace them to their sources, we should find, in all Languages,

the names, which stand for Things that fall not under our Senses, to have their first rise from sensible *Ideas*.[49]

Under the new dispensation, human mind is still considered to be universally the same, but whereas under the old code disciplined thought can only occur within pre-existent systems of linguistic categories, the new logic finds the categories of traditional logic useless encumbrances. Locke, for instance, thinks syllogistic reasoning is "Artificial Ignorance, and *learned Gibberish.*"[50] "Natural reason," he says, is "large, sound, round about Sense,"[51] the only instrument necessary to discriminate truth from falsehood: "Every Man carries about him a Touchstone, if he will make use of it, to distinguish substantial Gold from superficial Glitterings, Truth from Appearances. And indeed the Use and Benefit of this Touchstone, which is natural Reason, is spoil'd and lost only by assumed Prejudices, overweening Presumption, and Narrowing of our Minds,"[52] the inevitable consequence, he believes, of traditional methods of learned inquiry and discourse. The "proper business of the Understanding," says Locke, is "to think of every Thing just as it is in it self."[53]

The Royal Society, again prefiguring Locke, went so far in abandoning the methods of disciplined thought laid down by traditional logic that they refused to set any program of thinking at all in the conduct of their experiments. Though they were not yet ready to throw traditional logic out completely, as Locke would do, they had begun seriously to question its value. And their distrust of traditional logic lay squarely in their recognition that the old logic was bound in by language (divorced from material referents) and that language-bound syllogistic reasoning was a closed system.

> [The Royal Society has resolved] not to prescribe to themselves, an certain *Art* of *Experimenting* within which to circumscribe their thoughts; But rather to keep themselves free, and change their course, according to the different circumstances, that occur to them in their operations; and the several alterations of the Bodies, on which they work. The true Experimenting has this one thing inseparable from it, never to be a *fix'd* and *settled Art,* and never to be *limited* by constant Rules. This, perhaps, may be shown too in other *Arts;* as in that of *Invention,* of which, though in *Logick,* and *Rhetorick,* so many bounds and helps are given, yet I believe very few have argued or discoursed by those *Topicks.* But whether that be confin'd or no, it is certain that *Experimenting* is . . . never wholly to be reduc'd to *standing Precepts;* and may almost as easily be obtain'd as defin'd.[54]

Moreover, because the new code subordinated word to thing and mind to matter, the new referential discourse was valued for its ability to *do* something, to make things happen in the world, to change human behavior: "Thoughts being but Internall Actions and Actions but Externall Thoughts."[55] Just as the new philosophers question the usefulness of a language system that is self-referential only, so too do they question the use of a system of reasoning that is distant from experience. Boyle scorns traditional logic as a teacher of ethics because he considers it a battle of empty words, a merely clever linguistic pyrotechnics that achieves its effects nowhere but in the airy hollows of mind and memory:

> 'Tis a Mistake to think, that a large System of Ethicks, dissected according to the nice Prescriptions of Logick, and Methodically replenish'd with Definitions, Divisions, Distinctions, and Syllogisms, is requisite or Sufficient to make men Virtuous. Too many Moralists write as if they thought Virtue could be taught as easily, and much the same Way, as Grammar: and leaving our Rational Motives to Virtue, and Determents from Vice, with other things to have a Genuine Influence on the Minds and Manners of men, they fall to wrangle about the Titles and Precedence of the Parts of Ethical Philosophy, and things extrinsecal to Vice and Virtue; and they spend more time in asserting their Method, than the Prerogatives of Virtue above Vice; they ... are more Industrious to impresse their Doctrine on our Memories, than our Affections, and teach us better to dispute our Passions than With [sic] them.[56]

Just as the new learning strained against the limits of a logic shackled in language and an ethics divorced from life, so also did it begin to dispute the usefulness of a knowledge enclosed and confined by the past. The new thinkers were in search of a logic that could produce knowledge not yet known, and they believed that a strictly mimetic language was their life-line to the future: "By their fair, and equal and submissive way of Registring nothing, but *Histories* and *Relations;* [the natural philosophers of the Royal Society] have left room for others, to *change,* to *augment,* to *approve,* to *contradict* them, at their discretion. . . . By this, they have made a firm *confederacy,* between thier own *present labours* and the Industry of *Future Ages.*"[57] The validity of the new conception of knowledge is, as Karlis Racevskis argues of Enlightenment knowledge, established "according to the tautological procedure of the human sciences, which take the limitations inherent in empirical knowledge as the very proof of this knowledge's truth."[58]

Traditional logic–rhetoric carried the seeds of its own destruction within it, of course. Donatus, the fourth-century grammarian whose works were the elementary texts from which all seventeenth-century schoolchildren learned, said that words are air: "*vox est aer ictuus sensilibis auditu, quantum in ipso est*" [voice, or language, is air that has been struck, which exists only as long as its hearing].[59] Chaucer, in *The House of Fame,* tells us:

> every speche that ys spoken,
> Lowd or pryvee, foul or fair,
> In his substaunce ys but air.[60] [ll. 766-768]

And the fragility and mutability of language that led a Boyle or a Wilkins anxiously to question the foundations of logic were already well known to the sixteenth century. The Count in Castiglione's *The Courtier* is already questioning the word = immutable Idea equation when he muses on the fragility and mutability of words and the loss of whole languages to time: "time [doth] make those first wordes to fall, and vse maketh other to spring a fresh ... vntil they in like sorte consumed litle and litle with the enuyous byting of time, because at the last both wee and whatsoeuer is ours, are mortall."[61]

Ironically enough, the theories of language formulated by the natural philosophers and scientists of the Restoration period also carried the seeds of their destruction within them. Just as a Wilkins, Boyle, or Locke shook the foundations of pre-modern logic and language, so in the turning wheel of time do postmodern philosophers like Derrida and de Man come to challenge them.

> Philosophers like Locke and his latter day positivist descendents devote a great deal of their thought to establishing a discourse of dependably logical and referential meaning, such that philosophy can carry on its work undisturbed by the beguilements of rhetoric. And yet—to adopt one of Bacon's sayings— "drive metaphor out with a pitchfork, yet she will return." Deconstruction in the hands of a conceptual rhetorician like Paul de Man shows just how omnipresent and potentially disruptive are the effects of this "buried" figural dimension.[62]

In the postmodern age we have come again to zero point. The turn has come full circle and, once again, philosophers and rhetoricians are showing us that *all that is* is language, that all conception, perception, and reasoning always and inevitably are in and of language: "Deconstruction is first and last a textual activity, a putting-into-question of the root metaphysical prejudice which posits self-identical concepts outside and above the discriminating play of language."[63]

We did not, however, have to wait three hundred years for an assault on positivist language theory. In keeping with the destructive/constructive paradox of Restoration zero point, at almost the moment that the new semiotic code was being constructed a satire appeared to mock and undermine it. In 1683 an anonymous writer published *The Whores Rhetorick, calculated to the Meridian of London and Conformed to the Rules of Art. The Whores Rhetorick* is an "imitation" (in the Restoration sense of the term) of Ferrante Pallavicino's satire on logic and rhetoric, the Jesuits, and the magisterium of the Roman Catholic Church, *La Rettorica della Putane* (1642), for which, and other of his anticlerical writings, the author was beheaded in 1644. Pallavicino's satire is much in the manner of libertine deconstructive satire in that it attacks all institutions and social conventions as hypocritical; and, like *libertinage,* it reaches beyond social satire to explode as unreal all ideals of love and honor, all constructs of morality, all human pretentions to knowledge: "Like a Machiavelli writing on private instead of public life [Pallavicino] assumes that . . . all is a cover for some base aim."[64] Unfortunately, because Pallavicino ironically used sexual prostitution as a metaphor for intellectual and moral prostitution, his work has been mistaken for pornography, as indeed, the English imitation of it has been (and that as recently as the 1970s). Pallavicino's *Rhetorick* follows the design of a traditional rhetoric very closely. It consists in fifteen rhetorical disquisitions in perfect correspondence to the fifteen divisions of a formal textbook, and it arranges its parts to conform exactly with the parts and categories of a traditional rhetoric. The English *Whores Rhetorick,* which is double the length of Pallavicino's, is cast novelistically as loosely joined dialogues between the procuress, Mother Cresswell, and Dorothea, the young woman whom she is instructing in her art, who is the daughter of a noble cavalier, impoverished during the Interregnum by his loyalty to the king and left to languish despite the Restoration (a figure common in dramatic satire of the period). The looser structure of the English version broadens its scope. Its satire is more general and wider ranging. All classes and professions, their habits and their discourses, are fair game. It targets the court: "The wise *Italians* by *Courtegiano* and *Courtegiana* understand the Courtier and the Trading Lady, thereby intimating that a Whore ought to be furnished with all the Courtly qualities, she ought to be a Female sycophant, or the Courtier's Wife."[65] But it mocks the merchant class too, calling a whore the wealthy, retired merchant "who is grown old and tired with cheating, who has quit both Exchange and Coffee-House on the score of business, [and] only repairs thither sometimes for his consolation to rail at the Government, and smoak a Pipe" (p.32). The successful whore is mistress of all professions, for all professions so closely resemble hers: the clergy—"After you have suffered sufficient drudgery in the Pulpit, you shall rowle into a fat Bishoprick, and then pamper your self in Prelatical pomp and luxury"; the lawyers—"when you have ruined a million unhappy Clients, that have thrust their cause into your hands, and got a mass of money by bawling, cheating and lying: you shall then wrap your self up in lamb-skins, and take a nap on a lazy Bench"; and the doctors—"when you have acquired a plentiful fortune, by destroying many Legions of Wretched Patients: it will then be a good time to leave off killing and oblige posterity with some choice Receipts" (p.33). It takes potshots at the clerical Left—Mother Cresswell advises Dorothea to praise competitors she hates for hypocrisy's sake, "as Fanatick's pray for the King" (p.183)— and equally at the latitudinarian Right: "You must cloath your discourse with a meek, grave, and pious aspect, to make your sophistry pass for sincere and real" (p.60).

Social satire, however, is not the central aim of the *Whores Rhetorick*. The work is, rather, a complete mock-rhetoric, and, perfectly of its time, it is a double-edged weapon. It exposes the old logic-rhetoric as artful manipulation of empty language, and, at the same time it mocks the new experimental philosophers and their call for a positivist, mimetic discourse.

The *Rhetorick* is prefaced by a satirical "Epistle to the Reader" in which the fictional editor explains how he came upon "these documents" and the merit he deserves for "passing them on to the learned reader in the same manner (saving the academical Pedantry)." The heavily ironic "Epistle" mocks Ramist logic, which it often precisely parodies, as sheer sophistry:

> when I was at University, and entering on the Sophistical part of Logick, my Tutor . . . gave me this preliminary caution. *Young man, says he, you are now to receive my Instructions in a dangerous part of Learning. But before I proceed* (ne ignotis Sermo fit) *I must explain the nature and meaning of the Word.* [The first "place" of traditional logic-rhetoric is "Etymology"] . . . [It] *signifies no more in English than a Teacher of Wisdom. . . . It may be objected that this learning of Sophisms cannot be necessary, after knowing the true ways of arguing, in as much as contraries do illustrate one another* [a major principle of Ramus]. . . . *To this I must tell you, if Sophisms did appear in their own colours then that rule might very well hold. But alas! These false and deceitful Syllogisms, like Wolves in Sheep's Cloathing do ever appear in sincere and honest habiliments.*[66]

The satire here cuts two ways. The passage unquestionably mocks Ramus —and, as I have indicated, draws on specific Ramist doctrine in its parody— but it also clearly pokes fun at the alarms and anxieties of the new thinker's distrust of "false and deceitful Syllogisms."

In form the *Rhetorick* is a perfect mock-rhetoric; it imitates the traditional rhetoric or logic exactly in its twelve-category plan: ordering knowledge, method, subject, invention, probability, and so forth, exactly as a rhetoric textbook would. Mother Cresswell begins her instruction of Dorothea exactly as Wilson begins his *Art of Rhetoric* and his *Rule of Reason,* by laying down the whole design of her treatise:

> M.C. I have promised you a Rhetorick, and therefore to make good my word, I must observe some method, and limit my self to a certain order. . . . I will now

show you its object and the matter about which it is conversant. Interest is the subject of this art; and what ever an insatiable avarice can either pretend to, or desire, . . . the object thereof. Invention is principally necessary in this Art, to frame new pretexts, and a diversity of expressions, with reference to circumstances of person, time, and place: and to impose probabilities, or even things utterly false as certain, and true. [pp.38-39]

Her reference to "method," "order," "object," "subject," "invention," and "probability," mark Mother Cresswell as a disciplined thinker in, and master of, traditional school rhetoric. Moreover, like a university teacher, Mother Cresswell bolsters her categories and rules with numerous assertions of Ancient authority: "Dost know how *Seneca* excuses his repetition of the same Precepts? . . . Because people are again and again guilty of those Vices, which he was reforming. *Therefore* (says he) *my Precepts ought to be inculcated over and over*" (p.111).

Mother Cresswell sides with the old logicians in believing that memory is the intrinsic mirror of original "characters" in the mind; invention consists in exploration of the "places"; and disquisition is the artful arrangement of pre-existent linguistic constructs, or propositions:

> M.C. The Memory which belongs properly to you, is not so much an immense capacity, qualified to receive and retain all objects represented to the exterior, and thence introduced to the general interior sense; as an artificial ready remembrance of all points necessary to your own Trade, and the persuading power of your eloquence, which consists in timing your words and actions with a seasonable discretion, assigning every part of your art its proper place. . . . What we Rhetoricians call Disposition, is requisite in this place to regulate the several parts of interest to the best advantage. [pp.164-165]

In so describing the use of memory in "artificial," that is, artful, or according to the demands of the art/science which constitutes logical disquisition, Mother Cresswell is, again, following Ramus and Wilson.

In parody of traditional rhetoric's "colors" and its aspiration to "golden eloquence," the writer of *The Whores Rhetorick* reduces downward to matter. Verbal colors become material clothes—"I would have your Cloaths seem rather grave than gawdy . . . in their splendour shew something of the fantastical, and notwithstanding preserve decorum" (p.52)—and golden speech becomes golden coin—"In the sentiment of my Rhetorick, there is no music ought to sound more charmingly in a Whores Ears, as the sweet melody created by the clashing of Gold in her own purse." Dorothea, an apt pupil, recognizes the value of Mother Cresswell's instruction in guiding her way in the great world: "Why Mother, I think you design to make me a States-woman, as well as knowledge in the Rules of Rhetorick," she says (p.59).

However, although traditional logic comes under attack in this artful satire, *The Whores Rhetorick* takes the new logic and learning as its principal target and ridicules it as as great an intellectual whoredom as the old. Whores are the greatest of natural philosophers, Mother Cresswell says, for "Their business and Trade being universal, their cunning and industry ought to be so too. And indeed this general acquaintance, this multiplicity of experiments, is the readiest way, after the foundation of a good Theory, to make the Whore expert in her business" (pp.71-72).

"You talk Philosophically, Madam," Dorothea observes (p.72). And Mother Cresswell, with the fluency of a Boyle or Locke, goes on to develop her argument that *experience* is the only source of truth and knowledge, citing a modern authority to strengthen her argument: "Mr. *Hobbs,* child, says well, that Wisdom is nothing but Experience; so by consequence a Bawd must surpass all mankind in point of Wisdom, in as much as her experimental Knowledge does all others. She has read more Men than any mortal has Books" (pp.85-86).

Like the members of the Royal Society, Mother Cresswell throws out the language theory of "those silly Rhetoricks . . . that are commonly taught in Schools, as the four parts of Oration, Elocution, and the Doctrine of Tropes and Figures" (p.39). She says that her vast "stock of knowledge," like that of the natural philosophers, has been "imprinted in [her] by a long study in the theory, but likewise by many years of experience in the infallible practick part" of learning (p.19). Dorothea appreciates the mimetic fidelity and attention to particulars of her preceptor's language. "I thank you, good Mother," she says, "in that you are so sensible of my interest as to square your Discourse to my particular necessities" (p.41).

While the "Editor" in his "Epistle to the Reader" ascribes his love of sophistry to the traditional education he received at the University, Mother Cresswell blames her fall from star status in the practice of her art to the lesser position of teacher-bawd to her youthful enthusiasm for natural philosophy: "and it is but a just reward due to the non-observance of convenient rules. I was not so wise as to contain my self within the bounds of a Rhetorick; my vain curiosity transported me into the wild unpassable mazes of Philosophy, and to dive too far into the secrets of natural Philosophy to gratifie my own fantastical and giddy nature" (pp.19-20). At its best, as here, *The Whores Rhetorick* is multilayered as well as multivalent. The relation of the text to its fictional speaker, to the pre-texts to which it alludes and refers, to the theories of knowledge and language outlined in those pre-texts, creates layer upon layer of deconstructive irony. Dorothea's reply to Mother Cresswell's account of her downfall extends its satire upon the new learning even further. We will recall Sprat's argument that Aristotle and the other ancient formulators of traditional logic would have been better employed to hand down "histories of nature" and accounts of their experience than the vain imaginings that, in his view, constitute our inheritance from them. Or his notion that the discourse of the Royal Society is chosen especially to provide a foundation for future experimenters and future additions to knowledge. The writer of the *Rhetorick* clearly has such ideas as Sprat's in mind when he shapes Dorothea's response to Mother Cresswell's account of her youthful experience: "I ought gladly to build on the experience you have so dearly purchased, and rest satisfied with such practical Doctrines as you shall be pleased to impart to me; without entertaining any Metaphysical affections, I shall acquiesce in a knowledge of sublunary beings . . . I will not be solicitous to understand what substance the Heavens are made on; nor gratifie my ears with the Musick of the Spheres" (p.21).

In an interesting way *The Whores Rhetorick* exemplifies the Janus-faced nature of a zero point epistemological break, the continuity within discontinuity that we may overlook when we are considering such a rupture: "It is important to note that, paradoxically, these breaks serve mainly to underline the continuity in human affairs: the two periods separated by a break become comparable in terms of cognitive processes that adopt different strategies but serve the same purpose for each age. In other words the break does not change everything, but rearranges certain elements of the methodology through which humans gain an understanding of reality and try to justify their attempts to establish their control over it."[67]

TWO

The Semiotics of Restoration Deconstructive Satire

Such as with Railing Spirits are possess'd,
The Muses Frenzy, let them be suppress'd,
Allow no Satyrs which receive their Date
From Juno's Academy, *Billingsgate*;
No Banters, no Invective lines admit,
Where want of Manners, makes up want of Wit.
. . . Let those Eternal Poets be Condemn'd
To be Eternal Poets to the end.

Daniel Defoe, "The Pacificator"

With the exception of David Vieth's pioneer work and the more recent readings of Dustin Griffin, Kevin Cope, and Barbara Everett,[1] one may safely say that the universally accepted view of Restoration satire is that expressed by Raman Selden, who says,

> It is significant that the leading satirists of the day (Butler, Rochester, Oldham and Dryden) all ridicule deviations from a strongly held norm in the spheres of philosophy, religion, politics, or literature. It is true that the skeptical Butler and the Hobbesian Rochester themselves depart from that Augustan norm of rationality which was to be expressed definitively by Locke in the final decade of the century. Nevertheless they acted as front-line troops in the Augustan negative criticism of the 'irrational' beliefs and 'dangerous' dogmas of the past.[2]

We have not looked beyond the eighteenth-century binary model for satire, which determines that in order to *be* satire a text must direct us toward a positive norm, must contain, or, at least indirectly, uphold a clear *moral* "satiric antithesis." If a satirist does not fit the mold then his departure from it must be explained away, and, above all, he must be considered the exception that proves the rule. Therefore Rochester, who, in direct defiance of materialism, calls upon the "great Negative" to expose all "blind Philosophies," as we have seen, is labelled a "Hobbesian." And Butler's radical unravelling of epistemic constructs that Cope so well describes— "To dodge the evils of experience and philosophy Butler creates a model of behavior which corresponds to and is anchored in nothing"[3]—is dismissed as idiosyncratic skepticism. A *"strongly held norm"* of rationalism *must* somehow be upheld in Restoration satire, otherwise how can we call it satire?

Having cut the eighteenth-century, morally uplifting model for satire in stone, we do not allow that deviations from it call the model into question. On the contrary, we consider that exceptions confirm its rule. As I suggested earlier, we ourselves are products of the epistemology of modernism and in our thinking about the norms of satire we reflect eighteenth-century thinking, wherein "validity" "is established according to the tautological procedure of the human sciences, which take the limitations inherent in empirical knowledge as the very proof of this knowledge's truth. The knowledge thus constituted claims an unimpeachable prerogative to impose its norms as the universally applicable ideal for humanity."[4]

And just as we cannot abandon the notion that upholding a positive norm is the determining generic function of satire, neither can we give up the idea that satiric discourse is mimetic. Even a critic as astute as Everett Zimmerman, writing on a subject as problematic as Swift's narrative strategies, cannot rid himself entirely of the assumption: "Because satire assumes the prerogative of commentary on existents external and prior to itself, the interpretive strategy that it suggests is to define a historical author writing to a historical reader about historical events. In sharing, or pretending to share, a border with polemic, satire urges its reader toward a truth that appears outside the borders of its text."[5] Happily, the assumption of a mimetic function does not hinder Zimmerman's very intelligent and sensitive reading of Swift's texts, but it does often hold him back from accepting the full implication of his own interpretations. For example, Zimmerman cannot altogether acknowledge that there *is no* authorial "I" either within or behind a satire like *A Tale of a Tub*. On the subject of self in Swift he says, "writing is for Swift invariably an expression of self. But Swift does not, like Montaigne, use this perception to sanction the pursuit of self as the most legitimate object of writing. Instead, he attempts to counteract self by attending persistently to its deforming powers. . . . For Swift, self is a standpoint but not necessarily an enclosure."[6]

I shall argue that Swift's early satire, *A Tale of a Tub*, deliberately deconstructs "self" and explodes the idea that writing is "self-expression." The conceptions of a deep-seated internal arena, the locus of truth and font of self-expression, are the products of the new "natural philosophy" and discourse of modernism that are the *targets* of satire in *A Tale*. We have always had difficulty in trying to fit Swift's satire to the binary, moral-emendation model in satire. We have usually solved the problem by assuming that Swift was far in advance of his time, was, indeed, anticipating twentieth-century sensibility. Claude Rawson interestingly suggests that "Swift parodied both Sterne and Beckett in advance. . . . The fact suggests an intuitive understanding of the fragmentation of 'modern' sensibility and of the literary modes that this was to call forth."[7] I shall argue, rather, that Swift was *behind* his times, that (most especially in *A Tale*) his satire is a *throwback* to Restoration deconstructionist satire and for that very reason it resembles postmodernist works like the plays and novels of Beckett, the theoretical experiments of Derrida, and the semiological explorations of Eco.

For a deconstructionist a text "overruns all the limits assigned to it"; it is a *process,* a dubious system of signs having relation without positive terms, that can never arrive at closure, and that operates "to undermine everything that was set up in opposition to writing (speech, the world, the real, history . . .)."[8] The deconstructionist semiotician recognizes no empirical "reality"; there are for him, rather, various systems of signs that simultaneously inscribe and erase conceptual frames, which, because they too are linguistic, are inherently dubious. The task of the deconstructionist, as Gayatri Spivack puts it, is to demonstrate that "a certain view of the world, of consciousness, of language has been accepted as the correct one, and, if the minute particulars of that view are examined, a rather different picture (that is also a no-picture . . .) emerges."[9] That is because the "minute particulars" of the picture which is also no-picture are signs, and "the strange 'being' of the sign" is such that "half of it is always 'not there' and the other half 'not that'. The structure of the sign is determined by the trace or track of that other which is forever absent."[10]

We associate these conceptions with Jacques Derrida, and because Derrida has argued that "the history of the West" depends on "the determination of Being as presence in all senses of the word,"[11] we think of the deconstruction of signs and the discovery of the "not that / not there" component in signs as postmodern phenomena. But Derrida is wrong in asserting that Being = Presence throughout Western history. The presence of absence in the sign is a central principle in medieval language theory, the foundations of which were laid by Saint Augustine.

In *de Doctrina* Augustine says, "Now when I am discussing signs I wish it understood that no one should consider them for what they are but rather for their value as signs which signify something else. A sign is a thing which causes us to think of something beyond the impression the thing makes on our senses."[12] In *de Magistro,* an often playful and brilliantly ironic Socratic dialogue with his son, Adeodatus, Augustine again and again drives his demonstration of the non-identity between sign and referent. He has Adeodatus reduce a sign from a word to a single letter to a gesture—all in order to prove that a sign and its referent *cannot* correspond if a sign is to function as sign. For Augustine a sign—a word *or* thing—is a sign precisely because it indicates to the mind the absent *other-than-itself.* A key example with which he plays is *nihil,* which is *nothing* and is also *not what it signifies* since something is meant by it: "Instead of saying *nihil* signifies something which is nothing, shall we not say that this word signifies a certain state of mind when failing to perceive a reality, the mind finds, or thinks it finds, that such a reality does not exist?"[13] The Scriptures themselves, because they are words/signs, cannot designate knowable truth absolutely. Once written, once filtered through the mouth and mind of man, the word of God itself enters the inevitably dubious semiotic system and therefore cannot have positive value. In Book XI of the *Confessions* Augustine speculates upon this matter:

> Moses wrote this . . . [that God created heaven and earth]. He wrote it and went away; he passed hence . . . and now is not before me. For, if he were, I should hold him, and beg him, and beseech him through Thee to throw these words open before me. I would offer the ears of my body to the sounds bursting forth from his mouth. If he were to speak in Hebrew, it would impinge upon my sense to no avail, nor would any part of it reach my mind, but, if in Latin, I should know what he said. But from what source would I know whether he told the truth? And, if I did know even this, would I come to know it from him?[14]

Like any postmodern semiotician, Augustine allows for the *real presence* only of language: "nothing has been found, as yet, that can be shown by means of itself, excepting language, which, among other things which it signifies, signifies also itself: which yet, because itself is symbol, shows nothing that stands out clearly that can be taught without means of symbols."[15] For the medieval as for the postmodern philosopher everything that is perceived is a sign; all signs refer only and inevitably to other signs; and, inherent in the sign is the absent "other," the "not that" and "not there": "The play of difference supposes in effect syntheses and referrals which forbid at *any* moment, or in any sense that a simple element be *present* in and of itself, referring only to itself. Whether in the order of spoken or written discourse, no element can function as a sign without referring to another element which itself is not simply present."[16]

The persistent and pervasive influence of Augustinian thought in late seventeenth-century England has been so often and so amply demonstrated that it hardly needs to be reviewed here. Seventeenth-century writers knew Augustine so well that they quite often conducted their own philosophical speculations in conversation with him. And, most interestingly for our purposes here, Restoration writers frequently used Augustinian

semiotics to subvert both the materialist philosophy coming to dominance in their own day and the essentialist philosophy that was their inheritance from Augustine's time, the Middle Ages. Let me give a rather
complicated example of what I believe to be a three-way seventeenth-
century conversation with Augustine.

In the *Confessions* Augustine, in his usual brilliantly ironic manner, speculates upon the construct time and, in speculating upon it, erases it:

> What then is time? . . . if nothing passed away there would be no past time; if
> nothing were coming there would be no future time; if nothing were existing
> there would be no present time. Then, how do those two periods of time, the
> past and the future, exist, when the past is already not existing, and the future
> does not yet exist? And again, the present would not pass away into the past, if
> it were always present. . . . So, if the present, in order to be time, must be such
> that it passes over into the past, then, how can we say that it *is*; for the sole
> reason for its existence is the fact that it will stop being, that is to say, can we
> not truly say that time *is* only because it inclines not to be?[17]

Hobbes responds to Augustine from a materialist's perspective: "The *present*
only has being in Nature; things *past* have a being in memory only, but
things *to come* have no being at all."[18]

Rochester, in turn, uses the Augustinian reduction of temporality to
nothing and also uses the Hobbesian idea of *real* present to undermine the
constructs—self, love, and constancy—that convention, particularly the
linguistic constructs of pastoral literature, has written upon our consciousness.

I

All my past life is mine no more,
The flying hours are gone.
Like Transitory Dreams giv'n o'er
Whose images are kept in store
By Memory alone.

II

The Time that is to come is not;
How can it then be mine?
The present Moment's all my Lot;
And that, as fast as it is got,
Phillis is only thine.

III

Then talk not of Inconstancy,
False Hearts, and broken Vows;

> If I, by Miracle, can be
> This live-long Minute true to thee,
>   'Tis all that Heav'n allows.[19]

Consider the valences of this "conversation." Rochester is Augustinian in that he erases the construct time. Rochester is also Hobbesian in that he centers the only possible apprehension of time in the present moment. But the confluence of Augustinian and Hobbesian lines do not mingle in Rochester's poem; rather, they cancel one another out. Rochester goes a step further than Augustine in erasure. The discourse of both Augustine and Hobbes suggests an observer, a speaking "I." With greater comic irony than Augustine, Rochester *locates* inconstancy, or, more properly speaking, locates the collapse of temporality, in an "I" who is also "not-I," since, like all other entities, it has no duration in time.

> this ending makes of the lines a decisive handing over of the self to some unknown quantity, the "present" being only a knowledge of what is unknown. And this . . . self-offering is . . . able to suggest the perpetual existence of self as in a void, created from moment to moment as a poem is from line to line. For the poet of "Life and Love" has, by definition, nothing at all to call his own—neither past nor future, nor any present that he knows, beyond that Miracle of the poem's live-long Minute.[20]

Nothing exists except writing and the reader's response to an absolutely "open text."

For Augustine there are no things, only signs out of which the imperfect human mind creates and deconstructs fragile designs that are in no way reflective of the distant realm of pure Idea. There is no present "here." For Hobbes, and the "natural philosophers" of the Restoration (as in the motto of the Royal Society) there are "no Ideas but in Things." Hobbes's "present" has existence only because it exists in Nature, and is therefore empirically verifiable, for Nature—solid, material, changeless—is everything, and all that is. "The whole mass of all things that are, is corporeal, that is to say, body . . . also every part of body, is likewise body, and hath the like dimensions; and consequently every part of the universe, is body, and that which is not body, is no part of the universe: and because the universe is all, that which is no part of it is *nothing*; and consequently nowhere."[21] Restoration deconstructive satire made that "nothing" and "nowhere" its province. The deconstructive discourse of zero point used Augustinian semiotics to demonstrate the conventional nature of language and thereby to call all constructs, all laws, all values, all concepts—like "reason," "mind," or "truth"—into doubt.

However, for Augustine that illumination of "truth which presides over the mind itself from within"[22]—which *cannot* be captured by signs, but rather, whose existence can be inferred *only by the process of dismantling signs*—comes from God. Even the twelfth-century "radicalized sign theory" of Abelard, which "relegated to the realm of the contingent, relative, and historically determined that which once partook of the necessary, absolute, and eternal,"[23] left intact the unknowable, mysteriously centered, ordained cosmos. All signs, contingent as they are, by the very absence inherent in them, point toward that invisible, mysterious center, which alone is full. In the Restoration period, "an ordered world based on universally acknowledged laws [was] being replaced by a world based on ambiguity" in which "directional centers are missing and . . . values and dogma are constantly being placed in question."[24] Like twentieth-century post-structuralist thought, Restoration zero point confronts the emergence of a multivalue logic that *incorporates* "indeterminacy as a valid stepping stone in the cognitive process."[25] As Barbara Everett puts it, "The 1660s and 1670s . . . were something of a cultural no man's land, a pause in time equally out of touch with the past and the future, the medieval and the modern."[26]

Paul de Man has defined two kinds of irony that to my mind can be useful in distinguishing the two kinds of satire that were produced by the two discourses competing for dominance at the moment of epistemological rupture with which I am concerned. Both ironies arise out of a perception of difference. However, in the one case the difference is intersubjective; that is, it occurs "in terms of the superiority of one subject over another, with all the implications of will to power, of violence, and possession which come into play when a person is laughing at someone else— including the will to educate and improve." This, in my view, is the ironic perspective invoked by the discourse of modernism and the late Restoration and eighteenth-century satire it produced. The second irony which de Man discriminates differentiates the self from the world and "transforms the *self* out of the empirical world into a world constituted out of and in language."[27] That dislocated self thereby "exists only in the form of a language that asserts knowledge of . . . [its own] inauthenticity," and "before long the entire texture of the self is unravelled."[28] This is the ironic perspective evoked by Restoration deconstructive satire.

Restoration satire, which for so long was thought to be realistic, grossly physical, even pornographic, is, on the contrary, the most literary of modes. It exists nowhere but in language, for it is both *of* and *in* language. The collisions, the ruptures that it effects are among words, genres, and mental constructs to whose inauthenticity it calls constant attention. Moreover, this satire is most exemplary of what Eco calls the "open work" in that it makes complicit in its own deconstructive operations the mind and memory of the reader. And, because it does so, it calls "mind" itself into question and "brings to a crisis [its] relation with language."

Because we have so long believed Restoration satire to be mimetic and assumed in it a binary form that brings into collision an idealized antithesis and a thesis, which, however downwardly exaggerated, images the *real,* we have taken its fictional libertine personae, the grotesque goings-on in St. James's Park that it figures, or the prodigious sexual performances of King "Sardanapalus" as "real," as exaggerated but nonetheless reliable records of the degenerate times of Good King Charles's Golden Days. Indeed, biographers have invariably used events and images derived entirely from the literary products of their authors to construct their "lives."[29] For example, Willard Connelly's *Brawny Wycherley* is no more than a reconstituted "Plain Dealer," while the "real" Rochester is a more variously patched product, a combination of his own "Disabled Debauchee," Burnet's sinner reclaimed, and the literary imaginings of his dramatist contemporaries—a "Count Rosidore" or "Dorimant."[30] I have no quarrel with these biographers. I know from experience that there is simply not enough reliable, verifiable evidence from the Restoration period to produce a biographical narrative that could possibly pass for a "transparent record of documented knowledge." My interest in establishing the fictionality of the "real" and artifactuality of "truth" in Restoration satire is not aimed at discrediting work that has been done, but at demonstrating the semiotic, deconstructionist nature of Restoration satire.

The problem that such a project raises is this: after three hundred years there is no "real" that is not a fiction. Since any event or circumstance, once narrated, of necessity becomes fictionalized, and since the Restoration period especially has accrued to itself very highly colored, markedly biased imaging, it is not possible to extract a "real" representation of the times that is not tainted by literary conventions. How then to demonstrate that a Restoration satire *does not* put into collision an upwardly exaggerated fictional ideal and a downwardly exaggerated real (such as we find in an eighteenth-century satire)? How then to prove that the oppositions effected in a Restoration satire are among *equally fictional* constructs, and are designed to effect a *semiotic crisis* in the mind of the reader? An opponent of my argument might well ask, "Why isn't the extravagantly perverse sexual activity in 'A Ramble in St. James's Park' what really happened there? Why isn't the Whitehall of *The Plain Dealer* a perhaps exaggerated but nevertheless accurate depiction of the Whitehall of 1676? Who are you to say that Oldham's 'Cunt was the Star that rul'd [Sardanapalus's] fate' is not an exaggerated but an accurate assessment of the sensibility of the real Charles II?"

Dustin Griffin's brilliant book, *Satires against Man,* especially in its conversations with the invaluable work of David Vieth, can open a path that may enable us to deal with this problem. For instance, Griffin sees Rochester's "A Very Heroical Epistle in Answer to Ephelia" *neither* as an attack upon the "real" Mulgrave, the supposed satirical speaker of the poem, *nor* as a simple defense of the libertine philosophy espoused in it. Rather, he understands both Rochester's poem and the poem of Etherege, "Ephelia to Bajazet," to which it gives answer, in the context of the Ovidian model in which both poems exist: "When viewed in this light, as a devilishly cavalier answer to a complaining cast-off mistress, with a tradition of Ovidian love epistles in the background, the poems of Etherege and Rochester form a self-contained whole, requiring no external reference."[31] The point is that neither poem is mimetic; neither refers to "existents external and prior to itself" nor "urges the reader to a truth that appears outside its own border," as Zimmerman would say. Rather, individually and together, they call into question the Ovidian model in the context of which both poems exist; they deconstruct a genre, a mind-set.

Elsewhere in the book Griffin argues that "on one level" Rochester's "A Ramble in St. James's Park" is image-for-image a response to Waller's "On St. James's Park, as Lately Improved by His Majesty" (1661). Griffin says "on one level"; I propose to go further and to argue that not "on one level" only, but always and everywhere the aim of a Restoration deconstructive satire is to present violent collisions among images, genres, linguistic constructs. The effect of these collisions is much like the ending of Ionesco's *The Bald Soprano,* when conventional words and phrases jump out of narrative—almost, indeed, off the stage or page—to engage in senseless, chaotic battle. Even the very simplest "satiric antithesis" in a Restoration satire is never "real," is never mimetic. Whether Fidelia in *The Plain Dealer,* or the lines of Waller that Dorimant so often quotes, or the invisible Waller washtint pastoral fluttering behind "A Ramble in St. James's Park," in a Restoration satire satiric antithesis is 1) *always* literary and remote, and 2) *never* a behavioral norm from which satiric thesis measures deviation.

Earl Miner once said of Dryden's satire, "Between the cities of satire and those of Utopia there exists a real city; . . . Dryden [called] that reality 'nature.'"[32] However, much of Dryden's later satire, and most especially his theoretical *A Discourse Concerning the Original and Progress of Satire* (1695), are products of the new discourse and epistemology of modernism. As I shall later attempt to demonstrate, Dryden's practice of the 1680s and, most certainly, his late essay reflect the constructive movement at zero point, the emergence of a new language, a new conception of mind, "natural reason," a new conception of the "self," the Nation, the world. That is perhaps why we feel comfortable talking about "The Age of Dryden, Pope, and Swift," whereas we would be distinctly uneasy calling it "The Age of Rochester, Pope, and Swift" or "Wycherley, Pope, and Swift" even though both Wycherley and Rochester were thought by their contemporaries to be greater satirists than Dryden.[33] My argument is that in a Restoration deconstructive satire "between the cities of satire and those of Utopia there exists" *Nothing*. The collison among genres in a Restoration deconstructive satire are not designed to show us "nature"; they are designed to show us that we are "whore[s] in understanding."

To demonstrate this point let me take for preliminary analysis a rather simple example, Rochester's "Song," "Fair Chloris in a pigsty lay." Antithesis is established in the very first line of the poem between the supersensuous airy realm of pastoral and the gross arena of satire by the very words "Chloris" and "pigsty." The dichotomy runs in continuous contrast through the fabric of the poem. Pastoral images ("snowy arms," "ivory pails," "love-convicted swain"), pastoral rhetoric ("Fly nymph! Oh fly ere 'tis too late"), and pastoral dream vision are syntactically intertwined with "murmuring gruntlings," a lover who "throws himself upon" his mistress, a rape, and finally, among the "murmuring pigs," a masturbation. We slip from the wash-tint realm of pastoral landscape—which exists *nowhere but in our minds,* in the invisible horizon of expectation that the words "Fair Chloris" call up—into the *equally fictional* realm of libertine erotica:

> She hears a broken amorous groan
> The panting lover's fainting moan
> Just in the happy minute.

—which, again, exists *not* in the dreaming mind of Chloris, but in the literature-conditioned mind of the reader—and finally, we fall into the pigsty with the autoerotic swineherd. There is no nature here at all; there is simply the clash of literary stereotypes drawn from antithetical literary genres. Well, then, what is the point? Who or what is the target of this little satire? Two loaded words in the last line point the target: "She's *innocent* and *pleased.*" *We* are the targets of this little satiric song. It is the mind of the reader at which the poet has the last laugh, because that mind is exposed as a storehouse of junky stereotypes. Both our conceptions of innocence and our conceptions of pleasure have been shaped in us by empty words, by creaky literary constructs. That place in ourselves that we value so highly, the mind, is a windy, empty attic stored with nothing but whimsies spun out of words.

Michael Seidel has argued that "history covers up so that events proceed legally," while "satire creates a frenzy around points of terminus, penetrates to elaborate moments of regression where origins are ends and where . . . all efforts to continue come to nothing."[34] This is not true of all satire; much eighteenth-century satire, like Young's *The Love of Fame* (1725) for instance, is the very handmaiden of historical cover-up. However, Seidel does here describe admirably the deconstructive collapse of "zero point": Imperial Rome under Nero, Caligula and Domitian; Restoration England; and late twentieth-century America. There is such a striking similarity among these three "points of terminus" that I believe the procedure I shall adopt in demonstrating the semiotics of Restoration deconstructive satire is justified, though I admit that it is highly unorthodox in a scholarly examination of this kind. To my mind the best way to overcome the difficulty of establishing the fictionality of what we have supposed to be the Restoration "real" from a three hundred years' distance is to analyze the semiotic operation of a late twentieth-century "toward zero" satire as a step preliminary to analyzing a Restoration satire that employs the same methods. My examples for analysis will be Mel Brooks's *Blazing Saddles* and Rochester's "A Ramble in St. James's Park."

"Satire is all our own," Quintilian said.[35] That is because satire is a public discourse, a city mode. It was invented when Rome was the center of power of the whole known world. *Blazing Saddles* was made when America came to be the modern Rome: the superpower, the guardian of Western values. And just as surely as the *Aeneid* shapes the great cultural myth of the Eternal City, won after arduous trial and pilgrimage, wrought by divine destiny and providence, so too does the American Western movie shape the American cultural myth of origins: the Nation won out of the "wilderness" by Pilgrims in arduous trial, guided by "manifest destiny" and the hand of God to stretch "from sea to shining sea." At the simplest level *Blazing Saddles* is simply a mock-heroic poem that laughs at our nationalistic pretensions. But it is far more than that; closer inspection reveals it to be a deconstructionist satire, which, like all zero point satire, explodes the foundational constructs that comprise our culture: mind, reality, truth. Like "A Ramble" or any of the other Restoration satires we shall examine, *Blazing Saddles* is a "system where the central signified, the original or transcendental signified, is never absolutely present outside a system of differences."[36] There is no historical reality which it parodies; it exists in a system of differences from, and parallels and referrals to, other fictional, dubious sign systems.

We will recall that deconstruction demonstrates that "a certain view of the world, of consciousness, of language has been accepted as the correct one, and if the minute particulars of that view are examined a very different picture (that is also a no–picture . . .) emerges."[37] It is in its manner of examining the minute particulars of the picture that is also no–picture that *Blazing Saddles* reveals its deconstructionist intent. Let us take for example the very opening scenelet. Railroad track is being laid by a work gang of African- and Asian-Americans. Many are dropping in the heat of the sun, and an Asian who has fainted will be docked of his pay for sleeping on the job. On the surface the satire of this scenelet operates merely to contradict the horizon of expectation conditioned in us by the Western: 1) that the opening of the West was the heroic fulfillment of manifest destiny; 2) that the hardy pioneers who opened it, sons of the founding fathers, were good, heroic folk inspired by American democratic values. The equation at surface level is simple and binary: the West was opened not by home-spun pioneers, but by greedy, corporation power brokers. But, because it is a deconstructionist enterprise, *Blazing Saddles* opens the "minute particulars" of this simple contrast to view. The scenelet goes further than mock-heroic parody. The White gang bosses ride up and ask the Black workers why they are not singing spirituals: Stereotype 1 = the happy slave singing with joy as he works in the master's fields. Then the bosses ask the workers to sing a song composed by a White man in Black dialect, "De Camptown Races," and when the workers do not know the song, the bosses demonstrate—singing, clapping, and jigging in "darky" style: Stereotype 2 = the White mental image of Blacks is a White construct unknown to Blacks. The Black men finally agree to sing for the entertainment of their oppressors, and they render a Jazz Quartet version of "I get no kick from champagne." Stereotype 3 = Black people are more sophisticated and cool than Whites. (This stereotype is reinforced when the newly deputized Sheriff Bart appears in a Rodeo Drive outfit, complete with Gucci saddlebag.) In this small bit of business what is satiric antithesis? What is "satiric thesis"? Which is "real" or "true"? Where is the "norm of nature" here? There is none. Thesis *and* antithesis; expectation *and* the confounding of expectation; upward exaggeration (hypsos) *and* downward exaggeration (bathos) are all and equally empty stereotypes. Moreover, even among the stereotypes binary opposition is never constant, never fixed.

Like all great satires, *Blazing Saddles* aims particularly at the pillars of culture: authority and morality. The governor, for example, is a grotesquely exaggerated lecher, incompetent to govern because, like Sardanapalus, "Cunt [is his] sole Bus'ness and Affair of State." But the satiric treatment of the governor is not merely a mock-heroic, King-Fool binary opposition. Rather, the movie's imaging of authority calls attention to its own semiotic process and, consequently, extends beyond the simple disequation governor ≠ John Wayne to expose the emptiness of the "literary" conventions involved in our representations of authority. For instance, the public relations companies that shape the American consciousness of candidates for political office invariably picture candidates with their spouses and families. In America, as in Imperial Rome, the honor and reputation of a citizen depends upon his being a *paterfamilias.* (That is why Naevolus, the bisexual steward in Juvenal's *Satire Nine,* has to work so hard.) By the exaggerated fictionality of its semiosis *Blazing Saddles* mocks the fictionality of the real in American political consciousness. For instance, the presidential campaign of a decade ago, as conducted in television commercials, was a Battle of the Signs worthy of Brooks, or Swift. The image of one candidate riding in a tank gave challenge to that of the other surrounded by American Legionnaires; one candidate kissing his Hispanic grandchild attempted to erase the other as the Ascanius of American immigrant parents; a bronzed clean-living, good-guy Westerner image fell crushed beneath a tabloid photo of a man with a young woman on his knee. And the winner resurrected the "points of light" shining in the heavenly city as a beacon to the barbarians to crown his victory. These fictions shape our consciousness and move us to cast our votes—or, perhaps more accurately, to choose sides— in a continuous game that has neither beginning nor ending, but rather exists in a semiotic field of difference without positive terms.

Blazing Saddles is designed to expose the fictionality of cultural inscriptions which are altogether empty yet are powerful enough to move us to kill one another. There is no "nature," no "reality" in such a satire. Equally fictitious, equally conventional signs collide to expose the emptiness underlying them. Inauthentic constructs erase each other in a continuous process that exists for the sole end of undoing itself. The whole satire unpeels itself to expose fiction after underlying fiction. For example, the villain in the Western is fierce and implacably evil. Here Hedley Lamar, whose name makes him a fiction-in-opposition to the romantic fictional image of the movie glamour queen Hedy Lamar, is an exaggerated sign of the corporation hatchet man. At surface level he is a parody villain; that parodic mask is stripped to reveal a parody capitalist political operator who uses money and sex for gain; that parody falls before an effete little nasty playing with his froggie in the tub; that parody in turn falls to reveal an actor in the lobby of Grauman's Chinese Theater, who is shot/not-shot by another actor in a scene that spills over the borders of its narrative into a parody Busby Berkeley musical set, which, in turn spills into a fictional studio commissary where signs from every movie genre—storm troopers, chorus girls, cowboys, extraterrestrials—collide in pointless battle.

In the same way that authority is not simply overturned but semiotically eradicated, so too is morality. Maria von Schtupp is a parody of the dangerous and irresistible seductress image associated with Marlene Deitrich. On the simplest level the counterfeit mocks the original; the sexuality of romantic obsession is reduced to "They quote Byron and Shelley / Then jump on your belly / And break your balloons." But, as in "Fair Chloris in a pigsty lay," one generic stereotype does not simply cancel another; rather, the collision among *many,* various stereotypes (for example, the racial-erotic cliches subsumed under the cliches of sexual obsession) exposes the vacancy of the cultural consciousness shaped by them.

The climactic action of *Blazing Saddles* if, indeed, a plotless dramatic satire can be said to have one, consists in the exaggeratedly parodic townspeople foiling the exaggeratedly parodic villains by building a false facade replica of their town under the direction of their clever-possum sheriff. This action, itself a sign, is what Keir Elam calls "the gesture of putting on show the very process of semiotization involved in the performance."[38]

The semiotics of *Blazing Saddles* is designed not to attack "real" persons, or to ridicule "real" circumstances or behavior, but to attack our fatal tendency to believe that the empty fictions which govern and shape our consciousness are real. This is a satire entirely *in* and *of* sign, a satire that puts on show the duplicity that makes truth possible, thereby destroying "truth."

Dustin Griffin's analysis of "A Ramble in St James's Park" reads the satire as on one level a response to Edmund Waller's panegyric, "On St. James's Park, as Lately Improv'd by His Majesty" (1661). Griffin considers the satiric thesis in the poem downwardly exaggerated but, nevertheless, realistic, a depiction of things as they were: "Rochester's anti-pastoral satire . . . measures the distance between Waller's old ideal and present reality by parodying the panegyric."[39] I believe, rather, that the relation between Rochester's and Waller's poems is similar to the relation that Griffin observes between Rochester's "Heroical Epistle" and Etherege's "Ephelia to Bajazet" cited earlier. That is, in "A Ramble" Waller's and Rochester's poems speak to each other in the context of the pastoral *locus amoenus* tradition and "require no external referent." That there is, indeed, a St. James's Park and that it was a fashionable meeting place in the 1670s is no more significant to Rochester's satire than the *real* existence of the nineteenth-century American West and the historically verifiable existence of cowboys, settlers, and sheriffs is to *Blazing Saddles.* "A Ramble in St. James's Park" is not the realistic narrative of a libertine's encounter with his faithless mistress in the sexually licentious atmosphere of the park; it is rather a loosely organized collision among a variety of generic models, literary conventions, and mind-sets that assaults both its fictional speaker and its imagined reader as fashion-conditioned, convention-conditioned "whore[s] in understanding."

The title of the poem sets an initial dichotomy that runs as an underlying thread through the fabric of the text. This ramble stands in juxtaposition to Waller's stately romantic "lovers walking in the amorous shade" of a modernized pastoral landscape. However, the subversion of pastoral extends far beyond mere parody of Waller. The whole pastoral tradition of the "sacred grove"—from Virgil to Guarini to Fletcher—is deconstructed by Rochester's "all-sin-sheltering grove." Rochester's "sacred" place is "consecrate to prick and cunt." Here the priest of pastoral, who stands within his bower blessing the innocent shepherd-lovers as they pledge their platonic troths, is his fiction-in-opposition, a Sullen-Satyr figure who "would frig upon his mother's face." Furthermore, Rochester's "lovers" are "walking" to amorous encounters as forced, unnatural, and self-induced as that of their presiding genius.

Thomas E. Maresca has said, "Satire . . . is a protean creature. . . . It is not truly a genre. It actually has no fixed form. . . . It exists in and as flux, as the breakdown of canons or the deconstruction of forms."[40] Once again, I do not believe that this description is applicable to *all* satire, but it is very illuminating indeed of zero point satire, and it is particularly accurate as a description of the deconstructive process which constitutes "A Ramble." Rochester's poem does not measure the distance between the removed scene and style of pastoral and present reality. Rather, it is designed to fracture and subvert the constructs that the "serious" and "respectable" literary genres have written upon our consciousness. It makes chaos of genres, of conventions, of language itself.

Consider, for example, the operation of lines 10-32, which we would *expect* to be the opening of a narrative:

> There by a most incestuous birth,
> Strange woods spring from the teeming earth,
> For they relate how heretofore
> When ancient Pict began to whore,
> Deluded of his assignation
> (Jilting it seems was then in fashion),
> Poor pensive lover, in this place
> Would frig upon his mother's face;
> Whence rows of mandrakes tall did rise
> Whose lewd tops fucked the very skies.
> Each imitative branch does twine
> In some loved fold of Aretine,
> And nightly now beneath their shade

> Are buggeries, rapes, and incests made.
> Unto this all-sin-sheltering grove
> Whores of the bulk and the alcove,
> Great ladies, chambermaids, and drudges,
> The ragpicker, and heiress trudges.
> Carmen, divines, great lords, and tailors,
> Prentices, poets, pimps, and jailers,
> Footmen, fine fops do here arrive,
> And here promiscuously they swive.[41]

The passage begins by exploding the very idea of a "tale" of mythic origins, that is, the origination of the park in the time of the ancient Picts, which is a story "they relate." The mythic ancient priest of nature—in romance a figure who fosters and tends nature's life—is monstrified into a violator of his Mother Earth. Subversion of the cultural myth of origins is succeeded by perversion of the celestial-terrestrial order. Trees fuck skies not just to parody Waller's "bold sons of earth that thrust their arms so high" but also, shockingly, to overthrow our most basic spatial sense, our sense of cosmic order and balance. Having grotesquely inverted the relation of earth and sky, the poem turns to the creation of vegetable chaos. Branches grow deformedly, forcing themselves into Aretinian postures. From the convolution of vegetable nature we move to corresponding unnatural distortions in the human realm—"buggeries, rapes, and incests." Splintering the mirror of nature occurs in an explosive chain of descent: from mythic origins, to cosmos, to vegetable nature, to human nature, and, finally to social chaos: the "promiscuous" mixture of "whores," "chambermaids," "ragpickers," "great lords," "pimps," "footmen," "fops." Ring by ring, circle by circle, we tread the structural design of romance-epic, shattering as we go that highest of genres' claim to truth. In the last seven lines of the passage, as figure upon figure, image after image, pile up helter-skelter, and all the world "promiscuously . . . swive[s]," language itself abandons all pretense at orderly narrative or description. Words collide with words, images with images, in random, atomistic chaos.

Having deconstructed the epic/romance vision of cosmic and earthly *harmonia,* "A Ramble" turns our attention to Cavalier lyric. "When I beheld Corinna pass" constructs in order to deconstruct a perfect miniature Caroline lyric of the kind that in the idyllic age "before the Flood" would have celebrated *precieuse* "Platonick Love" concepts of love and honor. Rochester elegantly *works* the convention before, in the last line, he demolishes it. Lines 33 to 40 are worthy of Lovelace or Suckling. Moreover, the reversal—"But mark what creatures women are: / How infinitely vile when fair"—is itself *conventional*. Think, for instance, of Book II, Canto xii, Stanza 75 of *The Faerie Queene*, wherein a perfect *carpe diem* lyric is completely inverted by the substitution of a single word, "sin," for the word expected, "love." A single word, by confounding the reader's expectation, reverses the generic thrust of the lyric. The object of satire in this passage is not some "real" person, the mistress of Rochester, or of some other "real" libertine. What is at war is not a literary convention and a reality. Rather whole armies of literary conventions are in dubious battle on a darkling plain.

In an almost Aristotelian progression, "A Ramble" moves from the demolition of romance modes and conventions to those of the drama. The three "Knights o' the elbow" are conventional types from Restoration comedy/dramatic satire: the courtier/not-courtier; the Wit-would, who uses postures and language he learns from the stage to seduce his City landlady; and the adolescent Pinocchio-blade, who is learning the lore of his fake mentors. As in a dramatic satire of Etherege or Wycherley, these types are not "characters," not parodies of real social types. They are, rather, linguistic signs. The blades as well as Corinna's response to them are signs of the mental processes "A Ramble" is designed to deconstruct, the process by which the human mind "Converts abortive imitation / To universal affectation." A contemporary example may open the function of these signs to us. Two figures, male and female, execute a series of highly unlikely, highly artificial postures on a television screen. They mouth some unintelligible babble in which the word "obsession" is repeated several times. This enactment of what, in reality, would be a mental disease (obsession) is used as a seductive image of fashionably conceived sexual attractiveness to move the viewer to want to be *like* the figures on screen, empty as they are, and thereby move her to buy Calvin Klein perfume. The viewer is persuaded to this action by "neither head nor tail." Corinna's encounter with the fashionable empty signs of men is designed to expose this process whereby we are moved to act neither by generous "lust" nor by a spontaneous attraction to the Beautiful generated in understanding—neither by body nor by mind, but by empty conventions, by au courant "in" notions of what is sexy. The process corrupts us in body, for we are moved by empty, mutable, cultural inscriptions to enact mechanically and without feeling a natural act that thereby becomes unnatural. It corrupts us in mind, for we force our natures to the contours of empty images as surely as the grotesque St. James's Park trees force themselves into Aretinian postures. The process forces us to *create* the "artifactuality of the real" and to embrace "the fictiveness of truth."

Finally, the poem exposes its libertine speaker as yet another empty

shape, an artifact of literary invention. First, the speaker-libertine is revealed as a false libertine. He uses the language of libertine love lyric—

> When leaning on your faithless breast
> Wrapped in security and rest
> Soft kindness all my powers did move
> And reason lay dissolved in love! [129-132]

to disguise a process as mechanical and unnatural as Corinna's when she
goes off with the blades. The image of swooning lovers is false. By admis-
sion the libertine has been *forcing* to spend himself into what he considers
to be a sink. What is worse, he has used a convention-designed image of
the heroic love mistress to hide his compulsively mechanical action from
his understanding in a veil of language.

However, even to speak of the satiric spokesman of the poem in such
terms is to create a totally false impression of "characterization," of interiority and psychology in a satiric speaker that is, in fact, a linguistic sign, a
wholly conventional *literary* type. The curse that ends the poem discloses
the speaker as a convention centuries old in the native English satiric
tradition. He is the satyr-satirist, a highly complex persona. Tradition determines that this satiric spokesman 1) is guilty of the very vice he castigates, 2) uses language as a weapon because he is impotent to act, and 3) in
the act of cursing becomes what he hates. In "A Ramble" 's final curse the
extravagant, lashing language of the speaker is a substitute for action. Like
his enemy, he is a "whore in understanding," and he wills for the other—
insatiable longing that must turn to wild despair—the essential quality of
the libertinism he represents. "A Ramble in St. James's Park" ends by erasing the speaking "I," by demonstrating that the speaker exists nowhere but
in language, is a product solely *of* language.

THREE

No "I" and No "Eye"

I. "Author," "Speaker," "Character"
in Restoration Deconstructive Satire

Despite the warning Maynard Mack gave us over forty years ago we continue to labor under the misconception that the writer of satire and the speaker of satire are the same, or at least that the speaker reflects some aspects of the writer's "personality."[1] But the speaker of satire is a rhetorical strategy—whether, as in Restoration satire, s/he is a target, a mask, an empty space, or by turns all three; or whether, as in eighteenth-century satire, he is "I," a like-minded man of reason and common sense. The eighteenth-century concerned citizen, who stands at the center of a satire and whose aim is the reformation of real social ills, is, after all, an invention of discourse. However, that figure replaced an equally rhetorical but much more complex figure which had developed over centuries in native English satiric discourse and which was the Restoration writer's inheritance from Renaissance practitioners: the maddened, often morally deformed satyr-satirist, who hurls invective at his enemy to kill him, not to correct his morals or manners. We rarely look further back than Dryden for an understanding of what English satire is, and, as Johnson said, "Dryden may be properly considered as the father of English criticism, [because he was] . . . the writer who first taught us to determine upon *principles* the merit of composition" (ital. mine).[2]

Because Dryden aimed in his late essay, *Concerning the Original and Progress of Satire,* to establish principles of composition for satire—to make it a respectable, classical genre, a subspecies of epic—he repudiated the native tradition in satire. In turn, because we look back to Dryden as our seminal critical source, we respond to English satire of the medieval and Renaissance periods using Dryden's ideal model, a form produced by the *constructive* discourse of modernism which is concerned with existents external to the text and is designed to order the world and order the reader. Therefore we conceive of the satiric speaker of all satire—including premodern Renaissance satire—as an authorial "I." For example, Ian Donaldson assumes that the angry speaker of Ben Jonson's satire is Ben Jonson the man: "In invoking this unamiable tradition [of Archilochus, the killer-with-words] Jonson reveals an aspect of his own temperament and genius about which modern criticism has chosen to remain silent. We hear more nowadays of Jonson's rationality, self-containment and moral composure than of his anger and excess."[3]

Setting aside the more fundamental issue of whether there are not as many "Ben Jonsons" as there are genres in which he wrote—which is my view—we need only to compare Jonson's satire with that of his contemporaries (Marston, Wither, Hall, or Donne) to discover that the speaker in satire of the early seventeenth century is a trope, not a subject. Consider, for instance, the speaker of Jonson's "Apologetic Dialogue to the Reader," prefatory to *The Poetaster:*

> They know, I dare
> To spurne, or baffull 'em or squirt their eyes
> With inke or urine; or I could do worse,
> Armed with Archilochus' fury, write *Iambicks*
> Should make the desperate lashers hang themselves.
> Rime 'hem to death, like *Irish* rats
> In drumming tunes. Or living I could stampe
> Their foreheads with those deep and publick brands
> That the whole Company of *Barber Surgeons*
> Should not take off with all their art and playsters.[4]

The "speaker" here is a conventional figure that had been embedded in satiric discourse for at least two hundred years before Jonson wrote and is commonplace in late Renaissance verse satire. It is the mask that Hall, who mistakenly called himself the first English satirist, assumes when he writes his last three books of "byting satyres" (as opposed to his first three of "toothlesse satyres"), which he says "doth resemble the sour and crabbed face of Iuvenals."[5] The speaker's rage in Jonson's preface, therefore, is not that of the historical Jonson, but is an attribute of an emblematic figure, a linguistic sign, that of the "sharp fang'd" satyr-satirist, the same speaker we find in Marston's *The Scourge of Villanie:*

> My soul is vext, what power will't desist?
> Or dares to stop a sharp fang'd Satyrist?
> Who'll coole my rage? Whole stay my itching fist,
> But I will plague and torture whom I liste?[6]

Ira, rage unto uncontrollable madness, is called into play by the speaker as appropriate to the genre which he speaks, satire. Marston's speaker says,

>   my vexed thoughtfull soule,
> Takes pleasure, in displeasing sharpe controule . . .
> *Ingenious Melancholy*, take thy gloomy seate,
> Inthrone thee in my blood. Let me intreate.
> Stay his [the soul's, or poetic imagination's] quicke iocond skips,
> and force him runne
> A sad pac'd course, until my *whips* [the satirist's "rods"] be done.[7]

Moreover, Marston the poet makes it quite clear that the decorum of a particular poetic genre, and not his own "vexed soul," determines his raging discourse: "I will not deny that there is a seemly decorum to be observed, and a peculiar kind of speech for a Satyres lips, which I can willinglier conceive, then dare to prescribe; yet let me have the substance rough."[8] Similarly, Jonson the critic tells us that it is *poetry*—the genre, satire, and satiric discourse itself—that determines the angry, death-dealing "personality" of the satiric spokesman: "Shee [poetry] shall out of just rage incite her servants (who are *genus irritabile*) to spoute inke in their faces, that shall eate farder then their marrow, into their fames; and not *Cinnamus* the barber [an inhabitant of Juvenal's fictional Rome, not of Jonson's seventeenth century England] with his arte shall be able to take out the brands, but they shall live and be read, 'til the wretches die, as things worst deserving of themselves, in chiefe, and then of all mankind."[9] The enraged speaker of satire of the early seventeenth century, then, is an emblematic figure, a trope. As Raman Selden says, "Never has the satirist's persona declared itself so boldly as a fictional product, a reworking and development of a literary type."[10]

This raging satyr-satirist has a long and, I think, quite interesting history. There are two schools of thought regarding the origins of native English satire. One holds that the earliest English satire is goliardic—witty and gay. This joyful tradition, it is supposed, held sway until the fourteenth century when pulpit satirists, religious and social reformers following the manner of Saint Jerome and his idol, Juvenal, overwhelmed the good-natured native satire with their *saeva indignatio*. The second school, taking a longer view, rests its theory on the supposition of a relation between ancient English and Celtic satire (recall Jonson's lines on rhyming Irish rats to death). This school maintains that cruel and bitter satire is of native growth and finds its earliest English expression in the *niding* verses and *bismeorleod* of the Anglo-Saxon poet-magician. The aim of the first English satirists, this theory asserts, is the literal word-death or disfigurement of an enemy; the ancient satirist, it is supposed, was able "to destroy his victim flesh and bone, nerve and sinew, his victim's hounds, cattle, pigs, wife and children. . . . In other instances he meant to mutilate his victim's face so shamefully that he could hold no tribal office."[11]

As we have seen in both Marston and Jonson, the convention that language is a weapon that can kill or mutilate a victim's face and fame is deeply embedded in the discourse of satire. It is a generic determinant throughout the seventeenth century and remains strongly present in Restoration deconstructive satire. For example, we find deep traces of the ancient destroyer with words in the libertine-speaker's curse upon his faithless mistress in "A Ramble in St. James's Park"; in Manly's curse upon Olivia in *The Plain Dealer* (and, indeed, her relishing the curse as a malediction upon which witches thrive); and most strikingly in Oldham's "A Satyr upon a Woman," the last sixty lines of which are a single curse:

> I come to haunt her with the ghosts of wit
> My ink starts out, and flies on her,
> Like blood upon some touching murderer;
> And should that fail, rather than want I would,
> Like hags, to curse her, write in my own blood . . .
> Ye spiteful powers . . .
> Assist with malice and your mighty aid
> My sworn revenge, and help me rhyme her dead!
> Grant I may fix such brands of infamy,
> So plain, so deeply graved on her, that she
> Her skill, patches, nor paint, all joined can hide,
> And which shall lasting as her soul abide.[12]

By the fourteenth century satiric discourse found a new arena, the pulpit, and in consequence the persona of the satiric speaker was enriched and then problematized. When his stage became the pulpit the satirist's rage became generalized as *contemptus mundi,* his bitter cruelty justified as a necessary scalpel to cut away the disease of sin. The goliardic strain (probably Norman in origin) disappeared entirely from English satire: "If the [late fourteenth-century] satirist ever laughs at all, it is with a fierce laughter that bursts out suddenly without warning here and there, filled often with a spirit of mad exasperation and reckless despair."[13]

Curiously, however, while the fierce word-killer satirist emblem is ever more firmly established in the satiric discourse of the fourteenth century, the figure is also fractured and problematized. Satiric discourse comes to be double-edged, exposing its victim and its speaker at the same time. Duplicity enters into the figure of the satirist-reformer and complicates it. Chaucer's pulpit satirist, the Pardoner, provides a very good example of the complexity which the type achieved by the end of the fourteenth century. As a satirist-reformer, the official, declared ministry of a pulpit orator should be to scourge sin, and the force and efficacy of the lashing, abusive language Chaucer gives his Pardoner to speak is undeniable. His words, we learn, *do* reform his audience, but that reformation is an accidental effect, as "many a predicioun / Cometh ofte of yvel entencioun."[14] His "real intention" (and we must keep in mind that "he" and "real intention" are rhetorical strategies in a poem), the speaker says, is "to ben avaunced by ypocrisie," for "veyne glorie," and "for hate." In the process of the Pardoner's "self-disclosure," satiric discourse becomes exceedingly complex and multivalenced. We discover that language is this satirist's weapon *not* as he is a wielder of word-magic, but rather *because* he is impotent to attack by other means:

> For whon I dar noon other weyes debate
> Thanne wol I stynge hym with my tonge smerte
> In prechying ... [412-414]

Chaucer (whom Marston links with Persius and Juvenal in acknowledging his masters)[15] radically problematizes the persona, the satiric speaker. Like that of his predecessors, this speaker's language is sheer violence; reform is not his object but his mask: "Thus spitte I out my venym under hewe / Of holynesse, to semen hooly and trewe." Moreover the speaker is guilty particularly of the sins he attacks, and, more complicated still, he attacks them because he is incapable of enjoying them. The final effect of this process of problematization is a conception of linguistic attack as a *substitute for* action. The fifteenth-century Mystery Cycle Plays enlarged still further upon the highly complex satirist persona by making the most voluble and rhetorically brilliant speaker of satire the Father of Lies— who, doomed by his own sin, trapped in Hell and paralyzed, unable to release himself from his condition, uses language to bring others into it.

Operating upon one of the most fruitful etymological errors in the history of English writing, Renaissance humanists embroidered upon the multifaceted figure they had inherited in a most interesting way. In his preface to the works of Terence (used universally in Elizabethan schools), Donatus made the error of deriving the word "satire" from the Greek *satyros* rather than from the Latin *satura*.[16] Extrapolating from that error, he traced the origin of satire to the Greek satyr play. And thereby hangs a tale. A whole mythical history sprouted from the germ of an etymological error which conceived of the earliest satire as verbal attack delivered upon an audience by actors disguised as satyrs. And upon that "story" layer upon elaborative layer grew. For example, the very influential Elizabethan critic, Henry Puttenham, in his *Arte of English Poesie* (1589), provides not just "intention" but motivation for the satiric speaker's assumption of a satyr mask:"the first and most bitter invective against vice and vicious men was the Satyre: which to th'intent their bitterness should breed none ill-will ... and besides making their admonitions more efficacie, they made wise as if the gods of the woods, whom they called Satyres or Silvanes should appear and recite those verses of rebuke."[17]

The image of the satyr, superimposed upon the existent medieval satiric speaker, heightened certain facets of that already complex figure. The satirist's sadistic pleasure in hurting his victims, suggested in the Pardoner, is more deeply engraved when the "sharp-fanged" beast-man's features are added to it; as Thomas Lodge says, "those monsters [satyrs] were then as our parasites [court fools] are now adayes, such as with pleasure reprehend abuses."[18] More interesting still, attributing the purposeful assumption of a satyr's disguise, a mask, to the figure emphasized the duplicity already inherent in it. Renaissance writers of satire repeatedly call attention to the speaker's doubleness:"Though in shape I seem a man / Yet a satyr wilde I am." Add to the mixture the uncontrollable lechery traditionally associated with the satyr in pastoral and romance and the mask-face disparity assumes yet greater significance: bestial lust, it is assumed, is what the mask is hiding. By the Renaissance the hypocrisy and lust of the medieval figure becomes the satiric speaker's most salient characteristic:

> An Executioner am I
> Of Lust and Wanton Venery.
> Thus are vices scourged by me
> Yet myself from vice not free.
> Like to Sumners that cite others
> When themselves defile their mothers.[19]

When we apprehend the outlines of this early seventeenth-century speaker figure just below the surface of the "Libertine" "Character" (which is itself the product of a particular mode in discourse) we can begin to appreciate the rhetorical complexity of a narrator like that in "A Ramble in St. James's Park."

My object in providing this capsule history of the "speaker" in native English satire has been to demonstrate its fictionality. However, what is most interesting is to discover that this fiction, this product of language, which exists nowhere but *in* language, comes to *produce* language. As we have seen, Marston among others was quite sharply aware of the "decorum" that governs the particular kind of speech suitable to a "Satyres lips." The satyr-satirist speaker, engendered *in* and *by* satiric discourse, in turn engenders the kind of discourse demanded by the genre, satire. A self-reflexivity, or logical circularity comes into being: that is, this is the language suitable to a satyr's lips/*and also*/ this discourse—by its coarseness, by its marked instability, by the rough irregularity of its cadences—reveals itself to be satire. What is certain is that language and language alone generates satire; there *is no* external existent signified by it.

It is this self-contained, self-generating and self-reflexive property of poetic language that makes seventeenth-century writers of satire prefer Persius—for his "obscurity"—and Juvenal—for his irregularity, his "abundance," and his violent collisions of idiom—to Horace—with his soft-toned, urbane, and rational speaker, "I." "*Juvenal,*" says Henry Peachum in 1622, "of Satyrists is the best. In his Satyres [Horace] is quicke, round and pleasant; and as nothing so bitter, so not so satyrical as *Juvenal.*"[20] The sentiment is echoed again and again by early Restoration writers, for whom the Juvenalian style is the ideal model in satire. (Even when a Restoration satirist is writing an "Imitation" of a particular Horatian satire he will use the Juvenalian style—see, for example, Oldham or Rochester.) "I do not think great smoothness is required in a *Satyr,* which ought to have a *severe* kind of *roughness* as most fit for *reprehension,* and not that gentle *smoothness* which is necessary to *insinuation,*" writes Shadwell.[21] Robert Gould praises Oldham in a passage that not only clearly demonstrates the interpenetration of genre and discourse I have described above, but also indicates that it is that circularity between genre and discourse that explains the Restoration deconstructive writer's preference for Juvenal over Horace:

> How wide shoot they, that strive to blast thy Fame,
> By saying that thy verse was rough and lame;
> They would have Satyr by Compassion move,
> And writ so plyant nicely and so smooth,
> As if the Muse were in a Flux of Love:
> But who of Knaves, and Fops, and Fools would Sing
> Must Force and Fire and Indignation bring
> For 'tis no Satyr if it has no Sting.
> In short, who in that Field would Famous be,
> Must think and write like Juvenal and thee.[22]

Even Dryden, who in his later works reflects the beginning of a turn from Juvenal to Horace as favored stylistic model, and whose late *Original and Progress of Satire* is a critical milestone on the path to the new conception of satire—formal, mimetic, binary, "respectable"—recognizes the dominance of Juvenal in his own time and links the Ancient satirist with Wycherley: "Juvenal is a more vigorous and masculine wit [than Horace], he drives his reader along with him. . . . When he gives over it is a sign the subject is exhausted and the wit of man can carry it no further. *If a fault* can justly be found in him, it is that he is too luxuriant, too redundant, says more than he needs, like my friend The Plain Dealer, but never more than pleases" (ital. mine).[23] That Dryden considers *ira* and abundance a possible "fault" in 1690 indicates that the triumph of the analytico-referential discourse of modernism is complete and the binary, mimetic model in satire securely in place.

The magnetic attraction between the seventeenth-century satyr-satirist speaker and his Juvenalian model, as well as the circularity of determination between speaker and discourse have still greater significance. As Howard Weinbrot says, "Horatian satire affirms stability and the triumph of cogent but not haranguing argument between rational men."[24] Most usually the Horatian speaker and adversarius, easily distinguishable, *demonstrate* their rationality by the logical progression of their argument. Not so a Juvenalian satire. The abundance, the redundancy, the abrupt transitions and idiomatic instability, the furious, seemingly irrational pace of a satire by Juvenal proclaim satire's self-referential, linguistically self-contained nature. A Juvenalian satire is not a "cogent . . . argument between rational men"; it is a semiotic battleground. In a Juvenalian satire it is *language itself* that is in violent and always dubious turmoil. *Language,* rampant and vigorous, makes war with itself. Moreover, Juvenal uses every conceivable rhetorical device in the classical repertoire: thesis, apostrophe, exclamation, example, aphorism, question, anaphora, analepsis, in copious and chaotic abundance. Here is a *lanx satura* with a vengeance. Consequently, in the dialogue (if we can reasonably call it that) of a Juvenalian satire it is impossible to distinguish among speakers, or, indeed, to determine whether a speaker is directly addressing the reader, whether a speaker is exclaiming in wild apostrophe, or whether he is talking to himself—or, quite often, whether *all* of the above are not occurring in rapid, tumultuous succession. While the predominant idioms in a Juvenalian satire are the lofty, "literary" heroic, and the low, obscene vulgar, these two modes do not exist in constant or binary relation. As Selden says, "satiric effects are derived from the clash of styles and the resulting incongruity."[25] However, the clash itself is not simply a collision of binary opposites. It is more nearly an explosion in many directions.

The point is that Juvenalian satire is literary, self-reflexive, "open" in Eco's sense of an "open text," and, precisely because it is so, it *deconstructs* its speaker, the "I." Curiously, therefore, the satiric discourse that is generically *demanded* by the "speaker" of seventeenth-century satire *erases* that speaker. Like the Juvenalian style it incorporated, seventeenth-century satire is multivocal, heteroglossic, and dialogic. Its multiplicity of voices, clashing and jangling, issue as from a many-throated, carnivalesque crowd:

> Welcome all eyes, all eares, *all tongues to me,* [ital. mine]
> Gnaw peasants on my scraps of Poesie.
> Castilos, Cyprians, court-boyes, spanish blocks
> Ribanded eares, grenado-netherstocks,
> Fidlers, Scriveners, pedlars, tynkering knaves,
> Base blew-coats, tapsters, broad-cloath minded slaves
> Welcome I-fayth, but you may ne'er depart
> Till I have made your gauled hides to smart.[26]

Marston's many-tongued crowd—sometimes targets, sometimes speakers, sometimes both at once—and the catalogue of their promiscuous confusion, reminds us of "A Ramble in St. James's Park," especially in the lines we examined in the last chapter, wherein the vortex of satiric discourse sucks all constructs—mythic, moral, social, and linguistic—into the black hole of zero point.

The amalgamation of the satyr-satirist spokesman and the Juvenalian style that occurred in the English Renaissance determined the defining characteristics of satire and satiric discourse that Restoration writers inherited from their immediate predecessors. Its "suppressed transitions, intense brevity, rapidly shifting dialogue with undesignated speakers and veiled ambiguous expressions,"[27] worked to make the satiric speaker a grotesquely exaggerated, fictional mask that called attention to its own artifactuality, or to erase the speaker entirely, and usually to do both. And just as this highly dialogized discourse splinters or erases the illusion of an authorial "I," so too does it not admit a point of view, or even a consistent vantage. C.S. Lewis says of Donne's satire: "There is a complete absence of that cheerful normality which in Horace relieves the monotony of vituperation. In Donne if any similie or allusion leads us away from the main theme, it leads us only to other objects of contempt and disgust—to coffins, 'itchie lust,' catamites, death, pestilence . . . excrement, botches, pox, 'carted whores.' Instead of a norm against which the immediate object of satire stands out, we have vistas opening to corruption in every direction."[28] There can be no single "main theme" nor any "norm" against which an immediate object of satire stands out in a seventeenth-century satire because it has no single perspective—neither a central "I" *nor* a central "Eye." Like early seventeenth-century satires, the deconstructive satires of the Restoration period are multivalent and centrifugal: "Rochester's poetry [creates] a kaleidoscopic effect which establishes one tone only to shift suddenly to another and another. . . . Often the *coup de grace* of the effect comes when the poem's apparent note of completion is undermined, leaving the reader with competing perspectives which the poem as a whole does not resolve but holds in suspension."[29]

The atomistic, centerless, explosive mode in satire holds throughout the century whether in a verse satire of Marston or Donne early in the century, or of Oldham or Rochester later on, whether in a dramatic satire of Jonson in 1600, or of Wycherley in 1676. The fictionality and instability of the speaker, the dialogism and self-reflexivity of language, and the centerless, radical variability of perspective that Restoration writers inherited as the generic determinants of their mode equipped them particularly well for their task: designing the deconstructive, self-erasing satire of zero point.

Alexander Pope, master of the Horatian style of "talking on paper," who thought of satire as a *heaven-sent* "sacred Weapon" and a clarion "To rowze the Watchmen of the Publick Weal,"[30] in true eighteenth-century taxonomic style measured Restoration writers of satire on a stylistic scale that mounted toward a manner most like his own—ordered and ordering, mimetic and narrative—a style created and determined by the constructive discourse of modernism that was born in the Restoration period:

> **Pope** Oldham is *too rough and coarse.* Rochester is medium between him and Dorset. Lord Dorset is the best of all those writers.
> **Spence** What, better than Rochester?
> **Pope** Yes; Rochester has neither *so much delicacy nor exactness* as Dorset.[31]

Tom Brown, another eighteenth-century commentator, clearly reveals his own unconscious espousal of the same mimetic, public-spirited, moral-emendation model for satire that is Pope's ideal when he declares that Oldham's satire is probably too indelicate, furious, and inexact to qualify as satire: "both his thoughts were too furious and his style too bold to be correct. . . . His curses were cruel, and sometimes stretched to that degree, that his verses could be termed no longer satire, but rather the hot expressions of some witty madman."[32] And in our own day Ken Robinson explains Oldham's predilection for Juvenalian style as rooted in an affinity of *personality* between the two satirists: "In Juvenal Oldham found a writer who, like himself, was committed to values outmoded before his birth; each was *temperamentally* an outsider and unable to adapt to the society in which he found himself."[33] That we know absolutely nothing about Juvenal the man, not even the date or place of his birth, and that we have not a jot of evidence that Oldham, befriended and admired by Rochester and his circle, "was unable to adapt to the society in which he found himself," does not deter a critic of our time from locating the source of satiric discourse in the inner being, or "personality," of the writer of satire—even when we have clear evidence that Oldham deliberately and dispassionately chose his rugged style as a primary requirement of the poetic mode in which he was writing: "certainly no one that pretends to distinguish the several colours of poetry would expect that Juvenal when he is lashing at vice and villainy should flow so smoothly as Ovid or Tibullus when they are describing amours and gallantries and have nothing to disturb and ruffle the eveness of their style."[34] John Traugott, attempting to discriminate and locate one "true" perspective and one "real" voice in the dialogic polyphony that is *A Tale of a Tub* asks finally, "Are we in the presence of an aristocratic ironist mimicking egregious idiots or a satanic conjurer calling up the damned human race?"[35] To resolve the ambiguity that confronts him, Traugott, like Robinson, turns to the "deepest thoughts" of the author, Jonathan Swift. Ann Cline Kelly, too, looks to the "personality" of Swift for an explanation of his disturbing discursive practice: "One is never comfortable in Swift's presence. His perennial power to disturb derives in part from the unpredictable mixture of orthodoxy and heterodoxy that informed his life, his works, and his attitudes toward language. . . . To understand his linguistic theories and practice one needs to explore the other pole of his personality—his urge to violate the common forms."[36] I would argue to the contrary 1) that it is impossible to uncover the "deepest thoughts" of any person now living, much less one three hundred years dead, and 2) that we need to explore not the "personalities" of "authors"—Swift, Oldham, or Wycherley—but rather to understand the nature of satiric discourse and the linguistic and generic conventions embedded in it at the end of the seventeenth century to appreciate the furious irrationality of a verse satire by Oldham, the dark misanthropy of a dramatic satire by Wycherley, or the purposeful linguistic chaos of *A Tale of a Tub,* wherein "words are removed from their ordinary connotative context and volleyed about like balls to create ephemeral patterns like the arrangement, at any given moment, of atoms in a void or the shape of a cloud in the sky."[37]

II. Not Him: Oldham's "Aude aliquid. Ode"

A Tale of a Tub is, without doubt, *primus inter pares* among those deconstructive "texts of bliss [*jouissance*]" that constitute satire at the end of the seventeenth century, and is also doubtless the most striking achievement in the art of creating an author-who-is-no-author writing a book-which-is-no-book. But satire that destroys, erases, and grotesquely fictionalizes its speaker, and texts that exist in the process of undoing themselves, are the rule, not the exception, in the deconstructive satire of Restoration zero point. In his three panegyrics—"Aude aliquid. Ode" [Satyr Against Vertue], "A Dither-ambique on Drinking," and "Sardanapalus"—John Oldham provides us with three exceptionally good examples of satire which purposefully complicates its speaker and destabilizes its genre. Not until its *pirated* publication in 1679 was "Aude aliquid" called "A Satyr Against Vertue," a name which Oldham repudiated in his "Advertisement" to the only edition he authorized. The only good text published during Oldham's lifetime (1682) calls the poem simply "Pindarique," a title which is justified by the autograph fair copy, R2, and which we must assume was the poet's preferred choice of a title.[38] When Oldham wrote the poem in 1676 he called it "Ode" and prefixed its title with an epigraph from Juvenal: "Aude aliquid brevis Gyaris, et carcere dignum / Si vis esse aliquis" [If you want to be somebody these days, you have to be daring enough to commit a crime worthy of Gyaris, or jail] (I,73). He subtitled the poem "Suppos'd to be spoken by a Court-Hector at Breaking of the Dial in the Privy Garden." The incident to which the subtitle refers was reported in a newsletter of 26 June 1675: "My Lord Rochester in a frolick after a rant did yesterday beat doune the dyill which stood in the middle of the Privie [Gard]ing, which was esteemed the rarest in Europ." Aubrey's notes on the maker of the dials, Franciscus Linus, adds further significant information. They, the dials, "were broken all to pieces (for they were of glasse spheres) by the earl of Rochester, lord Buckhurst, Fleetwood Shepard, etc., coming from their revels. 'What,' said the earl of Rochester, 'doest, thou stand here to [fuck] time?' Dash they fell to worke."[39]

Brooks and Selden, the modern editors of Oldham, agree with Sharrock in thinking that "in social and moral satire of this period the sense of vivid contemporary immediacy is often the chief pleasure to be gained from the poem."[40] That is to say, the modern editors and one of the most serious scholars of Restoration satire agree that the value of Oldham's satire is its mimetic quality. I would argue to the contrary that "Aude aliquid" is not mimetic in nature. Its signified is not an external existent—Rochester's breaking the dials or some other "vivid contemporary event." Quite the contrary, the *event* is absorbed, and transformed, by the genre and discourse that comprise the *lens* through which we *"see"* the event. The central signified of the poem is its own generic form, the Pindaric ode, which, as the epigraph from Juvenal indicates, it satirically destabilizes. Indeed, we can better understand the subtle complexity of the secondary title the poem acquired, "A Satyr Against Vertue," when we realize that "virtue" here is Pindar's *arete,* an excellence of spirit which enables an Olympic victor to achieve the stature of a demigod: "The Greek word *arete* in other contexts often translated as 'virtue,' has a much wider meaning than the English word, and can apply to high merit in almost any activity that is praiseworthy and skillful."[41] The "virtue" here in focus is heroic, aristocratic *arete.* Moreover, it is not possible to understand Oldham's Pindaric satires without reading them through the lens of the Pindaric ode; and the Pindaric ode itself, as we shall see, is pointedly *not* a mimetic genre.

The fruitful collision of genres effected by Oldham's "pindariques" brilliantly fractures and fictionalizes their speakers. The "real" Earl of Rochester is neither the real speaker nor the real target of "Aude aliquid." Indeed, so delighted was the real Rochester by Oldham's virtuoso poetical performance that he promptly visited Oldham with a group of the court wits to praise him in person. It was with this circle of wits in mind as audience that Oldham wrote a whole series of subsequent deconstructive satires in the 1670s: "Upon the Author of a Play called Sodom," "Sardanapalus," "A Ditherambique on Drinking. Suppos'd to be Spoken by Rochester at the Ginny Club," and "The Dream."

In his article "Oldham, Pope, and Restoration Satire," taking the usual, evolutionary view of Restoration and eighteenth-century satire, Selden sees Oldham's complexity in "Aude aliquid" as a *fault,* which the unskillful writer tried in vain to mend: "Oldham's [*Satyr Against Vertue*] is both cruder and less controlled than Pope's [*Dunciad*]. While Pope's ironic praise of dullness is *stabilized by consistent inversion* of values, Oldham's attack on virtue is complicated by his desire to dramatize the libertine outlook of Rochester. His 'Apology,' appended to the published version, and his 'Counterpart to the Satyr Against Vertue,' published in the *Remaines* (1683) only *emphasize the instability of the first poem's irony*" (ital. mine).[42] It is Selden's ideal model in satire—Popean, regular, and "consistent" in its binary, closed form—that will not allow him to see that Oldham's destabilization of genre, his ambiguity and variability of perspective, and his complication of the satiric spokesman figure, are *purposeful.*

Geoffrey S. Conway, the modern editor and translator of Pindar, explains the literary-poetic, non-mimetic (or metaphoric) nature of the odes: "Though [Pindar's] Odes are concerned with particular achievements, his treatment of his subject-matter frees it from all local limitations, and his poetical genius raises the victor's achievement and the poem which celebrates it out of the sphere of every-day reality to the plane of the ideal. His myths, treating as they do of the legends of gods, heroes (demi-gods) and mortals of mythical antiquity and their more than human exploits, are in keeping with this idealizing tendency."[43] A Pindaric ode never describes or (re)presents the actual victory it celebrates. Rather it uses the occasion of victory to launch into the purely linguistic realm of myth: "The connection of the myth with the victory which the Ode celebrates is not . . . a close one, deriving sometimes from the reputed ancestral descent of the victor's family, sometimes with the mythical figures associated with early legends of the victor's city."[44]

The heart of a Pindaric ode, its central generic feature, is its myth, and most usually not a single myth but a series of skillfully interwoven myths. For example, *Olympian VII,* celebrating the victory of Diagoras of Rhodes, the winner of a boxing match, tells us nothing whatever about Diagoras or the boxing match. Rather it explores the mythic origin of Rhodes and the ancestry of her people in reverse mythic chronological order. The first myth Pindar uses is that of the coming of the Argives to Rhodes under the leadership of Tlepolemus, son of the man-god Heracles. Then follows the myth of an earlier time—the command of Helios, god of the sun, to his descendents, the earliest inhabitants of Rhodes, to set up the worship of Zeus and Athene in his city. Finally comes the originary myth, the story of how Helios, deprived of a territory in the original apportioning of the world by his absence from the Olympian council on the day the division was made, takes as his domain an island newly emerging from the sea. This last-first myth is recapitulated in the story of how Rhodes grew from the sea to become the special charge of Helios, who took as his bride the maiden, Rhodes, daughter of Aphrodite, and how from that union the original ancestors derived.

Two features of Pindar's use of myth here are interesting. The first is that the movement of the poem is to penetrate further and further through layers of story to origins; the second is that the myths are not related in logical narrative order, but are rather connected on the surface as myths of origins, and, below the surface, are even more subtly related in that each myth contains in germ a "fortunate fall"—a crime or misfortune that led to a happy issue. Tlepolemus killed his cousin, Licymnius, in Tiryns, and his subsequent exile brought him to Rhodes; the Heliadae failed to carry out the bidding of Helios but were nevertheless rewarded by a shower of gold from Zeus and the gift of craftsmanship from Athene; Helios suffered the mischance of being absent from the original territorial allotment but came through that disappointment to the reward of the gift of Rhodes. The ode is an "open text"; it is dependent upon active, continuous interpretive acts of the reader in order to exist. It is a linguistically self-reflexive text, a system of interacting symbolic configurations having difference without positive terms. It is a text that leads the reader *away* from the realm of the actual to the imaginary center of origins.

Now let us consider for comparison the *process* of Oldham's "Aude aliquid. Ode" as it operates in its first three stanzas. The heroic victory that this "pindarique" celebrates is a "Court-Hector['s] ... Breaking of the Dial in Privy-Garden." We will recall that the *reported* words of the court-hector as he made his attack upon the dials were "doest thou stand here to fuck time?" The court-hector's victory, then, consists in smashing human measurement: the human construction, time. This "event" is completely absorbed into the poetic process of the poem; as a particular act of negation, it is never described, but rather its central significance recurs in a host of similarly negating mythic acts which the poem recounts. In antithetical relation to an ode of Pindar, which in its opening would invoke an inspirational power—the sun, water, a deity—and would then recall the ancestors of the hero, this opening stanza begins with an apostrophic *curse* upon the whole tribe of

> "vertuous Fools
> who think to fetter free-born Souls
> And ty 'em up to dull Morality and Rules.

The hero-speaker—who is no hero and no Hector—smashes the constraints imposed by custom-governed fools of "Vertue" upon freeborn souls at the same "time" as he breaks the dials that would fetter time to human measurement. In ironic imitation of Pindar's manner "the athletic context celebrated by the [speaker—i.e., the dial-breaking] . . . is not directly described but . . . colours the metaphors and similies used."[45]

The second and third stanzas of Oldham, again following the Pindaric strophe-antistrophe pattern, begin to weave the mythic constellation that surrounds the banishment of virtue. The first lines of stanza 2—"Hence hated Vertue from our goodly Isle" to "Go, follow that nice Goddess to the Skies . . . Converse with Saints and holy folke above"—are an extended allusion to the fate of Virtue, or Chastity, in the opening passages of Juvenal's *Satire Six:*

> Credo Pudicitium Saturno rege moratum
> in terris visamque diu, cum frigida parvos
> praeberet spelunca domos ignemque Laremque
> et pecus et dominos communi clauderet umbra,
> . . . paulatum deinde ad superos Astrea recessit
> hac comite atque duae pariter fugere sowres.

[I believe that in the days of Saturn Virtue still lingered on earth, and could be seen from time to time, when people lived in cold caves and one dwelling place housed human beings, their herds and their household gods. . . . After that Astrea retreated to Heaven, with her comrade Chastity, the two sisters fleeing together.] [1-21]

Oldham's (or, more precisely, the satiric speaker's) Virtue too can abide only in "some unfruitful, unfrequented Land," a "lean, barren region"; and she is urged to follow her sister, Astrea:

> Go follow that nice Goddess to the Skies,
> Who heretofore, disgusted at encreasing Vice,
> Disliked the World and thought it too Profane
> And timely hence retir'd, and kindly ne'er return'd again:
> Hence to those airey Mansions rove,
> Converse with holy folkes above [43-48]

Stanza three, like the second strophe in a Pindaric ode, provides another
configuration of mythic associations for Virtue: Brutus's final abjuration of
the goddess to whose service he had devoted himself, and Juno's escape
from Ixion's attempted rape. In this third stanza Oldham, like Pindar, moves
through alternate renderings of myth. For instance, the image of Brutus's
devotion to, and final recognition of the hollowness of, virtue, moves
through two literary figurations to make its point.

> The greatest Votarie, thou ere could boast . . .
> Though long with fond Amours he courted Thee,
> Yet dying did recant his vain Idolatry;
> At length, tho' late, he did Repent with shame
> Forc'd to confess thee nothing but an empty Name [67-74]

These lines refer inward to two earlier literary inscriptions. Cowley's "Ode
Upon Brutus" praises the great ancient hero who made "Virtue" his "Life's
Center" until in his final defeat he spoke the "Tragick Word," that revealed
virtue to be "An *Idol* only and a *Name*."[46] But Cowley's ode itself refers
back to Brutus's dying exclamation, which is itself a *quotation* of a line
from a Greek tragedy translated by Dio Cassius as "Te colui (Virtus) ut
rem; ast tu nomen inane es."[47] Just as in Pindar, the process of the poem
departs from the realm of actuality to penetrate further and further into
fiction, into *writing*. Brutus's recognition of the hollow name of virtue is
embroidered upon by another mythic figuration of emptiness in the lines
immediately following:

> So was that Lecher [Ixion] gull'd, whose haughty Love
> Design'd a Rape on the Queen Regent of the Gods above [Juno];
> When he a Goddes thought he had in chace,
> He found a gawdy Vapor in the place,
> And with thin Air beguil'd his starved Embrace [75-79]

The subtlety and complexity of Oldham's deconstructive satire here is
breathtaking. A fictional persona, a libertine who is also no-libertine, as we
shall see, is speaking a Pindaric ode—in the classical canon the lyrical
genre that is twin to epic—that is, the most idealizing and elevating of

forms. He apostrophizes Virtue in precisely the manner of his model, using a concatenation of mythic accounts to adumbrate the ideal. However,
whereas Pindar moves along a line of interwoven myths to arrive at origins, Oldham, through his unreliable speaker, moves along myths to arrive
at Nothing, at the apprehension that virtue is no more than an empty
name, a beguiling sign written upon "thin Air."

Oldham's satire here is not merely paradoxical encomium, as Brooks
and Selden, following H.K. Miller,[48] would have it, for paradoxical encomium entails no more than a simple binary inversion. Oldham's poem is
not an inversion but a whirligig. The allusion to Juvenal that underlies the
apostrophe to Virtue of stanza 2, for example, is itself a double inversion,
for Oldham's Pindaric is not praising virtue, as an encomium or Pindaric
ode would; it is castigating Virtue. On the other hand, however, Juvenal's
satire, to which the lines allude and which *generically* is the opposite, or
inverse of ode, does not castigate Virtue, but obliquely mourns her absence. We arrive, then, at a generic reversal that is also no-reversal, or,
perhaps, is a double negative inversion.

The process of pursuing myth into the layers of constructs that constitute it to the point of NOTHING is even more striking and powerful in
the last four stanzas of the poem (comparable to the Pindaric epode). In
these stanzas the speaker, by aligning himself with a whole ancestry of
makers of nothing erases himself into the corner of ME, and at the close
of the poem erases that monument to nothingness as well.

The tradition of makers of nothing—Herostratus, Nero, Guy Falkes,
Satan, Cain—is constructed/deconstructed with absolute fidelity to the
Pindaric method of interconnection and interpenetration of myth. The
connection among the myths is that they all center upon a prodigiously
destructive act which ends with the destroyer "writing" his name, his word-
sign, on empty air. The first in the line evoked is Herostratus, and in the
stanza that describes him Oldham puts on show the process of deconstruction that Herostratus's and the succeeding acts entail—writing one's empty
name/fame on empty no-place, or anti-place.

> How gallant was that Wretch whose happy Guilt
> A Fame upon the Ruins of a Temple built
> Let Fools (said he) Impiety alledge,
> And urge the no-great Fault of Sacriledge;
> I'll set the sacred Pile on Flame,
> And in its Ashes write my lasting Name,
> My Name which thus shall be
> Deathless as its own Deity. [185-192]

Writing a *name*—which as the opening, anti-encomium stanzas on Virtue have shown, is in itself an empty sign—upon absence is the act which these words of Herostratus celebrate. But, underlying this story is another, fuller story of Herostratus that leads further into nothingness and also further complicates the stanza. Herostratus set fire to the temple of Diana at Ephesus in 356 B.C., he confessed, for no other reason than to immortalize himself. To punish his crime the Ephesians condemned his *name* to oblivion. The consequence, therefore, of writing one's name by an act of destruction is the erasure of that name.[49] The relation of the myth of Herostratus to the satiric speaker who praises him is also interesting because Herostratus becomes associated with libertinism in the 1670s. Shadwell's Don Antonio in *The Libertine* (1674), for instance, says of himself and the rest of Don John's company, "We are his [Herostratus's] rivals" (V,i).

Herostratus's story is the first in a series of myths, each of which concerns a heroic maker of nothingness. The progress from myth to myth is increasingly destructive—and therefore creative of *wider,* more significant negation—and yet, paradoxically, *narrower,* for each story moves closer to the center/no-center, the satiric speaker's ME. As Herostratus destroyed a temple and tried to make his name a deity, so Mausolus, King of Caria, and the Egyptian Pharoahs "idly did consume / Their Lives and Treasures to erect a Tomb" (195-196). They are followed by Nero, "who sacrific'd a City to a Jest" but did not, in the speaker's judgment, go far enough:

> Bravely begun! Yet pity there he staid
> One step to Glory more he should have made,
> He should have heav'd the noble Frolick higher,
> And made the People on that Funeral Pile expire,
> Or providently with their Blood put out the Fire.
> Had this bin done,
> The utmost Pitch of Glory he had won
> No greater Monument could be
> To consecrate him to Eternity
> Nor should there need another Herald of his Praise but Me. [97-105]

As nothingness grows wider and wider, from the destruction of Rome to the wished-for destruction of the whole race of Romans, so, in reverse movement, does focus simultaneously narrow to "me."

Next, in the style of true Pindaric, Oldham's stanza, listing Cain in the ancestry of heroic destroyers, refers back to, and mimics, Cowley's *Discourse . . . concerning . . . Cromwell* on Cain and the manner in which the first crime might have been magnified:

> 'Twas a beginning generous and high . . .
> So well advance'd, 'twas pity there he staid;
> One step to Glory more he should have made,
> And to the utmost bounds of Greatness gone;
> Had *Adam* too been kill'd, he might have Reign'd alone.[50]

The "alone" on which Cowley's verse ends points toward the satiric speaker's final lines in Oldham's satire, wherein he too praises "noble Cain" and is left at last alone in minus-Hell.

Moving ever more widely from Nero, to Guy Falkes, to Satan—the destroyer of Rome, the would-be destroyer of England, the destroyer of mankind—the speaker asks inspiration from their stories to commit a crime more daring than theirs, a crime "Unknown, unheard, unthought of by all past and present Time." He yearns to be "the bold Columbus . . . who must new Worlds in Vice descry." In a gesture worthy of the twentieth-century writer Jean Genet, the speaker desires to create a perfect act of negation, an act which would be, as Genet might argue, a crime that is a poem because it makes the devil God. In the vulgar many, the speaker says,

> Sin is a meer Privation of Good,
> The Frailty and Defect of Flesh and Blood,
> In us 'tis a Perfection, who profess
> A studied and elab'r'te Wickedness.

The poem ends with praise of

> The noble Cain, whose bold and gallant Act
> Proclaimed him of a more high Extract

Yet, even Cain, first murderer though he was, is "unworthy me [the speaker]," for, had fate put him in Cain's place, the speaker says, he would have done "some great and unexampled Deed" that would "show that Sin admits *Transcendency*" (ital. mine). Sin, which, as John Davies of Hereford says, is "naughty Nothing that makes all things nought," has mounted to transcendent perfection, and the speaker, moving in inverse direction, achieves a "merit more than Hell."

Conway tells us that "It is thought by some scholars that the practice of including myths in the epicinian Odes was adopted not only with a view to increasing the decorative effect of the poems but also to give to the Odes, and to the men in whose honour they were written, some share in the aura of timeless immortality which these legends enjoyed in the minds of the Greeks of those times."[51] The genius of "Aude aliquid. Ode" is to make *nothingness* timeless and immortal, to design zero, and to have its speaker/hero *descend,* rather than ascend, to the zone of minus–zero.

What does this radical destabilization of genre do to the figure of the satiric speaker? All that we can say with certainty is that by speaking in the manner of the most celebrated lyric poet of the ancient world, the speaker figures poet/*and also*/no-poet. But is he a modern *parody* of an ancient poet-aristocrat, of the kind Pindar himself was ("an aristocrat by birth" whose "preference for governments of aristocratic or oligarchic type" was well known),[52] as the poem's title, "Aude aliquid," might suggest? As a libertine—in the specifically seventeenth-century sense of the term—does the speaker's limit-breaking *arete,* his desire to be "A true and brave Transgressor" and "To sin with the same Height of Spirit Caesar fought" (167-168), *imitate* or *parody* the *arete* of the brilliant aristocratic athletes whose prodigious performances Pindar celebrates? Or is his brilliantly excessive *linguistic* performance *mock-action,* a verbal substitute that spends itself in "airey" words just as Ixion, in one of the myths the linguistic performance incorporates, "Idly spent his vigor, spent his Blood / And tir'd himself t'oblige an unperforming Cloud" (80-81). Is the speaker's desire to move beyond all human limit, to be "the wild Columbus . . . Who must new Worlds in Vice descry. / And fix the Pillars of impassable Iniquity" (272-274), a kind of heroic madness of the sort that Pindar himself describes:

> Yet for his valorous deeds [the hero] treads now
> The highest peak, touching from thence the far
> Pillars of Heracles. Beyond
> Is pathless for the wise
> Or the unwise. That road shall I
> Never pursue; name me madman else. [*Olympiad III,* ep.3.]

Or is the speaker mad in a less exalted sense? Is that which he speaks the "mad ranting and debauched specimens of poetry of this author Oldham" which "[Rochester] seemed much delighted in," as Anthony a Wood thought?[53]

As Harold Fisch has observed, "*Character* in Greek signifies a mark or token made by a writing or marking instrument. . . . In this it is like *type*—formed by another Greek word meaning to write or incise. . . . In such a usage we return to the notion of 'character' as something belonging essentially to *ecriture,* to a linguistic ordering of reality."[54] The speaker of "Aude aliquid. Ode" is a product *of* language, existing only *in* language. Even if we were to consider him a caricature of Rochester, his relation to the world would still be not mimetic/referential but linguistic/metaphoric for "the art of caricature . . . does not signify what is already in the world;

rather it imposes a mark on the world, and that mark is henceforward going to be indelible."[55] We must come to understand that the historical John Wilmot, Second Earl of Rochester as we know him exists only in the realm of *ecriture;* he is a product of Oldham's poems, of Etherege's *The Man of Mode,* of Burnet's *Life,* and so forth. But most particularly he derives from a conventional literary rhetorical figure, a Theophrastan "Character," "the Libertine." Oldham makes that "character," that linguistic sign, the speaker of his poem precisely because the central defining characteristic of the libertine is his disbelief in, and purposeful violation of, *all* moral, social, legal, intellectual, *even* "natural" constructs and inscriptions. "Libertinism . . . is not simply or exclusively concerned with the pursuit of pleasure. The libertine leant towards an intellectual skepticism, and he was particularly inclined to challenge the usual conceptions of nature and natural law, of society and social custom, and even accepted ideas and practices of religious belief."[56]

The Restoration "character" of the libertine was an extraordinarily complex figure. As Dale Underwood so brilliantly demonstrated, a wide variety of quite often contradictory philosophical positions met in the late seventeenth-century philosophy of *libertinage.* Moreover, those philosophical strains met not to join but to cancel each other: "with all the traditions of thought to which he was exposed, the libertine could find both something to his liking and something which he was obliged to reject, and . . . the consequences of his choice could add further paradox and inconsistency to his body of beliefs."[57] Our common simplification of the libertine into a mere anti-rationalist who followed the dictates of his senses is narrow and superficial to the point of error. The libertine *does* deny the power of man to conceive reality through reason, but he is not a materialist, for he also denies the existence of order in material nature. Because he denies the existence of a fixed order in nature—and consequently rejects the notion of *jus naturale*—he insists that human laws and institutions are "mere customs varying with the variations of societies."[58]

However, his Pyrrhonistic skepticism is far more radical than that; the Restoration libertine, following Montaigne, Charron, La Mothe le Vayer, *asserts that all knowledge is questionable,* "that both the senses and reason are in . . . respect [to the ability to receive or generate knowledge] unreliable."[59]

The libertine scorns the tepid, rationalistic skepticism of the Royal Society—in "Aude aliquid" he substitutes for a Royal Society dedicated to the empirical investigation of that which *is* a "Royal Society of Vice" dedicated to the creation of that which *is not*—because he distrusts the conception that there *is* an orderly reality "out there" to be investigated. The libertine scorns as well all human constructs as whimsical chimeras spun out of the purposeless activity of the human brain, and, therefore, he "scorns all conventional values regarding public life and institutions": those of the state, the church, the family, and so forth; and likewise all "the institutions, laws, and technology which man's 'art' or 'civilization' had produced."[60] Negating all that is, or can conceivably be thought to be or to have been, the libertine thereby negates him/her SELF, for "The irrational element in such a controlling impulse toward negation suggests not merely a disenchant-ment with, but a psychological and spiritual privation of what it seeks to destroy. The impulse must finally, therefore, be self-defeating."[61]

The speaker of "Aude aliquid," then, is no-self, or even, perhaps, anti-self. His/its function is to erase the very vantage point upon which we might expect a speaker, or narrator, to stand. Like a figure in an animated cartoon, he erases his landscape and also himself and, therefore, at last, adumbrates absence, or *néant*. He picks up, only to drop again a wide variety of philosophical positions. For example, adopting the primitivistic Epicurean stance, he negates as crippling (but also hollow) all the con-structs of law, morality, and religion:

> But damn'd and more (if Hell can do't) be that thrice-cursed Name,
> > Whoe're the Rudiments of Law design'd
> Whoe' re did the first Model of Religion frame,
> And by that double Vassalage inthral'd Mankind,
> By nought before but their own Power or Will confin'd.
> > Now quite abridg'd of all their primitive Liberty,
> And Slaves to each caprichious Monarch's Tyrrany. [13-19]

Then, using the Cynic's philosophical position, he erases moral delinea-tion: all "Epithets of Ill or Good / Distinctions unadul'trate Nature never understood." But he goes still further and, in radical Pyrrhonistic mode, erases the mental center that *generates* cultural inscriptions, declaring that conscience (a word which in the seventeenth century *includes* what we would call "consciousness") is itself a "wild Chimera," a "giddy airey Dream" (142-143). Any cultural value is merely a "Name," and the name-giving faculty too is dubious and untrustworthy. Oldham's deconstructive satire, then, is a text that exists in the process of undoing itself, which, as its central rhetorical strategy, creates a speaker/no-speaker whose function is to make himself an empty space.

III. *Not Them: Wycherley's* The Plain Dealer

Wycherley's *The Plain Dealer*, which Dryden called "one of the most bold, most general, and most useful satires which has ever been presented on the

English theatre,"[62] provides some of the most convincing evidence in support of the several arguments I am making here: that is, 1) that the discourse of Restoration deconstructive satire is Juvenalian, self-reflexive, self-propelling, and genre-determining, 2) that this satiric discourse *generates,* and is *not generated by,* its speaker(s), and 3) that the satiric speaker, a highly fictionalized, conventional figure, is capable of almost endless refraction, multiplication, and division.

Because *The Plain Dealer* is a dramatic, rather than a verse satire, and because, as I have argued elsewhere, we have been conditioned by the "naturalism" that was produced by the discourse of modernism to think of dramatic characters as fictional persons, like ourselves having interiority and psychology,[63] we have been very loath to acknowledge that the play is a dramatic satire, and not a "Restoration Comedy," and, more important still, to recognize that it is a play that has no "characters" in our post-Enlightenment sense of the term. I have argued in many places for many years that Wycherley's dramas are satires.[64] We need only to examine the epigraphs he appended to their titles, wherein he teases us for our literary-critical pretentiousness and points us to the places we must look to seek out the literary "influences" we like to find, and the "rules" we like to impose on literary texts—"lest . . . [we] should [not] find 'em out by the Play." All the epigraphs are drawn from the *theoretical* pronouncements of Horace, for as Juvenal was the supreme *model* for satiric writing during the seventeenth century so Horace was the supreme critical theorist. One of the epigraphs is from the *Ars Poetica,* one is from *Epistle II,* and deals with the proper stance for a modern poet to take in approaching the Ancients, and two of the epigraphs are drawn from the famous Horatian discussion of the rules for writing satire, *Satires, I, x.* The epigraph appended to *The Plain Dealer*—a play that Anne Righter calls "truly disturbing" and James Sutherland finds "much the grimmest of Wycherley's four plays"[65]—is "*Ridiculum acre / Fortius et melius magnas plerumque secat res*" [Ridicule can deal more forcefully and effectively with important things than severity can]. Like the Dedication to Mother Bennet, the procuress (which in itself is a small but perfect prose satire), the epigraph is there to make us aware that Wycherley is writing *satire,* for in Horace the lines begin a long description of the nature of satiric discourse. Wycherley was not interested in bringing his prose "within the range of realistic conversation," as Bernard Harris and many other twentieth-century critics would have had him do,[66] because *he was not writing mimetic comedy;* he was writing linguistically self-reflexive, deconstructive satire. The aim of such satire—in drama exactly as in verse—is not to imitate realistic conversation but to recreate the self-reflexive, self-propelling, deconstructive language we find in Juvenal.

In *The Plain Dealer* there is no attempt at realism of character or dialogue, for characters (who invariably are types) speak not to each other, in simulation of conversation, but rather directly to the audience. Satiric "exchanges" among characters do not function to reveal the characters' "personalities" but to create the same kind of chaotic, semiotic combat that language wages in a verse satire of Rochester or Oldham. The style of deconstructive satire, whether it assaults us from the page or the stage is declamatory, not conversational. Once freed from inherited preconceptions about the "realistic" dialogue of "Restoration Comedy of Manners," even the most cursory examination reveals that in a Wycherley play as in an Oldham "pindarique" satiric discourse, hurtling along at a furious pace, *creates* and is not *created by* its speakers. Indeed, discourse splinters among multiple speakers, who are often indistinguishable from one another in "personality." For example, Act II, scene i, consists *entirely* of satiric raillery among Olivia, Novel, and Plausible. The fast-paced, continuously broken satiric exchanges do not simulate conversation. Rather they call attention to themselves as rhetorical performance; they make us conscious of the self-generating, and self-reflexive nature of satiric discourse itself:

> **NOVEL** . . . but as I was saying, madam, I have been treated today with all the ceremony and kindness imaginable at my Lady Autumn's, but the nauseous old woman at the upper end of her table_____
>
> **OLIVIA** Revives the old Grecian custom of serving in a death's head with their banquets.
>
> **NOVEL** Ha, ha! Fine, just, i'faith; nay, and new. 'Tis like eating with the ghost in *The Libertine;* she could frighten a man from her dinner with her hollow invitations, and spoil one's stomach_____
>
> **OLIVIA** To meat or women. I detest her hollow, cherry cheeks. She looks like an old coach new painted, affecting an unseemly smugness whilst she is ready to drop in pieces . . .
>
> **NOVEL** But the silly old fury, whilst she affects to look like a woman of this age, talks_____
>
> **OLIVIA** Like one of the last, and as passionately as an old courtier who has outlived his office.
>
> **NOVEL** Yes, madam; but pray let me give you her character. Then she never counts her age by the years, but_____
>
> **OLIVIA** By the masques she has lived to see.
>
> **NOVEL** Nay then, madam, I see you think a little harmless railing too great a pleasure for any but yourself, and therefore I've done. . . .
>
> **NOVEL** If you would hear me, madam.
>
> **OLIVIA** Most patiently. Speak, sir.
>
> **NOVEL** Then we had her daughter,_____
>
> **OLIVIA** Ay, her daughter, the very disgrace to good clothes, which she always wears but to heighten her deformity, not mend it. . . .

NOVEL So! But have you done with her, madam? And can you spare her to me a little now?

OLIVIA Ay ay, sir.

NOVEL Then she is like_____

OLIVIA She is, you'd say, like a city bride: the greater fortune, but not the greater beauty for her dress.

NOVEL Well. Yet have you done, madam? Then she_____

OLIVIA Then she bestows as unfortunately on her face all the graces in fashion, . . . but as the fool is never more provoking than when he aims at wit, the ill-favored of our sex are never more nauseous as when they would be beauties . . .

OLIVIA But, Mr. Novel, who had you besides at dinner?

NOVEL Nay, the devil take me if I tell you, unless you will allow me the privilege of railing in my turn. . . . [II,i,170-223][67]

This free-floating word combat exists *for* and *in* itself; its speakers are as obviously fictional types as the Lady Autumns and ugly daughters of whom they speak. They are not differentiated *personalities;* they are undifferentiated "voices." It is of no consequence to the satiric effect that one speaker is called "Olivia" and the other "Novel" (the names themselves are one an allusion and the other an allegorical figuration), but only that there are two voices in competitive relation, indistinguishable by idiom. We might say that satiric discourse here generates speakers as boiling water makes bubbles. The bubbles appear, speak the lines that are required *to expose the hollowness* of their culture, and are simultaneously exposed as empty spaces, as mere word-catapults, by the epigrammatic raillery they speak.

Satiric discourse is complex and rugged in this play; like the satiric style of Juvenal, it very often uses even the *break* between speakers, an empty space, to produce its satiric effect, as, for example, in the "turn" between Manly and a "City Rogue:"

ALDERMAN Captain, noble Sir, I am yours heartily, d'ye see. Why should you avoid your old friends?

MANLY And why should you follow me? I owe you nothing.

ALDERMAN Out of my hearty respects to you, for there is not a man in England_____

MANLY Thou wouldst save from hanging with the expense of a shilling only.

ALDERMAN Nay, nay; but captain, you are like enough to tell me_____

MANLY Truth, which you won't care to hear; therefore you had better go talk with somebody else.

ALDERMAN No; I know nobody can inform me better of some young wit or spendthrift, that has a good dipped seat and estate in Middlesex, Hertford, Essex, or Kent; any of these would serve my turn. Now if you knew such a one, and would but help_____

MANLY You to finish his ruin.

ALDERMAN I'faith, you should have a snip_____

MANLY Of your nose! You thirty in the hundred rascal, would you make me your squire setter, your bawd for manors? [III,i,672-690]

There is not the slightest attempt at mimesis here. (Obviously, no villainous ruiner of the gentry would ever openly proclaim his intentions.) These speakers are not "fictional persons engaged in an action" of the kind that we have come to expect in a drama. In this particular exchange of "voices" there is a satirist position as opposed to a straight-man position. Throughout the play, character = line drawing, as in Novel's charge that Olivia is "Giving the character before [she] know[s] the man." The "character" can be a figure enacted by an actor, more precisely *spoken by* an actor, or can exist within the language that one of the actors speaks. For example, "Sir John Current" is not one of the dramatis personae, but is a figure evoked in a discursive satiric contest in which two of the dramatic characters engage. Sir John Current is one who "endeavors only with the women to pass for a man of courage, and with the bullies for a wit, with the wits for a man of business, and with the men of business for a favorite at court, and at court for good city security" (II,i,326-329). "Sir John Current," a *name only*, is a satirical device for exposing the arbitrary, hollow nature of social identity. He is, so to speak, an erasure of cultural forms *within* an erasure of cultural forms. But he is no less "real" than the Alderman, or Manly, in the exchange above. More importantly, they are no *more* real than "Sir John Current" merely because actors speak the lines that satiric discourse demands that two "voices" speak.

Language does not emerge from character nor does language exist to illuminate character. On the contrary, a "character" is generated *out of* satiric discourse as a rhetorical position, or as a launch pad, from which more satiric language can be volleyed. Consequently, *any* character in the play can be, at one time or another, a speaker of satire. For example, the Widow Blackacre is a *target* of satire, a grotesquely exaggerated, litigious, pseudo-learned virago. BUT she is also a very effective *speaker* of satire against marriage, against fashionable young rakes, and especially against *love language,* which would gloss over the hidden, ugly economic mechanisms of exploitation underlying courtship and marriage.

WIDOW [to Freeman] Marry come up you saucy, familiar Jack! You think with us widows 'tis no more than up and ride. God forgive me, nowadays every idle, young, hectoring, roaring companion with a pair of red breeches and a broad back, thinks he can carry away any widow of the best degree; but I'd have you know, sir, all widows are not got like places at court, by impudence and importunity only. [II,820-826]

Satire here explodes in three directions: it figures its speaker, the litigious virago; it re-figures its apparent target, Freeman, as an ugly, opportunistic jointure-hunting young rake; and it also unmasks court politics of preferment. As the widow is charactered by the discourse so too does she "character" other speakers, and in the process also destroys the pretentions to meritocracy of the cultural establishment. In like manner, in satirically charactering Major Oldfox the widow-as-satiric-spokeswoman attacks another bastion of the seventeenth-century socioeconomic structure, the January-May marriage, in swinging Juvenalian style:

> **WIDOW** First I say for you, major, my walking hospital of an ancient foundation, thou bag of mummy, that would fall asunder if 'twere not for thy cerecloths_____ . . . Thou withered hobbling distorted cripple; nay, thou art a cripple all over. Woulds't make me the staff of thy age, the crutch of thy decrepidness? Me_____
> **FREEMAN** Well said, widow! Faith thou woulds't make a man love thee now without dissembling.
> **WIDOW** Thou senseless, impertinent, quibbling, drivelling, feeble, fumbling, frigid nincompoop! . . . Woulds't thou make a caudle-maker, a nurse of me? Can't you be bed-rid without a bed-fellow? Won't your swanskins keep you warm there? Would you have me your Scotch warming-pan, with a pox to you? [II,i,864–882]

It does not in the least matter that in the very next bout of characterizing the widow will take the January position in attacking young Freeman, the position *directly antithetical* to that which she assumes here, because consistency of characterization plays no part at all in *The Plain Dealer*. Juvenalian "abundance" is the effect at which the Widow's diatribe against Oldfox aims. The discourse flies off from its speaker; indeed, it has little relevance to its speaker as she is a "character." All that satiric discourse demands is a female voice that will unmask the desire to exploit that lies hidden beneath the love lyrics with which an old man would go a-courting, and to uncover the nasty decaying brute that lies inside each of us under the tissues of falsehood with which we try to disguise it. This satiric language does not admit us into the psychology of its speakers; there *is no* interiority, no internal arena, in these figures. They are tropes, rhetorical strategies, continually variable positions that the rush of discourse assumes in making its multivalenced attacks. It does not permit us to wonder what the Widow "is really like" or whether the caricatures of Major Oldfox and Freeman are "true." Indeed, the words launched against Freeman from the Widow-position, so to speak, could very well appear in a verse satire of Oldham, Marston, or of Juvenal himself, as caricature of the libertine:

> **WIDOW** [to Freeman] Thou art some debauched, drunken, lewd, hectoring,
> gaming companion, and want'st some widow's gold to nick upon....Thou
> art a foul-mouthed boaster of thy lust, a mere braggadacio of thy strength
> for wine and women, and wilt belie thyself more than thou dost women,
> and art every way a base deceiver of women; . . . I say you are a worn-out
> whore-master at five and twenty both in body and fortune and cannot be
> trusted by the common wenches of the town lest you should not pay 'em,
> nor by the wives of the town lest you should pay 'em; so you want women,
> and would have me your bawd to procure 'em for you. [II,i, 913-928]

Like the Widow Blackacre, all the characters in the play are targets, the
conventional types of satire, but almost all the characters are also, to some
degree, *speakers* of satire as well. The advantage of the dramatic mode as a
medium of deconstructive satire is that it allows satiric discourse, which is
already multitextured, to become even more multivocal, more "dialogic"
in the Bakhtinian sense. Consequently, satire is more obviously centerless,
totally disallowing either an "I" or an "Eye."

It is impossible to single out one character as the sole satiric spokesman
in *The Plain Dealer*. However, the titular satiric spokesman, Manly, because
he *enacts* the role of the satyr-satirist whose development into, and preva-
lence in, the seventeenth century we have traced (i.e., he is a snarling
brute; he-becomes-what-he-attacks; and he-loves-what-he-hates-but-is-
impotent-to-enjoy) may be considered the play's fullest treatment, and
fullest analysis of that complex, conventional figure.[68] In precisely the sense
that Oldham's "The Eighth Satire of Monsieur Boileau Imitated," for example, *imitates* Boileau's satire, translating it into the cultural context of the
England of 1682, Wycherley's Manly imitates the early seventeenth-century satyr-satirist speaker. He is "a brutal," "a dogged, ill-mannered_____
. . . surly, intractable, snarling brute! A masty dog" (IV,ii,213-216). The
actor who plays Manly tells us what convention demands that his "part"
be before the play even begins.

> I the Plain Dealer am to act today
> And *my rough part* begins before the play. [ital.mine]

Our expectations are met in the opening scene, not just in Manly's treatment of Plausible, the flatterer, and of his own loyal men, but also in the
perspective Freeman gives us upon the Plain Dealer as the very satiric
discourse he espouses would "character" him:

> **FREEMAN** By the same reason [plain-dealing] too I should tell you that the
> world thinks you a madman, a brutal, and have you cut my throat, or worse,

hate me, what other good success of all my plain-dealing could I have . . .
[I,i,272-275]

The enemy of Manly, the plain dealer, is Olivia, his parody-self, his dark
shadow, who has seduced him in order to betray and expose him, and who
also, of course, figures the exposer-exposed both in the action of the play
and by virtue of her "part," the mock-plain dealer. Olivia is a parody satyr-
satirist; she has seduced Manly, she says, by pretending to be his mirror-
image

> **OLIVIA** I knew he loved his own singular moroseness so well as to dote upon
> any copy of it; wherefore I feigned an hatred of the world too, that he
> might love me in earnest. [IV,ii,209-211]

But the parody figure is also a no-parody, a reversal of a reversal. First of all,
as we have seen in the passages with Novel above, Olivia is a very effective
satiric speaker, but, more important, when the satyr-satirist Manly is the
open target of the parody-satirist's attack, the satire aimed against him
strips him and deconstructs his pose as a courageous truth-teller. It questions the validity of the plain-dealer posture and exposes it as a kind of
perverse self-love. Olivia demonstrates that the courage of the fearless
satirist *at best* is mere choleric humor and peevish pride—

> **OLIVIA** [to Manly] . . . I go on then to your humour. Is there anything more
> agreeable than the petty sulleness of that? Then the greatness of your cour-
> age, which most of all appears in your spirit of contradiction, for you dare
> give all mankind the lie; and your opinion is your only mistress, for you
> renounce that too when it becomes another man's. [II,i,626-632]

At worst the satyr-satirist's much vaunted courage is more disturbing; it is
hatred, cruelty, and disguised cowardice, as, indeed, it had been in this
problematic figure since the fourteen century:

> **OLIVIA** [Manly's courage,] Like the hangman's can murder a man when his
> hands are tied. He has cruelty indeed, which is no more courage than his
> railing is wit. [IV,ii,226-228]

Like an ancient English word-magician, Manly hurls curses—modernized and adapted to the Restoration cultural context—upon his victim:

> **MANLY** . . . may all the curses light upon you women ought to fear and you
> deserve! First may the curse of loving play attend your sordid covetousness
> and fortune cheat you by trusting to her as you have cheated me; the curse

of pride, or a good reputation, fall on your lust; the curse of affectation on
your beauty; the curse of your husband's company on your pleasures, and
the curse of your gallant's disappointments in his absence, and the curse of
scorn, jealousy, and despair on your love; and then the curse of loving on . . .
[II,i,755-764]

And because Olivia is his mirror-image, the parody figure that throws
back his reflection magnified and undermines his courageous posture, Manly
is cursed by his counter-satirist in turn—

> OLIVIA And to requite all your curses, I will return to you your last; may the
> curse of loving me still fall upon your proud, hard heart. [II,i,765-766]

The dramatic mode allows *enactment* of what verse satire can achieve only
in discourse. That is, Olivia *is* cursed by a good reputation falling upon her
lust, a husband's company on her pleasures, a gallant's disappointment in
his absence, and Manly is cursed with the pain of loving on. However,
enactment is secondary to discourse; action exists in dramatic satire to
gloss, or reinforce the effects achieved by discourse, as, for example, the
whole scene at Whitehall exists to make visible the attack upon the corruption of institutions and the decay of justice that satiric discourse is
launching.

The dramatic mode allows too for a much fuller exploration of the
problematic satyr-satirist figure than verse allows. The conventional attributes of the satyr-satirist—that he would enjoy the vice he castigates
but is impotent to do so, that he uses that which he scorns for his own
satisfaction, and, most important, that he *is*, or becomes, that which he
hates—are all embodied in Manly's discourse and actions. For example,
the Plain Dealer reveals his false pride, hypocrisy and duplicity in his own
speech:

> MANLY . . . I had almost discovered my love and shame [to Fidelia]. Well,
> if I had? That thing could not think the worse of me_____Or if he did?
> _____No_____Yes, he shall know it_____he shall_____but then I
> must never leave him, for they are such secrets that make parasites and pimps
> lords of their masters; for any tyranny is easier than love's. [III,i,69-75]

Manly makes Fidelia "pimp for [him]" (III,i,93) and at the same time he
hates and scorns her for being a parasitic pimp, and sarcastically snarls, "I
know you can do it handsomely; thou wert made for't" (96-97).

The instability of language, its breaks and abrupt transitions, in the
passage quoted above reinforce the shattering of the satiric speaker. The

speaker's own discourse will not allow us a single frontal view of him. It shows that the Plain Dealer is a double-dealer; it reveals that the truth-teller's blazon is an empty boast, an insidious lie. And that is the particular genius of the play. Throughout, *The Plain Dealer* consists in discourse in the process of undoing itself. In this play *language* undermines, subverts, and exposes the unreality of, language. Language reveals the impossibility of truth and the logical absurdity of the very conception of a "Plain Dealer." Language erases all possibility of truth, reason, or justice; indeed, language destroys matter and fact:

> **QUAINT** [the Widow's solicitor] I will as I see cause, extenuate or exemplify matter of fact, baffle truth with impudence, answer exceptions with questions, though never so impertinent; *for reasons give 'em words, for law and equity tropes and figures; and so relax and ennervate the sinews of their argument with the oil of my eloquence.* [ital. mine]

Language obliterates person:

> But when my lungs can reason no longer, and not being able to say anything more for our cause, say everything of our adversary, whose reputation . . . *with sharp invectives*_____ . . . with poignant and sour invectives, I say, *I will deface, wipe out, and obliterate* his fair reputation, even as a record with the juice of lemons. [ital. mine]

Language reveals that *all that is*—all truth, or fact, or history—is just a story written on the void:

> for the truth on't is, all that we can do for our client . . . is telling a story, a fine story, a long story, such a story_____ [III,i,163-178]

And, as Saint Augustine said, we can never know the "author" of the story: "He wrote it and went away; he passed hence . . . if he were [here], I should hold him, and beg him, and beseech him . . . to throw these words open before me. . . . But from what source would I know he told the truth?"[69]

Wycherley's satire deconstructs all cultural forms: "the arts and rules the prudent of the world walk by" (I,i,8). It ridicules all classes, spitting equally upon the "arrogant, big dull face of an outgrown knave of business" and "the gaudy fluttering parrots of the town, apes and echoes of men only" (I,i,575, 576). It demolishes all institutions: the court, "Where sincerity is a quality as out of fashion and as unprosperous" (I,i,64); Westminster Hall, which "the reverend of the law would have thought the palace or residence of justice; but [where she is] . . . besieged rather than defended by her numerous black guard here" (III,i,4-6); the Army, wherein officers "fall to making false musters; rather choos[ing] to cheat the King than his subjects" (III,i,22); the Houses of the Great, where a good-looking young man may "First fawn upon the slaves without, and then run into the lady's bedchamber," to make his fortune (III,i,54-59). This deconstructive satire collapses all binary oppositions between true and false, real and unreal: "all wise observers understand us nowadays as they do dreams, almanacs, and Dutch gazettes, by the contrary" (II,ii,43-44). This satiric discourse mocks itself—"for railing is satire, you know, and making a noise humour" (V,ii,209-210)—and it mocks its learned author: "There's Latin for you again, madam. I protest to you as I am an author, I cannot help it."[70] Finally, having destabilized the figure of a speaker of truth and demonstrated the incompatibility of truth and language, this dramatic satire deconstructs itself, and reveals itself as a text that "depends on its undoing to come into being,"[71] by ending exactly where it began— that is, an "honest, surly" Plain Dealer (in a kind of do-over) gives all his money to the only woman in the world he knows he can trust and embraces his *new* one best friend.

I have always believed that the best lens through which to see a Restoration satire is another Restoration satire. *The Plain Dealer* conforms in every particular to the wonderful description that David M. Vieth has made of Rochester's "A Letter from Artemisia in the Town to Chloe in the Country,"

> whose structure resembles a room full of mirrors endlessly reflecting one another. Which of the poem's many characters represents the truth? It may be the booby squire who dies in serene possession of "the perfect joy of being well deceived." Or it may be the whore Corinna. Or it may be the "fine lady" who argues so plausibly in favor of fools as lovers—although, as Artemisia observes, she 'knows everyone's fault and merit but her own.' Artemisia speaks self-righteously of the traditional spirituality of love, but she proves to be little more than a gossip-monger powerless against those who reduce love to a mechanical operation of the spirit and who conform so completely to fashion "that with their ears they only see.". . . Perhaps the norm is suggested by Chloe, Artemisia's correspondent, *who may stand for the reader, but whose presence is entirely the creation of Artemisia's words.*[72]

Just as we, the "Ideal Readers" of the "Open Text," *The Plain Dealer,* are created by its words.

IV. No-One, No-Place, No-Thing: Swift's Tale of a Tub

Jonathan Culler has said that "some literary works are violently explicit in their dealings with signs and signification, transgressing . . . all the linguistic and discursive conventions one can think of. As explorations both of the power of language to create thought and of the limits of discourse, works of this sort . . . show the impossibility of treating signification as a purely code-like phenomenon."[73] *A Tale of a Tub* (1697) is perhaps the greatest achievement in this mode. It is a purposeful explosion of the very possibility that signification is a codelike phenomenon, a complete demolition of the mimetic language theory of the "natural philosophers," or Moderns, particularly Bentley, and the theorist Bentley thought of as having "the largest and nicest knowledge of the English language of any Man now living," John Wilkins.[74]

Everett Zimmerman believes that, "in the *Tale,* Swift exposes the poverty of self by using Montaigne's method of examination: the external world is gradually subordinated to the perceiving subject. Yet the self that is revealed proves to be not Montaigne's in its ineluctable complexity but that defined by Hobbes. The increasing failure of form in the *Tale* mimes not the variousness of self but its chaos. It becomes energy without form, entropic. Ironically the narrator's attempt to create an identity through his book succeeds as his book fails."[75] My own view is somewhat different from Zimmerman's. The *process* in writing by which the "external world" is *absorbed into*—rather than "subordinated to"—the "perceiving subject" is a central *target of satire* in *A Tale of a Tub*. *A Tale* demonstrates that there *is no* external world, and the black hole into which all possible constructs of an "external world" are sucked, the narrator, is not a "perceiving subject" but an empty space. The narrator is neither the multifaceted self of Montaigne nor the material stable center of Hobbes; he is *nieman,* as his tale is no-tale, *néant.* The writer/no-writer is not a self of any kind, neither "I" (Self) nor "Eye" (single perspective). In this satire discourse is multivocal; language is at war with itself.

John Traugott has said, "The demonic joy with which Swift conjures up his repertoire of voices in the Tale and *speaks his deepest thoughts* in their tongues, the sheer invention and flamboyant virtuosity seem at times to define a game, civilized though pyrrhonistic and cynical, for would-be ironists, and we could accept it as such were it not for the deadly hatred and rage that show everywhere in odd, sudden bursts that it is not finally a game at all" (ital. mine).[76] But, of course, it *is* a game, the only game we humans have, the language game, a play of difference without positive terms. The repertoire of voices in the *Tale* do not "speak [Swift's] deepest thoughts" any more than the language of Genesis could speak Moses's "deepest thoughts" to Saint Augustine or the "sharp fang'd" speaker of *The Scourge of Villanie* speaks Marston's "deepest thoughts." Indeed, *A Tale* mocks the reader who would penetrate its surface to reach the presumed "deepest thoughts" of its writer: "There are certain common Privileges of a Writer. . . . Particularly that where I am not understood, it shall be concluded that something useful and profound is couch't underneath."[77]

In addition to exploding the Moderns' conception that there are "profound depths" and "deepest thoughts" underlying the surface of a text, *A Tale* ridicules to absurdity the notion that a reader can ever "become one" with an author by reading his writing. The Grub Street Writer poses the "identification" conception theoretically: "Whatever Reader desires to have a thorow Comprehension of an Author's Thoughts cannot take a better Method than by putting himself into the Circumstances and Postures of Life that the Writer was in, upon every important passage as it flowed from his Pen. For this will introduce a Parity and Strict Correspondence of Ideas between the Reader and the Author" (p.44). And then satire undercuts this lofty, abstract postulation by reducing it to crude practicality, saying that since the work the reader is reading was written in a garret, while hungry, "under a long course of Physick, and in great Want of Money," the only way for the reader to achieve "Parity . . . of Ideas" between himself and the author is to be hungry, poor, in a garret, and so forth: "Now, I do affirm, it will be absolutely impossible for the candid Peruser to go along with me in a great many bright Passages, unless upon the several Difficulties emergent, he will please to capacitate and prepare himself by these Directions. And this I lay down as my principal *Postulate*" (pp.44-45).

The "deadly hatred and rage" in *A Tale* are not the feelings of Swift the man, whom we can never know. Rather the rage, the indistinguishable multiple voices of the text, its linguistic incoherence and idiomatic collisions, are all rhetorical properties of late seventeenth-century deconstructive satiric discourse, exactly as they are in Juvenal. Indeed, even the false hiatuses, built-in empty spaces, are a feature of this satiric discourse: "Here is pretended [says the Bookseller-speaker] a Defect in the Manuscript, and this is very frequent with our Author, either when he thinks he cannot say anything worth Reading, or when he has no mind to enter on the Subject, or when it is a Matter of little Moment, or perhaps to amuse his Reader (whereof he is frequently very fond), or lastly, *with some Satyrical Intention*" (ital. mine). Like these purposeful gaps, the narrator too is an air bubble, both an empty sign and a sign of emptiness.

"Implicit in Swift's satire," Kelly says of *A Tale*, "is the idea that words are social conventions, not physical things."[78] *A Tale* drives the matter further; just as words are empty social conventions, it asserts, so too the social hierarchies and behaviors we build from them are tissues of falsehood:

They [the Three Brothers] talk'd of the Drawing-Room and never came there,

> Dined with Lords they never saw; whisper'd a Duchess and spoke never a Word
> . . . came ever just from Court and were never seen in it . . . Got a list of Peers
> by heart in one Company, and with great Familiarity retailed them in another.
> Above all constantly attended those Committees of Senators who are silent in
> the *House* and loud in the *Coffee-House,* where they nightly adjourn to chew
> the Cud of Politicks, and are encompass'd with a Ring of Disciples, who lye in
> wait to catch up their Droppings. [p.75]

And *A Tale* drives further still. Just as all social constructs, institutions, and
actions are empty, lying signs, so too are the people who make them empty,
covention-governed, convention-determined *signs,* micro-coats:

> those Beings which the World calls improperly *Suits of Cloaths,* are in Reality
> . . . rational Creatures, or Men. For is it not manifest, that they live, and move,
> and talk, and perform all other Offices of Human Life? . . . we see nothing but
> them, hear nothing but them. Is it not they who walk the Streets, fill up *Parlia-*
> *ment____, Coffee____, Play____,* and *Bawdy-Houses.* 'Tis true indeed, that these
> Animals, which are vulgarly called *Suits of Cloaths* . . . do according to certain
> Compositions receive different Appellations. If one of them be trimm'd up
> with a Gold Chain, and a red Gown, and a white Rod, and a great Horse, it is
> call'd a *Lord-Mayor;* If certain Ermins and Furs be placed in a certain Position,
> we stile them a *Judge,* and so, an apt Conjunction of Lawn and black Sattin, we
> intitle a *Bishop.* [pp.78-79]

There is nothing outside this arbitrary semiotic system. Language, *A Tale*
insists, cannot express inner feelings, define external existents, nor capture
eternal truth—"I profess to Your Highness [Prince Posterity], in the Integrity of my Heart, that what I am going to say is literally true this Minute
I am writing: What Revolutions may happen before it shall be ready for
your Perusal, I can by no means warrant" (p.36). Signs do not signify a
reality external to the linguistic system because there is none; nothing *is*
but mutability:

> If I should venture in a windy Day, to affirm . . . that there is a large Cloud near
> the *Horizon* in the Form of a *Bear,* another in the *Zenith* with the Head of an
> Ass, a third to the westward with Claws like a Dragon, and . . . [you] should in
> a few Minutes think fit to examine the Truth; 'tis certain they would be changed
> in Figure and Position, new ones would arise, and all we could agree upon
> would be, that Clouds there were, but that I was grossly mistaken in the *Zoog-*
> *raphy* and *Topography* of them. [p.35]

Language speaks only to language and in its self-reflexive combat offers us
glimpses of the void upon which it writes itself—only to be erased by
Time, "the Author of this universal Ruin. . . . Consider his baneful abomi-

nable Breath, Enemy to Life and Matter, infectious and corrupting. And then reflect whether it be possible for any Ink and Paper of this Generation to make suitable Resistance" (p.32).

A Tale of a Tub is at once a demonstration of the nature of semiotics and a deconstruction of "Modern" mimetic, word = thing semiotics—a satiric recapitulation of Augustine's theory of signs. Although, unlike Derrida, Augustine and Swift might have acknowledged the existence of a "truth which presides over the mind from within" and is from God,[79] *with* Derrida they assert that truth cannot be captured by signs, but at best can only be dimly perceived *in the deconstructive process of dismantling signs,* for, as *A Tale* has it, *"Words are but Wind, and Learning is Nothing but Words: Ergo Learning is Nothing but Wind."* The clumsy empiricism of the Moderns, their absorption with the "real" (so roundly mocked in section V), their assumption that language mimetically reproduces the material actual, their willful ignorance of the self-generative and self-reflexive properties of language, and their devaluation of Wit and Fancy, are all targets of satire in *A Tale,* as its title, which is drawn from an observation of Montaigne, would suggest: "What a Sottish and stupid People . . . are they, without Sense or Understanding, that make no Account either of Grammar, or Poetry, and only busie themselves in studying the Geneologies and Successions of their Kings, the Foundations, Rises, and Declensions of States, and such Tales of a Tub."[80]

A Tale uses the duplicity and multivocality of its speaker and the continuous and violent variability of his language as the principle rhetorical devices by which to rivet our attention upon its own semiotic nature and bring "to a crisis [our] relation with language." For example, within a single paragraph, ostensibly aimed at demonstrating that satire is ineffectual, the speaker begins in the position of a catapult from which satire is launched and ends as the object of satire in a series of rapid rhetorical executions that demonstrate the astonishing versatility and range of deconstructive satiric discourse doubling upon itself, simultaneously asserting and denying its own authenticity, and never for a moment losing its headlong, hurtling momentum. The attack begins as an attack *upon* English satire for being an empty rhetorical exercise:

> in England . . . you may securely display your utmost *Rhetorick* against Mankind in the Face of the World; tell them, *'That all are gone astray; That there is none that doth good, no not one'* [from Psalm XIV]; *That we live in the very Dregs of Time; That Knavery and Atheism are Epidemick as the Pox; That Honesty is fled with Astrea* [the fictional Bookseller in a marginal note cites Horace as the source of this line; it is, as we have seen, from Juvenal's "Satire Six"] with any other Common places *equally* new and eloquent, which are furnished by the *Splendida bilis.* [pp.51-52]

Weaving together a concatenation of inherited, *authoritative* voices—the Psalmist's, Horace's, Juvenal's—the speaker simultaneously draws the inherited *Splendida bilis* voice into his own discourse *and also* ridicules it as an empty cliche. Then, in an abrupt change of direction and tone, the speaker moves from mocking the satiric language of the past to obliquely attacking and exposing centers of power and influence in the present:

> Nay farther; It is but to venture your Lungs, and you may preach in *Convent-Garden* against Foppery and Fornication and *something else;* Against Pride, and Dissimulation, and Bribery at *White Hall*: You may expose Rapine and Injustice in the *Inns of Court* Chappel: and in a *City* Pulpit be as fierce as you please, against Avarice, Hypocrisy and Extortion. [p.52]

Then, abruptly stopping on a dime from the end of one sentence to the beginning of the next, the speaker *jumps* from a strong and effective attack on the institutions of power to undermine the attack he has just made, exposing it as mere word-game: "[Satire is] but a Ball bandied to and fro and every Man carries a *Racket* about Him to strike it from himself among the rest of the Company" [p.52]. Then, executing another, equally abrupt turn, the speaker leaps forward to occupy yet another, quite conventional rhetorical role: the Juvenalian "What happens to a satirist who dares to tell the truth" that we have already observed in operation in *The Plain Dealer:*

> But on the other side, whoever should mistake the Nature of things so far as to drop but a Single Hint in publick, How *Such-a-one,* starved half the Fleet and half-poison'd the rest; How *Such-a-one,* from a true Principle of *Love* and *Honour,* pays no debts but for *Wenches* and *Play*. . . . Or, how *such an Orator* makes long speeches in the Senate with much Thought, little Sense, and to no Purpose; whoever, I say, should venture to be thus particular, must expect to be imprisoned for *Scandalum Magnatum;* to have *Challenges* sent him; to be sued for *Defamation; and to be brought before the Bar of the House.* [p.53]

Satiric discourse here is faceted and subtle in the extreme. The speaker is adopting a position conventional from ancient Roman satire—that of the fearless satirist who exposes himself to danger by attacking powerful people. He argues, obliquely, that the only effective satire consists in attack aimed at particular external existents—that is, mimetic satire. Yet that is *not* what he is speaking in this passage; his use of "such-a-one" makes his satiric attack anonymous. Consequently, his attack is no-attack; it is as clearly a word game as the general satire he has just debunked and declared to be ineffectual. Yet, conversely, the general satire he has debunked has also functioned powerfully as satire since it has exposed the hollowness and hypocrisy at the heart of cultural centers of power. Satire becomes the object of satire and, in a double-turn, reveals its entirely linguistically self-reflexive nature.

At last, in a final abrupt leap, the speaker springs to a position that is *generically* directly antithetical to *all* of the satiric-voices and satiric-postures he has severally assumed: the anti-satiric, sentimental position: "BUT I forget that I am expatiating on a Subject wherein I have no concern, having neither a Talent nor an Inclination for Satyr; On the other side, I am so entirely satisfied with the whole present Procedure of human Things that I have been for some Years preparing materials towards *A Panegyric upon the World*" (p.53). In a single long paragraph the satiric speaker has incorporated five different, but all equally fictional and conventional, personae, all bubbles on the surface of boiling satiric discourse. There is the speaker-prophet condemning all mankind with his stilted sententiae/and also/the detached speaker who mocks him; there is the Juvenalian angry satirist who attacks the hypocrisy and vice of "society"/and also/built into what he says the voice that exposes his attack as ineffectual; there is the beleaguered Plain Dealer; and finally there is the sentimental Modern, who loves "the whole present Procedure of human Things." The "voices" do not blend into a single, however eccentric, voice, nor do they express a single consistently identifiable perspective. Rather, there is a profusion of linguistic and idiomatic collision; there is dialogism in the furthest degree; there are abrupt, often synaptic transitions. These features of the discourse shatter any possibility of a cohesive view, of one voice, of one focal center. The satiric speaker is not merely duplicitous; his "voices" are like scattered shards of a broken mirror, each fragment reflecting in many directions at the same time.

A Tale of a Tub is unquestionably a demonstration in the art of deconstruction. It *begins* in four prefatory false starts, the last of which, the "Dedication to Prince Posterity," calls attention to its own inability to begin: "I am sufficiently instructed in the Principal Duty of a Preface if my Genius were capable of arriving at it. Thrice have I forced my Imagination to make the *Tour* of my Invention and thrice has it returned empty" (p.42). It *ends* in a "pause," a synaptic empty space: "Therefore, I shall here pause a while till I find, by feeling the World's Pulse and my Own, that it will be of absolute Necessity (for us Both) to resume my Pen."

Its margins, or "digressions," are central and its center, or allegorical tale, is marginal; indeed, its arrangement is entirely fluid and is open to rearrangement by its reader:

> The Necessity of this Digression will easily excuse the Length, and I have chosen for it as proper a Place as I could readily find. If the judicious Reader

can assign a fitter, I do here impower him to remove it to any other Corner he please.

It *designs* zero:

> I am now trying an Experiment very frequent among Modern Authors: Which is to write upon *Nothing;* When the Subject is utterly exhausted to let the Pen still move on.

By satiric mockery and inverted, convoluted self-mockery, *A Tale* deconstructs the institution, and the "official" language upon which it rests:

> The Wits of the present Age being so very numerous and penetrating, it seems the Grandees of *Church* and *State* begin to fall under horrible Apprehensions, lest these Gentlemen, during intervals of a long Peace, should find leisure to pick Holes in the weak sides of Religion and Government . . . it was decreed that in order to prevent these *Leviathans* from tossing and sporting with the *Commonwealth* (which of it self is too apt to *fluctuate*) they should be diverted from that Game by a *Tale of a Tub.* [p.39–41]

A Tale is a text which erases the authority of authorial intention, for its Author is not its writer, Jonathan Swift, but is Swift's subversive and duplicitous *sign* of a writer who is also no-writer. The writer/no-writer's *semiotics,* "the Physio-logical Scheme of Oratorical Receptacles"; his *linguistic theory* "That Air being a heavy Body and therefore (according to the system of *Epicurus*) continually descending, must needs be more so when loaden and press'd down by Words; which are also Bodies of much Weight and Gravity"; and his *"Histori-theo-physi-logical" explanation* of how word = thing equivalency came into being—"*Zeal* . . . first proceeded from a *Notion* to a *Word,* and from thence, in a hot Summer, ripen'd into a *tangible Substance*"—hilariously, and quite comprehensively, parody the mimetic language theory of John Wilkins's *Toward a Real Character.* So effective is the parody that it exists, like a photographic negative, as a deconstructive erasure of positivist semiotics. And, just as a mimetic theory of language is the necessary handmaid to the Moderns' conception of universal and changeless human understanding, so *A Tale's* parody of mimetic semiotics is accompanied by broad ridicule of the very notion that human wit is either durable or universal: "nothing is so very tender as a *Modern* Piece of Wit, and which is apt to suffer so much in the Carriage. Some things are extremely witty *to-day,* or *fasting,* or *in this place,* or *at eight a clock,* or *over a Bottle,* or *spoke by* Mr. What d'y'call'm, or *in a Summer's Morning:* Any of which, by the smallest Transposal or Misapplication is utterly annihilate" (p.43). Moreover, human minds, indeed human beings, are not the *creators,* but the *creations* of insubstantial, constantly mutable social inscriptions: "About this Time it happened a Sect arose whose Tenets obtained and spread very far especially in the *Grande Monde* and among every Body of good fashion. They worshiped a sort of Idol, who, as their Doctrine delivered, did daily create Men by a kind of Manufactory Operation" (p.76).

However, it is in its treatment of the relation between criticism and story that *A Tale* is most complex, a deconstruction of deconstruction. As we have begun to see, the mimetic, analytico-referential discourse of modernism created a linguistic climate favorable to trade, empire, and science. It also created instrumentation for the newly born "profession" of literary criticism, which *A Tale* scorchingly ridicules. Literary critical and philosophical commentary upon, and digressions from, what should-be/but/is-not the "history," the tale told (the allegory of Peter, Martin, and Jack), *consume* that story. The expected center of *A Tale,* therefore becomes its periphery, and the structure of the whole text (if, indeed, it can properly be said to have a structure) is constituted in a continuous process of turning inside out. The story of Peter, Martin, and Jack, the satire demonstrates, is a story which *should not be told.* We do not need to retell ("Here the story says") a critical-historical justification of the authority of Scripture; the use of our inheritance is not to provide a specimen for study. Swift's fictional mock-footnote ascribed to Wotton makes the point both in what it says and in its manner of saying it: "by the Coats are meant the Doctrine and Faith of Christianity, by the Wisdom of the Divine Founder fitted to all Times, Places, and Circumstances" (p.75). The footnote is irrelevant, for the coats that are given to us at baptism are meant to be *worn* only. We are not meant to tell the story of how we got them, or to analyze them, or to pick them or their "history" apart in learned treatises. We are meant to wear them without commentary. All writing about, saying about, telling about, them is pointless word-volleying, is designing zero. The three Brothers fall to grief when, failing to recognize that human happiness is a matter of ephemeral, empty social forms—"as human Happiness is of a very short Duration, so . . . [are] human Fashions, upon which it entirely depends" (p.84)—they attempt to rewrite a text:

> They Writ and Railleyed, and Rhymed and Sung,
> and Said, and said Nothing. [p.74]

The story of Peter, Martin, and Jack exists to demonstrate that it is unnecessary, that it is without historical or moral use. Historically, recounting a tale of religious controversy is not only useless but of dubious intention:

Martin cautions Jack that "it was not their Business to form their Actions by any Reflection on Peter's." Furthermore, the story has no moral use. The writer is mocked by the satire's sarcasm when he thinks that the end of religious writing is the consolation of its reader: "[Martin] would have delivered an Admirable Lecture of Morality, which might have contributed to my Reader's Repose of Body and Mind" (p.89).

To reveal its purpose in its process the fable of Peter, Martin, and Jack is continually broken in the telling. "And so leaving these broken Ends, I carefully gather up the chief Thread of my Story, and proceed" (p.81), the Writer-Narrator says, and then picks up the thread only to resume his deconstructive process of unravelling. The fable is an allegorical emblem, an enlarged sign of the failure of signs. It inscribes the Augustinian contrast between the word of God (re)spoken by a creature in time and the "eternal Word in its silence."[81]

Although I agree with Claude Rawson that in *A Tale of a Tub* Swift anticipates Beckett—and I would add, anticipates postmodernism—it is my contention that *A Tale* does so not because it was ahead of its time but, most particularly, because it was *behind* it. *A Tale* is not an eighteenth-century, mimetic, binary satire, designed to correct our manners and morals; it is a deconstructive, Restoration, Juvenalian satire that points toward zero. Moreover, it is a text that puts the process of semiotization on show to the end of invalidating it. Zimmerman has said that in this satire Swift attacks the "house of fiction" for its refusal "to look into the 'glass of Nature.' " *A Tale,* he says, "mimes the author's attempt to create a structure independent of nature, to attach the authority that the poem borrows from God to a small construction that opens inward on emptiness rather than one that opens outward on a universe."[82] I would say rather that in *A Tale* Swift attacks the house of *words,* fully acknowledging that it is the only house we have. There is no "nature" to reflect; there is no "outward" universe. Emptiness is inward—if we can legitimately suppose the existence of such a domain in a satiric speaker—but emptiness is outward as well. This satire not only discloses the underlying nothingness that all "Institution[s]"—"the Pulpit, the Ladder, and the Stage-Itinerant"—attempt to cover, but also exposes as empty fictions "reality," the "world" ("Look on this Globe of Earth, you will find it to be a very complete and fashionable Dress"), "culture" (the "Doctrine delivered [that does] daily create Men"), and even Man himself:

> what is Man himself but a *Micro-coat,* or rather a compleat Suit of Cloaths with all its Trimmings? As to his Body, there can be no dispute; but examine even the Acquirements of his Mind, you will find them all contribute in their Order

towards furnishing out an exact Dress: To instance more: Is not Religion a *Cloak,* Honesty a *Pair of Shoes,* worn out in the Dirt, Self-love a *Surtout,* Vanity a *Shirt,* and Conscience a *Pair of Breeches,* which tho' a Cover for Lewdness as well as Nastiness, is easily slipt down for the Service of both. [p.78]

For Derrida the task of deconstruction is to undermine "everything that was set up in opposition to writing." Swift, as a deconstructionist satirist goes further than Derrida. He exposes even writing itself as a senseless, frantic, automatic nervous tic of scribbling, mad humankind.

FOUR

Genders, Sexualities, and Discourse at Restoration Zero Point

all . . . active experiences and practices which make up so much of the reality of a culture and its cultural production can be seen as they are, without reduction to other categories of content, and without the characteristic straining to fit them . . . to other and determining manifest economic and political relationships. Yet they can be seen as elements of a hegemony: an inclusive social and cultural formation which indeed to be effective has to extend to and include, indeed to form and be formed by, this whole area of lived experience.

Raymond Williams, *Marxism and Literature*

Foucault has said, "Things attain to existence in so far as they are able to form the elements of a signifying system."[1] In the atmosphere following the "Glorious Revolution" of 1689—a social atmosphere dominated by the Societies for the Reformation of Manners and Morals—two phenomena "appeared" which to the consciousness of postrevolutionary Englishmen seemed to be entirely *new* in English culture and also seemed to be foreign importations. Both phenomena had had widespread, verifiable *historical existence* in England before the Revolution and both had not only been known to exist, but had existed extensively in writing as well as in "fact." Postrevolutionary ideology gave new *signification* and new *significance* to them. The phenomena are homosexuality and masquerade, and they are interestingly related because both threatened a new, postrevolutionary ideologically-determined conception of gender identity and a new politically and economically determined notion of sexuality.

In *The Second Charge . . . to the Grand Jury of . . . Westminster* Sir John Gonson argued that homosexuality "till lately rarely appeared in our histories or records."[2] Richard Smalbroke said that if it had ever, indeed, existed in England before his own time, which he very much doubted, it must have appeared only "among monsters and prodigies." What is more, even in his present time the practice was not native to England but was being "transplanted from hotter climes to our most temperate country."[3] Thomas Bury believed that he was sounding a warning clarion to the nation when he wrote in 1709 that "the Sodomites are invading our Land."[4]

And while one influential critic, Nahum Tate, held the stage responsible for promoting the licentiousness that was believed to be destroying the newly reforged, postrevolutionary "Nation"—"all endeavors for a national reformation . . . would prove ineffectual without a regulation of the Stage"[5]—another, equally influential critic, John Dennis, curiously enough argued in *favor* of immoral plays as deterrents to the newly emergent threat, homosexuality, "the like of which was never heard of in Great Britain before."[6]

The question is, why does homosexuality become so *visible* and so threatening in the last decade of the seventeenth century? How could a practice be thought *new* and of *foreign importation* that had been so publicly present only twenty years earlier—when, for example, Sir Charles Sedley "stood naked on the balcony of an inn and in full daylight 'showed his nakedness'; 'acting all the postures of lust and buggery that could be imagin'd' . . . and preached that he had a powder to sell 'as should make all the cunts in town to run after him.'"[7] Discussing the incident, one of Pepys's acquaintances remarks that "buggery is now grown almost as common among our gallants as in Italy . . . the very pages of the Town begin to complain of their masters for it."[8] Further, how could a *drama critic* as interested in the plays "of the last age," as Dennis was, not know of the existence of the notorious mock-heroic play, *Sodom* (ca. 1670), which, since it had been attributed to Rochester, was widely known in the Restoration period both in itself and also as it was the target of such satires as Oldham's "Upon the Author of a Play called *Sodom*"? How in the 1690s and early 1700s could homosexuality be thought a startling innovation when only a few decades earlier Rochester could casually send his young valet as a gift to his friend Savile with the endorsement, "the greatest and gravest of this court of both sexes have tasted his beauty."[9]

One might reply to the questions I have put with "Well, yes, but homosexuality had been considered a sin in Christian Europe since the twelfth century, and since after 1689 England was engaged in a general moral reformation, it is reasonable to expect that homosexuality, like any other sin, should be attacked." But the issue is not that homosexuality was *attacked* as a vice after 1689—it was as often a target of the moral reformers as blasphemy or profaneness. What is important to my argument is, first, that homosexuality is considered *new* in the 1690s-1700s, and, second, that it is considered to be a threat to the *nation*. Interestingly, *masquerade* was thought to be similarly dangerous and as *new*: "The masquerade was considered to be another innovation in spite of its having been one of the popular forms of diversion at Whitehall in the reign of Charles II. . . . According to a virtuous correspondent of the *Spectator*, this amusement was 'wonderfully contrived for the advancement of cuckoldum.' High and low could attend, the duchess and the streetwalker. Here was the perfect occasion for all the most shockingly wicked persons to cavort in anonymity."[10] As we have seen, the most serious threat presented by wit to newly emerging modern culture was that it was linguistically *destabilizing;* in like manner homosexuality and masquerade were *socially* destabilizing. They threatened certain newly-fixed *boundaries,* newly forged mental and cultural constructs. When in 1726 George I gave his approval for a masquerade "so infamous that even some of the great patrons of the diversion were scandalized by it,"[11] the bishops were so alarmed that they warned the king that official approval of such activities as masquerades had caused civil war in the past and could do so again. It is clear that, like homosexuality, masquerade presented a *national* threat after the "Glorious Revolution"; in large measure that is because that revolution fixed solidly into place a new nationalism, and, to bolster that newly conceived nationalism, a new morality. "Virtue . . . is the keystone of a nation's constitution, 'Tis righteousness that establishes a kingdom and exalteth a nation," Robert Drew preached in 1735.[12] Conversely, nothing is so dangerous to the state as "vice unpunished and prevailing."[13] Englishmen who practiced immoral acts were *traitors to their king,*[14] and their actions were a *national* danger.[15] The threat could come to the nation from within, in subversive sexual practices, or it could come from without, as those practices could be used as instruments in the hands of an enemy power: "Bishop Gibson believed that the French ambassador in Queen Anne's time had introduced the masquerade *in order to enfeeble the nation by licentiousness and effeminacy,* which he thought these entertainments encouraged" (ital. mine).[16]

In his interesting essay, "The Birth of the Queen: Sodomy and the Birth of Gender Equality in Modern Culture," Randolph Trumbach traces the progress in the late seventeenth to early eighteenth centuries by which male homosexuals came to be considered and to consider themselves, to be designated and to designate themselves, effeminate. In early years of the Restoration period (1660-1688) homoeroticism was associated with libertinism and therefore with the deconstructive thrust of zero point. The libertine, who, as we have seen, defied all boundaries and considered all cultural inscriptions, customs, and laws to be ephemeral whimsies written upon air, pursued sexual pleasure with men as well as women. Rochester's "Disabled Debauchee" recalls the height of his youthful libertine power, which he declares will not be forgotten in the annals of heroic sexuality:

> Nor shall our love-fits, Chloris, be forgot,
> When each the well-looked linkboy strove t'enjoy

> And the best kiss was the deciding lot
> Whether the boy fucked you, or I the boy.[17]

The libertine's homoeroticism was, for reasons I shall discuss, a sign not of *effeminacy,* but of *super-masculinity.* Like their Renaissance predecessors, Restoration writers thought that excessive *heterosexual* activity made a man effeminate. For example, Oldham's spokesman satirically comforts Sardanapalus by telling him that he is not to worry if he is accused of effeminacy for his prodigious heterosexual feats:

> Cunt was the star that rul'd thy Fate,
> Cunt thy sole Bus'ness and Affair of State,
> And Cunt the only Field to make thee Great. . . .
> Som Saucy Pedants and Historians idly Rail
> And thee *Effeminate* unjustly call. [ital. mine][18]

Fops, who were decidedly sexually interested in women, were also decidedly effeminate in the eyes of their Restoration contemporaries precisely because they preferred the company of women to that of men: "For none but easy ffops to Cunt will bow," as the play, *Sodom,* puts it.[19]

> In the three generations between 1660 and 1750, public attitudes toward the fop changed dramatically by generation. Between 1660 and 1690 the fop was firmly rejected in favor of the rake [libertine]. After 1690, however, the rake himself fell to the power of romantic marriage on the stage, and the fop's domesticated interests came to be more highly valued. But between 1720 and 1750 the fop's effeminacy came under a new kind of criticism. . . . After 1720 the fop's effeminacy, in real life and on the stage, came to be identified with the then *emerging role of the exclusive adult male sodomite— known in the ordinary language of his day as a molly, and later on as a queen.* [ital. mine][20]

The effeminization of the male homosexual and the new visibility of homosexuality as a national threat are the result of a new post-Revolution gender differentiation, a new semiotics of sexuality, for "gender, understood as the social construction of sexuality, mediates between sexual identity and social identity—it binds the former to the latter and roots the latter in the former."[21]

Phyllis Rackin, very persuasively arguing the historical difference between early seventeenth-century and modern gender differentiation, draws upon numerous examples from Shakespearean discourse to establish her thesis: that the Renaissance model of sexuality coded homoerotic love as heroic masculinity and excessive heterosexual love as effeminizing.[22] *Coriolanus,* for example, greets his general on the battlefield with the cry,

> O, let me clip ye
> In arms as sound as when I woo'd, in heart
> As merry as when our nuptial day was done
> And tapers burnt to bedward! [I,vi,29-32];

while Aufidius, the sometime enemy of Coriolanus, welcomes his heroic
rival to his camp with the declaration,

> Know thou first,
> I lov'd the maid I married; never man
> Sigh'd truer breath; but that I see thee here,
> Thou noble thing, more dances my rapt heart
> Than when I first my wedded mistress saw
> Bestride my threshold. [IV,v,106-111]

On the other hand, a man's desire for a woman, unless carefully restrained,
makes him effeminate; Romeo complains, "O sweet Juliet thy beauty hath
made me *effeminate* and in my temper softened valor's steel," while the
excess of love that Antony and Cleopatra exchange renders the sexuality
of both ambiguous: "[Antony] is not more manlike than Cleopatra nor
the queen of Ptolemy more womanly than he." As Rackin observes, in the
Renaissance model, "Desire for another man, then, fails to compromise
masculinity; instead it reaffirms it. Desire for a woman, by contrast, incurs
the risk of feminization."[23]

The Renaissance model for men holds true as well for women. Just as
excessively heterosexual men are effeminate, masculine women are het-
erosexually promiscuous: compare Joan in *1 Henry VI,* or the "collegiates"
in Jonson's *Epicene.* And later in the century, just as Sardanapalus leaves
himself open to the charge of effeminacy by his excessive heterosexual
behavior, so "the Duchess of Cleveland" and "Counselor Knight" assume
a masculine air and statesmanlike posture as they plan their heterosexual
foray into "Little Sodom," the red-light district in Restoration London
("quoth the Duchess of Cleveland to Counselor Knight," ca. 1671-76).
What is important to keep in mind for the argument I shall make is that
homoerotic love is *heroic* in the model which the Restoration inherited
from the Renaissance, for, as we have already seen, highly elevated, heroic
constructs were particularly subject to mock-heroic demolition in Restoration deconstructive satire: compare, for example, "Aude aliquid. Ode."

The Renaissance coding of sexuality persisted into Restoration culture
and discourse until the 1690s, when—along with other constructs, principles, and cultural inscriptions—postrevolutionary culture fixed into place
a new, "modern" model of sexuality. Phyllis Rackin describes the differ-

ence between seventeenth-century and modern inscriptions of gender
difference and sexuality extremely well:

> Both attempt to rationalize and ground a public ideology of gender on a private
> experience of sex, but our assumptions, unlike the assumptions that seem to
> inform Shakespeare's discourse, are based on models of sexual *orientation*. Those
> [seventeenth-century] models construct a kind of metaphysics of desire that as-
> sumes, first, that it is the norm to desire *either* men or women and, second, that
> desire thus specialized, defines personal identity. According to the prevailing
> norms of *our* culture, a person—either male or female—who desires women is
> defined as masculine, and a person—either female or male—who desires men is
> defined as feminine. A person who desires both men and women, we call "bi-
> sexual." In the latter case, the desiring subject is conceived as divided (*bi*sexual) in
> order to maintain the ideologically motivated categories as inviolate.[24]

It is clear, then, that modern, ideologically motivated categories of sexuality have a history. What is that history? What is the ideology that demands
that the categories be kept "inviolate"? And why does the birth of modern culture signal the death of the super-masculine homoerotic libertine
and "the birth of the queen?"

In a masterly analysis of the demographic data collected by Wrigley
and Schofield,[25] Henry Abelove finds an interesting correlation between
the startling increase in population and the almost exactly similar increase
in production during the "long eighteenth century" (1680-1830). Abelove
offers a fascinating suggestion to explain the correlation: "What does seem
to me at least conceivable . . . is that the rise in production (the privileging
of production) and the rise in popularity of the sex act which uniquely
makes for reproduction (the privileging of 'intercourse' . . .) may be aspects of the same phenomenon. Viewed from different perspectives, this
phenomenon could be called either capitalism or the discourse of capitalism, or modern heterosexuality or the discourse of modern heterosexuality."[26] As Abelove fully acknowledges, heterosexual intercourse had been
valued in every European society before the long eighteenth century, but,
as he says, it is also true that production was valued in every European
society before the "long eighteenth century."

> What happens to production in the late eighteenth century in England is
> nevertheless new. While production increases importantly it also becomes dis-
> cursively and phenomenologically central in ways that it had never been be-
> fore. Behaviors, customs, usages which are judged to be non-productive . . .
> come under extraordinary and ever-intensifying negative pressure. If I should
> be right in speculating that the rise in popularity of "sexual intercourse" . . . in
> late eighteenth century England is an aspect of the same phenomenon that

includes the rise in production then we should expect to find that "sexual intercourse" . . . becomes at this time and in this place discursively and phenomenologically central in ways that it never had been before.[27]

The "long eighteenth century" begins in 1680, and, although Abelove focuses his attention on the last forty years of the eighteenth century because the data supporting his hypothesis is most heavily concentrated there, we may legitimately think of the Blumenbergian zero point with which we are here concerned—"the zero point of the dissolution of order and the point of departure of the construction of order"[28]—as the period of "imagining" eighteenth-century sexuality. We have already observed the privileging of production and the discourse of production of which Abelove speaks in Defoe's and Blackmore's writings of the 1690s. Recall, for example, Blackmore's dictum: "the Labour of the meanest Persons that Conduce to the Welfare and Benefit of the Public are more valuable, because more useful, than the Employments of those who apply themselves only, or principally to divert and entertain the Fancy."[29] Furthermore, we have always known that marriage assumes a privileged position in the drama from the late 1680s onward—that sentimental, "conscious lovers" replace witty, combative ones as objects of our approval and admiration, that rakes may from time to time "relapse" but are always brought back to good, matrimonial behavior by the absolute fidelity and devotion of their virtuous wives, and that a new masculine ideal finds definition in the *husband* (in every sense of the term) rather than the sexually voracious, libertine lover. We have in the past attributed this change to an inexplicable birth of a new sentimental sensibility, a new warm-heartedness that arose in England toward the beginning of the eighteenth century, or we have traced the genesis of the "man of feeling" to latitudinarian preachers and their doctrine of a benevolent "human nature."[30] We have not looked for the economic ideological underpinnings of the change to sentimental sensibility largely because, until quite recently, we have tended to compartmentalize discourses, and to read literary and philosophical writing in isolation from other kinds of writing. However, discourses were not so compartmentalized at the end of the seventeenth century. For instance, William Popple, secretary to the Board of Trade of 1696, did not find it in the least incongruous to use one of the most romantic of lyrical forms, the rondeau, to write with a lover's fervor his paean to the new mercantilism:

RONDEAU

Business of Trade
Has been for private Gain

> Of my past Life the fruitless Pain
> But now kind Heaven, in Recompense has made
> Th'Employment of my Age
> For Publick Good, on Publick Stage,
> Business of Trade
> And may Success attend
> Tho' mine still fail that Publick End,
> For since therein my Country's Weal is laid
> I above all things prize
> That which all Publick Wants supplies
> Business of Trade.[31]

Popple's use of a high romance lyric form to give expression to the discourse of capitalism lends credence to Abelove's speculations. However, the strongest evidence supporting Abelove's hypothesis is to be found in one of the earliest textbooks on macroeconomics, Charles Davenant's highly influential and important work, *An Essay upon the Probable Methods of making a People Gainers in the Ballance of Trade* (1699). "The People being the first Matter of Power and Wealth, by whose Labour and Industry a Nation must be Gainers in the Ballance, their Increase or Decrease must be carefully observ'd by any Government that designs to thrive; that is, their Increase must be promoted by good Conduct and wholesome Laws, and if they have been Decreas'd by War, or any other Accident, the Breach is to be made up as soon as possible, for it is a Maim in the Body Politick affecting all its Parts."[32]

It is by no means coincidental that in the very same year that Davenant, a key member of the powerful Board of Trade, is calling for "wholesome laws" that will turn the sexual energies of Englishmen to the service of capitalist production, the first mass arrests of homosexuals in London and Windsor took place, nor that by 1707 the Societies for the Reformation of Manners were sending secret agents to infiltrate their recognized meeting places on London-bridge and the Arcades of the Royal Exchange.[33] Homosexuality had to be searched out and destroyed. Homosexuals, now effeminized and hardly to be *named* without scandal—"a new society . . . call'd S——d——ites; men worse than goats, who dress themselves in petticoats"[34]—had to be arrested and brought to punishment or transported. And why was this? Surely *not* because homosexuality was a sin; like avarice, pride, gluttony, or any other kind of lust, it had been a *sin* since the twelfth century. It became a serious *crime* at the end of the seventeenth century because *homosexual practices are sexual acts that are nonproductive*, and, as Abelove says, "behaviors, usages, and customs which are judged to be non-productive . . . come under extraordinary and ever-intensifying nega-

tive pressure" once capitalistic production "becomes discursively and phenomenologically central in ways that it had never been before."[35] As Defoe
had so concisely put the matter: "Multitudes of People make Trade, Trade
makes Wealth, Wealth builds Cities, Cities enrich the Land around them,
Land enrich'd rises in Value, and Value of Land enriches the Government."[36]

Like the proposals for a mimetic language, the "man of feeling," too, is
a product of the discourse of modernism, which was designed to promote
trade and empire as well as "natural philosophy." Locke designed for the
Earl of Shaftesbury's Council of Trade, the precursor of the Board of Trade
of 1696, a whole theoretical program which insisted that "Trade ... was an
affair of policy: members of the council must be able to distinguish and
understand the ends that are pursued by them as different from the ...
private designs of merchants."[37] In exactly the same way that trade could
no longer be considered a matter of private interest in the Restoration
reconstruction of culture, neither could sexuality.

Charles Davenant writes, "a large Proportion of the Females remain
unmarried tho' at an Adult Age, which is a dead Loss to the Nation, every
Birth being as so much certain Treasure; upon which Accompt, such Laws
must be made for the Publick Good, as induce all Men to marry whose
Circumstances permit it."[38] (The resemblance between Davenant's voice
and that of the "Projector," the narrator of *A Modest Proposal,* is uncanny, is
it not?) Just as laws against homosexuality must be strictly enforced and
violations of them severely punished, so too must sexual adventuring of
any kind be sharply curbed and penalized because any kind of libertinism,
any sexual behavior unamenable to state control threatens stable marriage,
and marriage is the best mechanism for the production and maintenance
of "hands" for the "Mr. Bounderbys"—the captains of capitalism who
were coming into ascendance in the last decades of the seventeenth century: "The securing the Parish for Bastard Children is become so small a
Punishment and so easily Compounded, that it very much hinders Marriage. The Dutch compel Men of all Ranks, to marry the Woman whom
they have got with Child; and perhaps it would tend to the farther Peo-
pling of *England,* if the Common People here, under such a certain Degree, were condemn'd by Law to suffer the same Penalty."[39]

The discourse of capitalism and the discourse of heterosexuality meet
and intersect in the "official language" of nationalism, and all the "juridico-
political contracts it guarantees." For Davenant, as for the reformers whose
pronouncements we have read above, the only virtue is "publick virtue."
And Davenant advocates "virtue"—by which he quite openly says he means
heterosexual behavior strictly confined within the bounds of marriage—exclusively to the end that it promotes and insures nationalism, class stability,

and growth in the gross national product: "we shall venture to affirm that if this Nation should ever be under any great Disorder, the truest course to mend it, will be to plant in the Minds of the better sort Morality, and the Shame of doing ill to their Country, and we shall presume to assert that observing the Rules and Dictates of Virtue, does not only lead to Heaven and a blessed State hereafter, but is the very best way of securing to a People in general, Prosperity, Peace, Safety, Power, and Happiness in this present World."[40]

Charles Davenant claimed that reading was of no use to him at all, for only mercantile experience could provide the basis of a political and economic program as comprehensive as that which he proposed. However, if the hardheaded economist's discourse openly calls for a recodification of gender differentiation and sexual behavior in the service of capitalism, literary discourse, though perhaps more subtle, was no less effective in instilling the new cultural inscriptions in the minds of late Restoration men and women. Fully confirming Abelove's hypothesis, marriage "becomes at this time in this place discursively and phenomenologically central in ways that it had never been before." Instead of the linguistically self-contained literary play that we found in the interrelation of works of the 1670s—such as Rochester's "A Very Heroical Epistle in answer to Ephelia" *speaking to* Etherege's "Ephelia to Bajazet," both poems playing in the environment of an Ovidian model—we find the externally referential discourse of modernism shaping didactic exchanges on the serious subject of marriage. For example, "The Virtuous Wife: A Poem in answer to 'The Choice,' That would have no Wife" (1700) not only makes the case for marriage, but provides a model of the new female gender characterization. The perfect new woman at the seventeenth century's end is a perfect wife—agreeable, rather than beautiful, reasonable rather than witty, prudent rather than romantic, and rationalistically commonsensical, indeed latitudinarian, in matters of religion.

> A Wife, whose Fairest *Character* should be
> Agreeable *Mien* and *Modesty* . . .
> *Reading* good *Books* and Needlework should be
> Her whole Diversion and Felicity.
> The *Lady's Calling* [a contemporary conduct book] teaches no *Romance,*
> For fond *Intreagues of Love* or *Modes of France.*
> But *solid Wit* and *Virtue's* still secure,
> Against *Temptation* and against *Amour;*
> A Wife well-read in *Books* of Sacred Note;
> Ingenious, but not *Witty* to a *Fau't* . . .
> No *Bigot* in Devotion; not *Confin'd*
> Against the *Laws* and *Libertys* of Mind;

Above all, the new woman must be the direct antithesis of her female progenitors of the last generation:

> Not such a *Lady* of the Rampant Age
> As loves her *Footman, Butler,* or her *Page.*[41]

Umberto Eco has said that the author and reader, or play and audience are "textual strategies," metaphors that refer "to the discursive and interpretive processes that constitute social communication; the two do not represent the points of origin and arrival of a textual message but rather *nodes* of intersection . . . of the various social discourses that transverse the text."[42] The discursive and phenomenological centrality of heterosexual productivity and capitalism, and the unity of the two that Henry Abelove describes begin to appear in literary texts—particularly dramatic—at the start of the "long eighteenth century," in the late 1680s, and become increasingly emphatic at the turn of the century. There is an inextricable knot, a central textual node, at which the discourses of marriage and capitalism meet in satiric texts of the 1690s and 1700s. The celebrated "proviso" scene in one of the most famous of them, *The Way of The World,* provides us with an excellent example. The proviso scene between Mirabell and Milliamant is what we would call in the 1990s a prenuptial agreement. It is a *contract* between "sentimental" lovers, who, no matter how elegant the witty *surface* of the language they speak might suggest otherwise, are in pursuit of *marriage* and *money* throughout the course of the action. Milliamant's dowery depends upon her aunt's consent to her marriage—"half her Fortune depends upon her Marrying with my Lady's Appobration" (I,i)[43]—and the action of the play *turns* upon the acquisition of that consent. The provisos the lovers make are intended to insure a stable, (re)productive marriage. The language the characters are given to speak is not the self-combative, self-deconstructive language that we have seen operating in *The Plain Dealer* and *A Tale of a Tub.* Rather it is the "official" language of which Derrida speaks in "Living on the Borderlines." It is a language designed to *uphold* the institution and "all the juridico-political contracts" upon which it rests:

> **Milla.** . . . Ah! I'll never marry unless I am first made sure of my Will and Pleasure.
> **Mira.** Would you have 'em both before Marriage? Or will you be contented with the first now, and stay for the other until after Grace? . . .
> **Milla.** . . . And d'ye hear I won't be call'd Names after I'm Marry'd; positively I won't be call'd Names.
> **Mira.** Names!
> **Milla.** Ay, as Wife, Spouse, my Dear, Joy, Jewel, Love, Sweet-heart, and the rest of that nauseous Cant, in which Men and their Wives are so fulsomely

familiar— . . . don't let us be familiar or fond, nor kiss before Folks. . . . Nor
go to *Hide-Park* together the first *Sunday* in a new Chariot, to provoke Eyes
and Whispers; And then never be seen there together again; as if we were
proud of one another the first Week, and asham'd of one another ever after.
. . . Let us be as strange as if we had been marry'd a great while; and as well
bred as if we were not marry'd at all.

Mira. Have you any more Conditions to offer? . . .

Milla. Trifles,_____As Liberty to pay and receive Visits to and from whom I
please; to write and receive Letters, without Interrogatories or wry Faces
on your part; to wear what I please. . . . To have my Closet inviolate; to be
sole Empress of my Tea-Table, which you must never presume to approach
without first asking leave. And lastly wherever I am, you shall always knock
at the Door before you come in. These Articles subscrib'd, if I continue to
endure you a little longer, I may by degrees dwindle into a Wife.

Mira. . . . Well, have I Liberty to offer Conditions_____That when you are
dwindled into a Wife, I may not be beyond measure enlarg'd into a Husband. . . . *Inprimis* then, I covenant that your Acquaintance be general; that
you admit no sworn Confident, or Intimate of your own Sex; no she Friend
to skreen her Affairs under your Countenance. . . . No Decoy-Duck to
wheadle you a *fop—scrambling* to the Play in a Mask_____. . .

Milla. Detestable *Inprimis!* I go to the Play in a Mask!

Mira. *Item* I Article, that you continue to like your own Face, as long as I shall:
And while it passes currant with me, that you endeavor not to new Coin it.
. . . *Item,* I shut my Doors against all Bauds with Baskets and penny-worths
of *Muslin, China, Fans* . . . .*Item,* when you shall be Breeding_____. . . .
Which may be presum'd, with a Blessing on our Endeavors_____. . . . I
denounce against all strait Lacing, squeezing for a Shape, 'till you mould my
Boy's Head like a Sugar-loaf; and instead of a Man-Child, make me Father to
a Crooked-billet. Lastly, to the Dominion of the *Tea-Table* I submit_____
But with *proviso* that you exceed not your Province; but restrain yourself to
native and simple *Tea-Table* drinks, as *Tea, Chocolate,* and *Coffee.* . . . _____
But that on no Account you encroach upon the Mens Prerogative, and
presume to drink Healths, or toast Fellows; for prevention of which I ban-
ish all *Foreign Forces,* as *Orange-Brandy* . . . and *Barbado's-Waters.* . . These
Proviso's admitted, in other things I may prove a tractable and complying
Husband.

Milla. O horrid *Proviso's!* filthy strong Waters! I toast Fellows, Odious Men! I
hate your odious *Proviso's.*

Mira. Then we're agreed. Shall I kiss your Hand upon the Contract? and here
comes one to be Witness to the Sealing of the Deed. [IV,v,31–152]

Despite the lightly bantering style in which the provisos are made—which
functions to make what they inscribe seem *natural,* agreeable, and charm-
ing—the conditions laid down in this passage design the power structure,

space, and function of the newly formulated *bourgeois* marriage. For instance, the wife has dominion over the domestic sphere—the tea-table, dressing room, and bedroom—so long as the activities conducted in that sphere do not admit any excursion into, or invasion from, the outside world that might threaten the inviolable boundaries of marriage—bawds disguised as petty tradeswomen, confidantes who encourage *masquerade* excursions to the theater and flirtation with fops, or "male" tavern activities like drinking and toasting. The central "endeavor" of the married pair is "breeding," and it is solely to the ends of that endeavor that the woman's beauty is put. She therefore need not use cosmetics nor "squeeze for a shape," for her beauty is serving its proper function and need not be "re-coined" as long as it "passes currant" with her husband. (We should note the discourse of capitalism breaking through the surface of the discourse of courtship in that line of Mirabel's.) The "contract" incises and inscribes the contours of gender roles, and the distinct separation, as well as the hierarchic relation, between them. The perfect male, "beautiful-looking" (Mirabel), is the *husband,* caretaker, provider, and governor general of the domestic space in which his perfect wife, "thousand charms" (Millamant), luxuriously nests and reigns as lieutenant governor. Libertinism has become the role of the adulterous villain, Fainall, the foolishly aggressive "professed whoremonger," Petulant, or the fop, Witwoud. Recognition of marriage as the ideal is the infallible sign of true wit and goodness of heart; failure to uphold the ideal signals falsity, perverted wit or intelligence, and evil nature—"Fainall" and "Marwood." Witwoud, for example, apologizes to Fainall for having asked after his wife: "I beg pardon that I shou'd ask a Man of Pleasure [i.e., the new, debased, idea of the libertine] and the Town, a Question at once so Foreign and Domestick. But I talk like a Maid at a Marriage. I don't know what I say" (I,iv, 26-29).

It is the *civic duty* of every good man to marry while he is still young enough to beget children—"Methinks Sir *Willful* shou'd rather think of marrying than travelling at his years. I hear he is turn'd of forty" (III,viii,12-14). And *unproductive* female sexual desire is the object of continuous ridicule and contempt: "My Lady Wishfort . . . who publishes her Detestation of Mankind, and full of the Vigour of Fifty-five declares for a Friend and *Ratafia;* and let Posterity shift for itself, she'll breed no more" (I,i,66-71). "Virtue" consists in prudence in matters of sex and money. For example, in providing marriage for a former mistress while also securing her money, Mirabel has secured Fainall as a husband for Mrs. Fainall to tidy up after his affair with her—"A better Man ought not to have been sacrific'd to the Occasion; a worse had not answer'd to the Purpose" (II,iii,29-31)— and he also saves the day for himself and all the "good" characters by having held her fortune in security. On the other hand, *prodigality* with love and money, traits inseparable from the ideal of "Honor" in the culture of the 1660s and 1670s, are the telltale marks of the now-villainous libertine. In response to Marwood's accusation that he has bankrupted her, Fainall replies, "Your Fortune has been bestow'd as the Prodigality of your Love would have it, in Pleasures which we both have shar'd" (II,ii,109-112). Pleasure is no longer an acceptable justification for love; and *expensive* pleasure is doubly criminal. Deception is evil only when it is used by evil characters, for the new, binary model in satire distinguishes "good" from "evil" entirely in terms of that which upholds, as opposed to that which deviates from, the *cultural ideal.* For example, Mirabel may use any means—a staged deception, or his own sexual allure—to dupe Lady Wishfort without compromising his honor because his *end* is marriage to her niece. However, it would be immoral for him actually to satisfy Lady Wishfort because *her* sexual desire is nonproductive:

> **Mira.** I did as much as Man cou'd, with any reasonable Conscience; I proceeded to the very last Act of Flattery with her, and was guilty of a Song in her Commendation. Nay I got a Friend to put her into a Lampoon, and compliment her with the Imputation of an Affair with a young Fellow, which I carry'd so far, that I told her the malicious Town took notice that she was grown fat of a sudden; and when she lay in of a Dropsie, persuaded her she was reported to be in Labour. The Devil's in't, if an old Woman is to be flatter'd further, unless a Man shou'd endeavor downright personally to debauch her; and that my Virtue forbad me. [I,i,77-90]

The greatest "flattery" that can be bestowed upon a woman is to be told she is thought to be capable of *productive* sexuality; the greatest folly in a woman is to have sexual desire, or to allow it to be known that she has, when she is no longer capable of bearing children.

The discourse of heterosexuality and the discourse of capitalism, of marriage and of money, are the warp and woof of this text. "Marry her, marry her!" Fainall deceitfully cries to Mirabel; "there's such Coupling at *Pancras,* that they stand behind one another, as 'twere a Country Dance," the Servant says, reporting Waitwell's marriage to Foible. "Excellent Foible, Matrimony has made you eloquent in Love," Mirabel exclaims. The villain *is* a villain because he hates his wife, but he uses a promise of marriage to enlist his mistress as an accomplice in his evil designs: "I'll hate my Wife yet more, Damn her, I'll part with her, rob her of all she's worth, and we'll retire somewhere, any where, to another World. I'll marry thee." The power of marriage and money together can be a *weapon*—"Starve him, Madam, starve him; marry *Sir Rowland* and get him disinherited"—or, a *lure,* or a baited *trap:*

> **Mrs. Fain.** So, if my poor Mother is caught in a Contract, you will discover the Imposture betimes; and release her by producing a Certificate of her Gallant's former Marriage.
>
> **Mira.** Yes, upon Condition that she consent to my Marriage with her Niece, and surrender the moiety of her Fortune in her Possession. [II,iii,40-44]

Or, it can be the only reliable proof of love:

> **Wait.** I am charm'd, Madam, I obey. But some Proof you must let me give you:—I'll go for a Black Box, which contains the Writings of my whole Estate, and deliver that into your Hands. [IV,xv,75-79]

The "writings" of capitalism can signal either a fall from grace—as the "Black Box" would be for Lady Wishfort in Waitwell's hands—or, can signal deliverance, as they finally are for Lady Wishfort when the "Black Box" is in Mirabel's hands. The discourses of heterosexuality and capitalism *design* ideal good. Money and marriage are goods in themselves, and are also the rewards for good behavior. Mirabel's reward to Foible for marrying Waitwell is money, and to Waitwell for marrying Foible is a lease:

> **Mira.** Your Diligence will merit more—in the mean time_____[Gives Mony]
> **Foib.** Oh, dear Sir, your humble Servant.
> **Wait.** Spouse.
> **Mira.** Stand off Sir, not a Penny_____Go on and prosper, Foible_____The Lease shall be made good and the Farm stock'd, if we succeed. [II,viii,32-38]

Conversely, sexual indulgence outside of marriage and a lack of money are equally causes of social disgrace. The greatest insult that Lady Wishfort can hurl at Mirabel is the imputation that he has been imprudent with money—"I warrant the Spendthrift Prodigal's in Debt as much as the Million Lottery" (III,v,69-71). And Marwood is as furious with Fainall for misusing her money as for abusing her honor. Her most potent weapon against him is the threat to expose him as a bankrupt:

> **Mar.** . . . I'll publish to the World the Injuries you have done me, both in my Fame and Fortune; with both I trusted you, you Bankrupt in Honour, as indigent of Wealth. [II,iii,104-108]

The villain's conduct in relation to women and money is *the exact inverse* of the hero's—as the new binary model for satire demands.

The Dedication to *The Way of the World* points us toward three most important characteristics of the text: 1) that its satiric design is binary—intended to teach us to discriminate "betwixt the Character of a *Witwoud*

and a *Truewit*" (p.337), 2) that it presupposes mimesis as the ground of
dramatic representation, and, correlative to these, 3) that it assumes "emulation" as the mechanism of audience response to artistic representation.
We have observed in the deconstructive satires we examined—*The Plain
Dealer, A Tale of a Tub,* or "Aude aliquid. Ode," for example—that the speakers
of this kind of satire are either "positions" from which satiric discourse is
launched, or "bubbles" that self-propelled boiling satiric discourse throws
up only to puncture in the course of its chaotic, self-combative movement. The speakers in *The Way of the World* are quite different; they are
"characters" in the modern sense of the term. They are fictional representations of people, designed to create the illusion that they have interior
"life" and to arouse in audiences sympathetic, empathetic, or antipathetic
responses to their "feelings." We have observed in *The Plain Dealer* that
speakers of satire are also invariably *targets* of satire, types stock in satire
since Juvenal: the brutal satyr-satirist, the rapacious lawyer, the virago, the
libidinous, greedy seductress. Deconstructive satire does not admit of the
existence of warmhearted eccentrics, or indeed, of interior landscapes,
warm or cold, within the human self. "Man" is a "micro-coat," a bag of
wind, an empty space. *The Way of the World,* on the other hand, is not
figured with shapes of folly; it is peopled. Moreover, folly itself is not (as in
deconstructive Restoration satire) endemic to despicable humankind, a
race of "whore[s] in understanding." Rather, in this new-style, binary satire, follies are correctable errors in judgment that cause essentially benevolent beings to deviate from the ideals that the binary model upholds.

> Those Characters which are meant to be ridicul'd in most of our Comedies,
> are of Fools so gross, that in my humble Opinion they shou'd rather disturb
> than divert the *well-natur'd and reflecting* Part of an Audience; they are rather
> Objects of Charity than Contempt; and instead of moving our Mirth, they
> ought very often to *excite our Compassion.*
>   This Reflection mov'd me to design some Characters, which shou'd ap-
> pear ridiculous not so much thro' a natural Folly (which is incorrigible, and
> therefore not proper for the Stage) as thro' an *affected Wit,* a Wit, which at the
> same time it is affected, is also false. [ital. mine; Preface, pp.336-337]

This is a satire that not only upholds the central values of the institution—
money and marriage—but instills those values in the audience. Moreover,
like an Horation satire, it is addressed to the pillars of society and solicits
their approbation: "Poetry in its Nature, is sacred to the Good and Great;
the Relation between them is reciprocal, and they are ever propitious to it.
It is the Privilege of Poetry to address them, and it is their Prerogative
alone to give it Protection" (p.339).

The new, morally amending, binary satire depends upon what I have elsewhere called "psychologically associative, emulation theory," that is, a conception of the manner in which a reader or spectator is led to emulate the exemplary models of "good behavior" s/he perceives in a work of art.[44] In the 1680s new ways of conceiving human nature arose—particularly among latitudinarian divines. For example, in *A Demonstration of the Divine Authority of the Law of Nature* Samuel Parker not only locates Good within the individual human being, but argues that it is a "law" of our nature to contemplate our inner goodness with pleasure. Moreover, our pleasure is doubled when we see the connection between the sentiments that enliven us and the universal law, established by divine authority, that governs our "nature" and all of "nature": "All men feel a natural Deliciousness Consequent upon every Exercise of their good-natur'd Passions; and nothing affects the Mind with greater Complacency, than to reflect upon its own inward Joy and Contentment. So that the Delight of every vertuous Resolution doubles upon itself; in that it first strikes our Minds with a direct Pleasure by its suitableness to our Natures and then our Minds entertain themselves with pleasant Reflections upon their own Worth and Tranquillity."[45] Ideas about human nature like Parker's wedded to ideas about human understanding like Locke's not only gave rise to new ideas about perception but also generated an associationist theory of aesthetic perception that is the philosophical basis of the affective theory of emulation: we *become* what we see with pleasure; if we see pleasing examples of "good" behavior, we are led to imitate them and thereby to become "good." "[Locke's] analysis suggested that explanation and control of human behavior might be achieved by an approach that focussed attention upon directly observable stimuli and responses."[46] Therefore, in 1709 Addison could argue that "Amendment" of the "people" was

> only to be made ... by encouraging the representation of ... noble characters ... from whence it is impossible to return without strong impressions of honor and humanity.... How forcible an effect this would have upon our minds, one needs no more than to observe how strongly we are touched by mere pictures; who can see Le Brun's Picture of the Battle of Porus, without *entering into the Character* of that fierce, gallant man, and being accordingly spurred to an *Emulation* of his constancy and courage.... If a thing painted or related can irresistably enter our hearts, what may not be brought to pass by seeing generous things performed before our eyes.[47]

And, more generally describing the mechanism, Pope in his Prologue to Addison's *Cato* writes that the function of dramatic representation is

> To wake the Soul by Tender Strokes of Art,
> To raise the Genius, and to mend the Heart,
> To make Mankind in conscious Virtue bold,
> Live o'er each Scene, *and Be what they behold:*[48]

In this new modern model the "Virtue" which we are to be brought to emulate is, of course, *public virtue.* Like the drama, or any other representational art, binary satire must promote "the Religion, the Government, and the Public Worship of its Country."[49] All three of these became the handmaidens of capitalism. As Collier said in 1697, "If an Ecclesiastick intends to keep Fair with the World . . . If he is in the City, he must avoid haranguing against Circumvention in Commerce, and unreasonable Imposing upon the Ignorance of the Buyer."[50]

There is an inescapable correlation between, on the one hand, libertinism and deconstructive discourse and, on the other hand, the discourse of heterosexuality, mimetic representation, and the emulation theory of moral amendment by literary example. That is, I think, because libertinism, like the Augustinian semiotics examined in chapter 2, admits of *no reality external to language.* All that there *is* are signs and signs refer only to other signs; language can refer only to other language, for only language *is.* This, in capsule, is the basic conception in Augustinian semiotics, the formula upon which linguistically self-reflexive literary representation rests. And, as we have seen, libertinism assumes that "reality" consists entirely in cultural inscriptions that are both ephemeral and empty. Mimetic representation, on the other hand, conceives of language as a second-order construct that is always entirely dependent upon a first-order *material* reality external to language. The emulation theory of moral emendment by literary example seeks to *move* and *change* material reality, that is, "real" human behavior, by means of language.

We find an interesting demonstration of the correlation I have outlined in the practice of Aphra Behn. In the 1670s Behn creates two *libertine* heroines of irregular greatness—Angelica Bianca in *The Rover* I (1677) and Laura Lucretia in *The Feign'd Courtesans* (1679)—both courtesans of heroic temper and high romantic soul, whose fiery greatness breaks through the boundaries of conventional morality and who scorn marriage as a mercenary contract suitable only to the mean of spirit:

> **Lau.** Honour, that hated Idol, even by those
> That set it up to worship! No,
> I have Soul, my Boy, and that's all Love;
> And I'll the Talent which Heaven lent improve. [II,i][51]

These figures step straight from the pages of French romance by way of the heroic drama; they are *literary types*. In the same period of her career Behn writes in the "Epistle to the Reader" prefatory to *The Dutch Lover* strongly arguing *against* the notion that plays are morally reforming:"Plays have not done much more to the amending men's Morals, or their Wit, than hath the frequent Preaching, which this last age hath been pester'd with . . . nor can I once imagine what temptation anyone can have to expect it from them; . . . Comedie was never meant either for a converting or conforming Ordinance."[52] Only fourteen years later Behn wrote *The Lucky Chance* (among the first "problem plays" in English) in which she adapted a stock, bed-trick comedy of the Caroline period, Shirley's *The Lady of Pleasure,* to the serious and sober consideration of a real social issue, forced marriage. The discursive nexus of Behn's play is marriage and money. For example, Lady Fullbank and Letitia are forced into marriage with feeble despised old husbands not, as in a heroic romance, by a cruel king or wicked stepmother, but by economic necessity:"Want compell'd thee to this wretched Marriage" (II,ii,217).

A stock figure, a trope, from Jacobean and Caroline comedy, the rake down on his luck and at the mercy of his City landlady, is transformed into an outcast sentimental lover, doomed to poverty by the forced marriage of his beloved. And the conditions of his poverty are mimetically reproduced—that is, material "reality" is described, or delineated, by language, which is subordinate to, and entirely dependent upon it.

> **Bred.** [Lady Fullbank's servant] . . . at the door [I] encountered the beastly thing he calls a Landlady. . . . I asked for Mr. Wasteall [the name the lover has assumed to cover the shame of his economic disgrace] and she began to . . . so rail at him, that what with her *Billingsgate* and her husband's [a smith's] hammers, I was both deaf and dumb . . . —I was sent up a Ladder rather than a pair of Stairs. . . .
>
> 'Tis a pretty convenient Tub, Madam. He may lie a long in't, there's just room for an old join'd Stool besides the Bed, which one cannot call a Cabin, about the largeness of a Pantry bin, or a Usurer's Trunk; there had been Dornex Curtains to't in days of Yore; but they were now annihilated, and nothing to save his Eyes from the Light, but my Landlady's Blue Apron, ty'd by strings before the Window, in which stood a broken six-penny Looking Glass. [I,iii]

This is the discourse of *things*—a room as small as a tub, a bed like a pantry bin, tatters of curtains that were sleazy material to begin with, a joint stool, a little cracked mirror. It is the discourse of the novel, the literary form that is the very child of the discourse of modernism. Moreover, the language is designed to draw us into sympathy with the character whose situation it represents, and into empathy with Lady Fullbank, who listens to the report and who is responsible for his situation. Typical of the whole play is its opening, wherein Lady Fullbank contemplates her "inner feelings" about her married state; at the very center of her soliloquy the discourses of sexuality and of money that transverse the text intersect:

> **L. Ful.** Oh, how fatal are forc'd Marriages!
> How many Ruins one such Match pulls on!
> Had I but kept my Sacred Vows to *Gayman*
> How happy had I been—how *prosperous* he,
> Whilst now I languish in a loath'd embrace
> Pine out my Life with Age—Consumptions Coughs. [III,i]

As in *The Way of the World,* the nonproductive sexual desire of the old is ridiculous, contemptible, and in this play is even *immoral.* The young lover, Bellamour, disguised as a ghost, frightens his beloved's aged husband away from the marriage bed—a stock theatrical joke for a hundred years. However, here the highly artificial stock trick is accompanied by a moralizing tag:

> Old Man forgive me—thou the Agressor art
> Who rudely forc'd the Hand without the Heart.
> She cannot from the Paths of Honour rove
> *Whose Guide's Religion, and whose End is Love* [III,iii]

In the Dedication to *The Lucky Chance* Behn reveals a complete reversal from the position she had held in 1673 on the question of the power of plays to effect moral improvement by providing examples for emulation. Now, in 1687, her view is that plays are "the Schools of Vertue.... They are secret Instructions to the People, in things that 'tis impossible to *insinuate* into them any other way. 'Tis *Example* that prevails above Reason or DIVINE PRECEPTS (Philosophy not understood by the Multitude); 'tis *Example alone that inspires Morality,* and best *establishes Vertue.* "[53]

That this transformation in Behn's discourse and in what she perceived her intention as a playwright to be occurred in so short a period of time demonstrates particularly well the suddenness of the epistemological break that occurred at Restoration zero point and the rapidity with which the new epistemic constructs arose upon the ruins of the old. It is clear that it is *the new episteme and the new discourse of modernism* that determine both Behn's practice and her critical stance in 1687, for in her *personal politics* Behn was most notoriously an extreme Tory. She would never consciously or intentionally have subscribed to the principles of natural philosophy that informed the thinking of "the great Whig philosopher" Locke, nor to the mercantile principles of the Whig economist Charles Davenant.

We will recall that "The zero point of dissolution of order and the point of departure of the construction of order are identical."[54] While the Restoration period is the point of departure for the construction of a new order and a new coding of gender and sexuality, it is also the point of dissolution of order, and therefore of the deconstruction of medieval/Renaissance codes. Louise O. Vasvari has said that "Certain literary modes —like parody, pastiche, and burlesque—are defined by their refusal to grant privileged status to official and hierarchical truth. . . . While the topsy-turvey world [of inverted verbal forms] might be considered to be a simple bundle of motifs, it can more profitably be placed in *the category of anti-genre* given its deliberate attempt to empty meaning from every primary genre with which it comes into contact" (ital. mine).[55] In the dawn of modernism, at the very moment that the premiere literary vehicle of mimetic discourse, the novel, was coming into being, "literature was flooded with parodies and travesties of all the high genres (parodies precisely of *genres,* and not of individual authors or schools)."[56] An extremely interesting case of a topsy-turvey, anti-generic "attempt to empty meaning" from the dominant "high genre" of the heroic drama is presented to us in the deconstructive dramatic satire *Sodom* (ca. 1670). As we have seen, homoeroticism was identified with heroic masculinity in the heroic genres of the Renaissance and early seventeenth century. That coding remained central in the heroic drama of the 1660s, especially in the motifs of male friendship, admiration of a heroic rival in love and war, and duty to the heroic code. *Sodom,* because it is a parody of a *genre* and not of an individual author or single text, deconstructs the heroic drama and consequently the Renaissance codes of heroic sexuality which that genre incorporates.

The text exists in an unknown hand in the manuscript "The Plays and Poems of Rochester" (Princeton MS AM1440); in *Sodom, or the Quintessence of Debauchery,* the pirated "1680 Antwerp edition"; and in an edition derived from the Antwerp edition, published in Hollywood in 1966.[57] It is important to note that it was not until 1689-90, in the immediate aftermath of the "Glorious Revolution" that English publication of the play was suppressed, and "The Stationer's Company instructed their messenger to prosecute at their expense the printers Benjamin Crayle and Joseph Streater; Crayle was summoned before the Earl of Shrewsbury on 11 February 1690."[58]

If one chooses to read *Sodom* on microfilm at the New York Public

Library, one must flip through twelve genuinely pornographic works to get to it. Yet far from being "The Quintessence of Debauchery," *Sodom* is not even pornographic. The fault in our so categorizing it lies in our own, post-eighteenth-century consciousness. Pornography is the quintessential emulation-evoking mode; it is writing designed to arouse the feelings and sensations of the reader; and, because a pornographic text is *always* a "closed text"—a text which aims "at eliciting a sort of obedient cooperation from the reader"[59]—it seeks to change the reader's behavior. *Sodom* is the very antithesis of pornography. Its representation is not mimetic, but wholly metaphoric. It not only exists "in conversation" with other literary texts, but its very existence, its very meaning–draining meaning is *entirely dependent upon* a highly defined literary genre. To take a very brief example, two central motifs in the heroic genres are the army's love for, and absolute loyalty to, their heroic leader or king, and the heroic love between warriors that we saw expressed above in the quotations from *Coriolanus.* Consider the ways in which these *literary* motifs are absolutely necessary pretexts for the mock-heroic satire of the following passage. Buggeranthos, the general, reports to Bolloxinion, the king, on the army's response to Bolloxinion's proclamation of total sexual freedom and of the superiority of sodomy among sexual practices.

> **BUGGERANTHOS**
>
> _____Great Sir, your Soldiers
> In double duty to your favour bound,
> They own it all, and swear and tear the ground;
> Protest they'll die in drinking of your Health
> And creep into the other World by Stealth,
> Intending there amongst the Gods to vie
> Their Sodom King with immortality.
> **BOLLOXINION**
> How are they pleased with what I did proclaim?
> **BUGGERANTHOS**
> They practice it in honour of your name;
> If lust present they want no woman's aid,
> Each buggers with content his own comrade. [I,i]

Compare the discourse of this passage with that which figures exactly the same motifs in *The Indian Queen,* the kind of heroic drama *Sodom* is designed to deconstruct:

> **Mess.**   that Great Man that carries Victory
> Where ere he goes; that mighty Man . . .
> The Troops gaze on him, as if some bright Star

> Shot to their Aids; call him the God of War;
> Whilst he, as if all Conquest did of right
> Belong to him, bids them prepare to fight. . . .
> At this the Army seem'd to have one voice,
> United in a Shout, and call'd upon
> The God-like Stranger *Lead us, lead us on!* [I,ii][60]

The parodic mechanism in the passage from *Sodom* is not simply to deflate by bringing to the ground the elevated "sacrosanct language" of the heroic genres—as, for example, the double entendre of Shakespearean clowns or the love duets of the puppet Hero and Leander in *Bartholomew Fair* do. Rather, parodic usage here causes heroic discourse to write over itself, so to speak; heroic language is the instrument of its own undoing.

Moreover, *Sodom* is an "open text." The reader's continuous interpretive action is required by it. The satiric effect of the passage above, then, is to undermine, or erase, inscriptions that already exist in the reader's mind, which s/he brings to the text. Therefore, simply to MEAN *Sodom* must depend upon the reader's familiarity with such heroic dramas as *The Conquest of Granada* and *Tyrannic Love,* and, beyond that, upon the reader's knowledge of the entire epistemology and coding of the heroic genres. We are not, as in a pornographic or in a modern "affective" text, drawn into *feeling with* the characters; indeed, we cannot possibly conceive of these parodic figures as "characters" at all. Certainly, we are not drawn to emulate them any more than we would be drawn to emulate figures in a comic strip. As Wolseley asked in reproof of Mulgrave's simpleminded equation of obscenity with pornography, "Does he think that all kind of obscene Poetry is designed to *raise Appetite*? Does he not know that obscene Satyre (of which nature are most of my *Lord Rochester's* obscene Writings, and particularly several of his Songs) has quite a different end, and is so far from being intended to raise, that the whole force of it is generally turn'd to restrain *Appetite*. . . ."[61]

Sodom is by no means a great satire. However, it *is* an anti-generic, deconstructive satire, and, in my judgment, it is often the case that an imperfect or mediocre text can better reveal the discursive strategies it employs than a masterpiece does. I do not agree with J. W. Johnson's attribution of *Sodom* to Rochester; as intelligent and informative as Johnson's argument is, the evidence upon which he bases his case is, finally, not definitive. However, I can understand the temptation to make such an attribution because there are Rochesterian touches in the work. My own hunch (which is quite unsupportable and entirely subjective) is that *Sodom* is a Restoration *Oh, Calcutta!,* the work of a group of wits, which might have included Rochester, members of a small circle who in writing the piece are sharing a literary joke. I think that in part the exercise was to ridicule the leading box-office genre of the time—an intention obvious from the opening lines, which parody the opening lines of *The Conquest of Granada*, "one of the finest of English heroic tragedies [and] . . . for well nigh half a century the most popular."[62]

> **BOABDELIN**
> Thus in the Triumph of soft Peace I reign
> And from my Walls, defy the Pow'rs of Spain [*Conquest of Granada*, I,i,1-2]
> **BOLLOXINION**
> Thus in the Zenith of my Lust I reign:
> I eat to swive, and swive to eat again. [*Sodom*, I,i,1-2]

However, *Sodom* is not a parody of one particular work, or of one particular poet; it is a continuous topsy-turvey inversion of the high heroic genres and the "love and honor" codes they incorporate, a persistent draining of meaning from what Vasvari calls "official and hierarchical truth." At "zero point," as we might expect of a time during which an epistemological order is collapsing, literature was flooded with parodies of all the genres sacrosanct in the Renaissance, precisely the high heroic genres, epic, and its seventeenth-century form, heroic drama.[63] J.W. Johnson observes, "Several such efforts at heroic parody can be dated at the approximate period when Buckingham, Sprat, Clifford, and Butler were working on *The Rehearsal* (acted in December 1671): Butler's "A Caterwauling" and *Dildoides*, Dorset's "Tarsander," the first version of *Sodom*—all derive from the era of Dryden's *Tyrannic Love* and *The Conquest of Granada* (1669-1671)."[64] The satire in *Sodom* is, however, somewhat more complex than that in the texts Johnson cites (including, in my judgment, *The Rehearsal*) for, like "Aude aliquid. Ode," *Sodom* uses libertinism to demolish heroic inscriptions but also, reflexively, as an instrument of self-destruction.

Just as is the case in the relation of "Aude aliquid. Ode" to the Pindaric ode, *Sodom* has as its heroic pre-text, or, more precisely, pre-genre, a literary form that is itself *not mimetic*. As I have demonstrated elsewhere, the heroic drama of the 1660s figures Idea; it does not (re)present even a heightened version of the "actual." Rather, "the function of the [heroic] drama is to lift the minds of its audience to a truth that is not discernible in experience. The design of a play does not consist in its events or rest upon the actions of its personae. Rather, [the expressed intention of such a play is] to elevate the understanding to an apprehension of Ideas of truth. Love and honor are the chosen vehicles of imaginative transcendence because . . . [in the coding of the Middle Ages and Renaissance] love 'excites in the Soul a remembrance of the Intellectual, [and] raiseth her from this terrene of life to the eternal; by flame of love refined into an Angel,' while honor, or heroic virtue, is [in this same coding] 'a habit of Mind . . . inspir'd from above' that elevates a man 'above mankind, and as much as human nature could bear, it render[s] him like a Deity.'"[65]

Heroic *desire,* then, is metaphysical aspiration. As the philosopher Thomas Stanley puts it in mid-seventeenth century, "Those employed in corporeal office [i.e., human beings in their bodies] are depriv'd of Contemplation borrowing science from sense, to this wholly inclin'd, full of errors: Their only means of release from this bondage is the amatory life; which . . . raiseth [the soul] from this terrene of life to the eternal."[66] Given this coding, the discourse of the heroic genres is intended to be a conduit to the ideational, metaphysical realm. Dryden says in the preface to *Tyrannic Love,* "By the Harmony of words we elevate the mind . . . as our solemn Musick, which is inarticulate Poesie, does in Churches."[67] Language is the medium, the movement, and the means of transcendence. Consequently, the speakers in heroic drama are not "characters." Rather, they are constantly changing, grouping, and regrouping *positions* in a continuous dialectic, a system of signs moving in dialectical progression to the refinement of an essential Idea.

We have long recognized that the discourse of the Restoration heroic genres have their roots in Caroline *précieuse* love and honor codes. "Platonick Love," or the *précieuse* religion of love, was born in the rarified atmosphere of such French romances as Honoré d'Urfé's *L'Astrée* (I, 1607), (II, 1610), (III, 1619), (IV and V, 1627); was cultivated as a highly artificial courtly code of behavior intended to effect "the purification of the language and of relations between the sexes," in the famous salon of the Marquise de Rambouillet;[68] and was brought to England by Henrietta Maria. In the coding of *précieuse* Platonick Love, heroic lovers, both male and female, are too "great of soul," their passion too elevated, for the restraint of such mundane customs as marriage. Davenant's *The Platonick Lovers* (1635) which, like his masque, *The Temple of Love,* was written at the request of Henrietta Maria and which was among the first plays to be revived and regularly presented at the opening of the theaters at the Restoration, includes a most interesting exchange between Phylomont, a heroic warrior, and his king and soul-pledged closest friend, the equally heroic warrior, Theander. Phylomont has asked Theander's permission to marry; the king responds to the request with horror:

> **PHYL.** This is strange, being married, is't not lawful, sir?
> **THEA.** I grant it may be law, but is it comely.
> . . . Think on't [love] a noble way. You two may live,

And love, become your own best arguments . . .
Be ever beauteous, fresh, and young, at least
In your belief. . . .
PHYL. But who shall make men, sir: shall the world cease?
THEA. . . . if such deeds [as heterosexual intercourse]
Be requisite, to fill up armies, villages,
And city shops; that killing, labour, and
That coz'ning still may last, know, Phylomont,
I'd rather nature should expect such coarse
And homely drudgeries from others than
From me. [II,i][69]

The female platonick lover, Eurithea, is of as high and aspiring a spirit as her soul mate, Theander. At the suggestion that she marry and mate with Theander because "custom will be obey'd," she replies,

> **EU.** Never by us. We'll live to be examples,
> Not, sir, to follow those we cannot like. [IV,i]

These passages, though their partly comic intention is clear, nevertheless reveal conceptions that are discursively central in the codes of gender and sexuality that obtain in the heroic genres of the Renaissance and early seventeenth century: for example, 1) that greatness of soul, or heroic passion, is elevating, metaphysical desire; 2) that such desire can neither be restrained nor directed by "custom," and 3) that marriage is the mechanism of a sexual productivity that is "homely drudgery," suitable only to the coarse or mean of spirit.

The relation between early seventeenth-century Platonick Love and later seventeenth-century libertinism is obvious. Libertine desire—whether *in men* or *in women,* whether *for men* or *for women*—is boundless. The libertine is a "wild Columbus . . . who must new Worlds in Vice descry" ("Aude aliquid. Ode," ll.272-273). The libertine is transcendentally heroic; in his system of belief,

> A true and brave Transgressor ought
> To sin with the same Height of Spirit Caesar fought.
> ["Aude aliquid. Ode," ll.167-168]

Libertinism scorns custom and boundary, first, because they are ephemeral, empty whimsies, and, second, because libertine desire, metaphysical in scope and intensity, is not containable. Paradoxically enough, the libertine cannot really be thought to be a simple materialist; his/her body and the bodies of others are for him merely instruments for the expression of transcendent metaphysical desire. The libertine's *way* is, of course, different from the Platonick Lover's, but only in that for the latter the body, the "corporeal office," is not a medium for, but an obstacle to, transcendence. It is this space between two closely parallel codes, platonistic préciosité and libertinism, that *Sodom* exploits. It is at this juncture that its heroic discourse dissects and becomes a single discourse running on two parallel tracks in mock-heroic contradiction of itself. For example, if from the following passage, which is Bolloxinion's declaration of the nature of his heroic kingship, only the *two words italicized* were removed, the passage could be inserted otherwise unchanged into any heroic drama, or high romance of the 1660s:

BOLLOXINION

Let other Monarchs, who their Scepters bear
To keep their Subjects less in love than fear
Bee slaves to Crownes, my Nation shall be free_____
My *Pintle* only shall my Scepter be:
My Laws shall Act more pleasure than command
And with my *Pr——k,* I'll govern all the Land.
[I,i, Princeton MS AM1440]

The name "Bolloxinion" parodies "Maximin," a character in Dryden's *Tyrannic Love.* Maximin, "vastus corpore [et] animo ferus," is the sign of power in the world, while Saint Catherine is the opposing, spiritual sign, which Maximin can neither conquer nor possess.[70] The play begins with Maximin in complete ascendence in the world. The "Martial Monarch" has by strength of arms conquered as far as his desire has reached. The figure images egoistic heroic power—the strength, rage, and personal valor that are the mark of "the Herculean hero."[71] In the course of the play Maximin becomes completely enamored of his captive, Saint Catherine of Alexandria. He loves her to the greatest height his worldly soul can reach, but the power he figures cannot reach the heavenly sphere where Saint Catherine's spirit dwells and to which her heroic martyrdom takes her. Maximin's "tyrannic love" is great but not great enough to transcend the body. Saint Catherine's heroic love of God, makes her spurn all earthly crowns (Maximin offers two), and lifts her to a sphere too high for Maximin. *Tyrannic Love,* to which in several places *Sodom* specifically alludes (the daemons of the air sequence, and the fall of Maximin, for instance), is a prototypical heroic drama, an almost perfect realization of the *genre* which *Sodom* is designed to deconstruct. When *Sodom* begins, Bolloxinion has sexually conquered as far as his desire can reach in the "inferior" heterosexual realm. Like Theander in *The Platonick Lovers,* he finds heterosexual activity a "homely drudgery." But the course he chooses to escape it is not *précieuse* platonism, but its sister philosophy, libertinism. He declares for

the "superior" pleasures of sodomy. Moreover, being a heroic prince, he
extends to his people the libertine freedom he has chosen for himself:

> **BOLLOXINION**
> [to Borastus, his general]
> Now onward Borast, set the Nation free
> Let conscience have its force of Liberty
> I do proclaim that Buggery may be us'd
> Thro' all the land so Cunt be not abus'd
> That, the proviso, this shall be your trust
> All things shall to your order be adjust
> To Buggeranthos let the grant be given
> And let him bugger all things under heaven. [I,i, Princeton MS AM1440]

(We might note incidentally that although Buggeranthos does, indeed,
bugger all things under heaven, he is also so prodigiously heroic in heterosexual performance that it is to him that the queen, Cuntigratia, applies to
supply her needs when she is neglected by the king. The libertine way is
to pursue maximum erotic pleasure with men and women equally.) As
discourse both Bolloxinion's declaration and the response of his courtiers
to it exist on the "distanced plane," and are couched in the "sacrosanct
language"[72] of the heroic genres:

> **POCKENELLO**
> [in reply to Bolloxinion]
> Your Grace at once hath from the Powers above
> A princely wisdom, and a princely love;
> Whilst you permit the Nation to enjoy
> That freedom which a Tyrant would destroy.
> By this your Royall Tarse will credit more
> Than all the riches of the Kings of Zoar. [I,i, Princeton MS]

The textual strategies in passages like these, which prevail throughout the
text, are complex. First of all, heroic discourse does not cease to be heroic
discourse; rather, it runs on two tracks of meaning at once, and thereby
cancels itself, or, more precisely, drains itself of meaning. Consequently, the
whole fantasy of heroic *arete*—in itself and also as it is a component of the
libertine code of heroic power and transcendence—is cracked open and
exposed as a mere tissue of words: empty, fancy language.

In the same way that heroic discourse unravels itself, so too do the
"turns," the rhetorical stema, or stations of classical rhetoric, in "love and
honor" debate form a dialectic by means of which the upward movement
of the dialectic is effected. The following are just four examples from among

the many absolutely conventional heroic turns that are satirically sub-
verted in *Sodom:* 1) A plot against the king is designed by a trusted courtier
who is driven to his disloyalty by love:

> **POCKENELLO**
> [to the king]
> Great Sir, when last yourself you did intomb
> Within the strait of Fuckadilla's womb . . .
> **BOLLOXINION**
> And what of that_____
> **POCKENELLO**
> _____I would a Plot reveal.
> **BOLLOXINION**
> Against my honour, Pockenello, tell.
> **POCKENELLO**
> No wonder she not swives as she was wont
> Pine had been familiar with her Cunt.
> **TWELY**
> My Liege, hee swiv'd her in the Tyme of Terme
> I saw him wipe the gleanings of her Sperme . . .
> Seeking to shelter his bold treacherous act.
> **BOLLOXINION**
> Alas, poor Pine, I cannot blame the deed
> When Nature prompteth by impulse of seed.
> **POCKENELLO**
> But 'twas a Trepass, without leave to swive
> Upon his Sovereigns Prerogative. [I,i]

2) A beautiful, heroic lady is torn between love and honor, loyalty to her
friend and duty to her king:

> **FUCKADILLA**
> [to the queen]
> What woman can a standing Pr—— refuse
> When love makes courtship when it might command. . . .
> He prest it hard, I wou'd have turn'd the Spring
> But that my duty was to obey my King. [II,i, Princeton]

3) A queen, caught between obedience to her monarch–husband and the
demands of love, is advised to obey love's higher law:

> **CLYTORIS**
> [to the queen]
> Madam I wonder such a noble Mind
> Should be to singularity inclined, . . .

OFFICINA
[to the queen]
Were I as you a Pintle I should have
Tho' it deprived me of the Crown he gave
Tho' he a Tyrant to your Honour be
Your Cunt may claim a subject's Liberty. [II,i]

4) A powerful, heroically wicked queen, led by uncontrollable desire, attempts to seduce a respectful, but reluctant hero (cf., Zempoalla in *The Indian Queen,* or Lyndaraxa in *The Conquest of Granada*):

BUGGERANTHOS
Your favours, madam, are so far above
The utmost merits of your vassal's Love,
That should I strive in Letchery to obey
And in obedience swive my soul away,
All my Endeavors would at last become
A poor Oblation to your Royal Womb.
CUNTIGRATIA
Still from my Love you modestly withdraw,
You are not by my favour kept in aw,
When friendship does approach, you seem to fly
Do you do so before your Enemy? [IV,i]

In the heroic drama there are no scenes of action; the plays consist entirely in the exchange of rhetorical set-pieces or soliloquies. The stately postures of the soul are shaped in elegant verse tableaux, rhetorical minuets. This is exactly so in *Sodom* as well; however, in *Sodom* this kind of representation by rhetorical embroidery affords yet another opportunity for satiric demolition, for the *irony* is that in the super-sexual, super-heroic arena of the play there is *no action at all,* only talk. Like the great deconstructive satires we have already examined, *Sodom* mocks itself for consisting entirely of empty words.

As there are no characters and no action in *Sodom,* so also there is no place. The semiotic representation of the text turns the wash tint landscapes of pastoral romance, which are inscribed upon our consciousness, to anti-generic topsy-turvydom. For example, in countless pastoral romances, the dejected, rejected heroine—a faithful shepherdess—retreats to a bower to lament her lost love. Act II, scene 2 of *Sodom* opens with the following description of scene:

A faire Portico joyned to a pleasant
Garden and adorned with many statues

> Of naked men and women in various postures
> in the middle
> Of the Garden a naked woman
> representing a fountain standing
> and Pissing Bolt upwards
> Soft musick is plaid to the purling
> water after which is sung this Song
> that follows by a smal voice in a
> mournful key
> Song
> Unhappy Cunt and Comfortlesse
> from swollen plenty faln into distresse . . .
> Divorst and banisht from itts Dearest Ducke
> That Proselite to Pagan Fucke. [II,ii, Princeton]

Finally, the "fall" of Bolloxinion exactly parodies the final destiny of Macbeth in the Davenant-Dryden *Macbeth,* and of Maximin in *Tyrannic Love.* Both heroes and mock-heroes "of irregular greatness" die defying the gods themselves:

> **Max.** . . . shoving back this Earth on which I sit
> I'll mount_____and scatter all the gods I hit.
> *Dyes* [*Tyrannick Love,* V,i,634-635]
> **BOLLOXINION**
> I'll then invade and bugger all the Gods
> And drain the spring of their immortal Cods
> Then make them rub their arses 'til they cry
> You've frigged us out of immortality. [*Sodom,* V,i]

Representation in *Sodom,* then, is entirely literary, entirely metaphoric. Conventional signs, and configurations of signs refer only to other signs and sign systems. Satire dissolves Renaissance heroic codes of gender and sexuality, and deconstructs the shapes of "official" truth engendered by the epistemology that is collapsing at Restoration zero point. *Sodom* explodes the conception of an "amatory life" that can raise the "soul from this terrene of life to the eternal"; it shatters the code of a heroic virtue that elevates mankind and "renders him like a Deity." It destroys the inscriptions of the heroic genres by demonstrating that their "harmony of words," lifting to divine truth, are so much hot air—are, indeed, "Mountains of whimseys, heaped in [man's] own brain," pretty embroideries upon Nothing.

FIVE

The Discursively Central "I" and the Telescope of Discourse

I. "The Proper Study of Mankind is M(E)"

For almost two centuries the European mind has put forward an unprecedented effort to explain the world so as to conquer and transform it.

Mircea Eliade, *Forgerons et alchimistes*

According to Foucault, the central epistemological construct of the modern age is the conception "Man." That construction, in my view, grew out of a late seventeenth-century coding that reformulated the idea of Self, invented "interior space,"[1] and relocated "truth" to that inner human arena. For Renaissance thinkers the inmost human self was furthest removed from God, the still center of the cosmic *harmonia;* "Poor soul the center of my sinful earth," Shakespeare's sonnet laments. The human mind, as we have seen, was the mirror of truth only when it was burnished to reflect metaphysical "characters" inherent in itself, in language, and in eternity. For the new Restoration modernism, on the other hand, the locus and the *font* of truth is the inner arena of the self, and the human mind is most worthily engaged when it contemplates its own operations. Boyle says, "Amongst the great Variety of Employments which I have fancy'd to take up my thoughts with, I have scarce found any more noble nor more worthy of them than the Contemplation of themselves."[2] Locke who as we have seen said that he had modelled *Concerning Human Understanding* upon the operations of his own mind,[3] considers self-reflexive observation of our own internal mental operations the basis of all human understanding: "Our Observation employ'd either about *external, sensible Objects; or about the internal Operations of our Minds, perceived and reflected on by our selves, is that which supplies our Understandings with all the materials of thinking.*"[4] Descartes, who declared that his whole system of logic stemmed directly from an adolescent resolve "no longer to seek any science than knowledge of myself, or the great book of the world,"[5] located the human spirit in the pineal gland.

As they dealt with mind, so too did the new philosophers and thinkers of Restoration modernism deal with feeling. For Renaissance thinkers sense is, of course, an obstacle to understanding, though passion, properly directed, can be a vehicle for transcending the sense-bound self: "Those employed in corporeal office [i.e., enclosed in fleshly bodies] are depriv'd of Contemplation, borrowing science from sense, to this wholly inclin'd, full of error;Their only means of release from this bondage, is the amatory life, which by sensible Beauties exciting in the Soul a remembrance of the Intellectual, raiseth her from this terrene of life to the eternal; by flame of Love refin'd into an Angel"[6]—as we have seen in chapter 4.Thinkers like Locke, as we have also seen, consider sense and inner reflection on "sensible ideas" the sole access to truth.

Not only the new logicians and scientists like Locke and Boyle consider the contemplation of our own inner arena of mind in operation our primary access to truth, but latitudinarian divines, the architects of theories of natural benevolism, also look to the inner arena to observe the operations of the spirit and the laws of nature. Samuel Parker in 1681 argues that "All men feel a natural Deliciousness consequent upon every exercise of their good-natur'd Passions; and nothing affects the mind with greater Complacency than to reflect upon its own inward Joy and Contentment,"[7] and Isham seeks the operations of the "Law of Nature" in the "natural Motions wrought *within us* and moulded into our very Frame" (ital. mine).[8] Just as adherents to the new "natural philosophy" looked outward to the mechanical operations of material nature to chart the "laws of nature," so too, paradoxically, did they look *inward* to the Self, the seat of "natural reason," to discover them.

Curiously enough, in this model the movement inward, once it has reached the locus of truth in the deepest self, reverses direction, and the Self, or what might better be called the discursively central "I," the "rational" mind of the knowing subject, "claims an unimpeachable prerogative to impose its norms as the universally applicable ideal for humanity."[9] As we have seen in Locke's letter to Stillingfleet, the new thinker looks inward to his own mind and then projects what he finds there outward as a universal standard.The method is in germ Cartesian. Descartes' first maxim is "never to accept anything for true which I did not really know to be such . . . nothing more in my judgment than what was presented to my mind so clearly and distinctly as to exclude all ground of doubt." His third maxim is to create outward from that center a whole *order* of thought, "that by commencing with objects the simplest to know, I might ascend by little and little, to knowledge of the most complex; assigning in thought a certain order even to those objects which in their own nature do not stand in a relation of antecedence and sequence."[10]

The inner self becomes not just the locus of truth, but *also* the measure of truth and the *source* from which truth emanates. "I" becomes the discursive center from which all order arises, then to be projected and imposed upon the external world. As Timothy J. Reiss puts the matter, in the period with which we are concerned,

> a discursive order is achieved on the premise that the syntactic order of semiotic systems (particularly language) is coincident both with the logical ordering of "reason" and with the structural organization of a world given as exterior to both these orders. The relation is not taken to be simply one of analogy but one of identity. Its exemplary statement is *cogito-ergo-sum* (reason-semiotic mediating system-world). . . . Its principal metaphors will be those of the telescope (eye-instrument-world) and of the voyage of discovery (self-possessed port of departure-sea journey-country claimed as legitimate possession of the discoverer).[11]

From that cohesive unity, the self, emerge increasingly expanded models that are enlargements of the human self: the nation, the empire, the world. Davenant constructs his model of the body politic upon the human body, bringing into confluence as he does so the discourses of commerce and the new science:

> Knowledge of the Sinews, Muscles, Arteries and Veines, with the late discovery of the Circulation of the Blood and all the parts of Anatomy, conduce very much to render this dark Science [medicine] more plain and certain. In the same manner, such as would understand the Body-Politick, its true Constitution, its State of Health, its Growth or Decay, its Strength or Weakness, and how to apply Remedies to the various Distempers to which it is incident, must study and look narrowly into all the distinct parts of the Commonwealth, its Trade, its Current Mony (which is its flowing Blood) the Arts, Labour and Manufactures, and the number of its People; with many other things which altogether are the Members of which the great Body is compos'd.[12]

We will recall from the Introduction the sixteenth-century description of London, the generic "City" modelled on the body of Christ, and the Ebstorf world map which also is projected upon the body of Christ (his head at the top of the map, his hands on either side, his feet at the bottom). In the new conception the *human* Self/Body has replaced Christ's as the archetype pattern and inscription of reality.

Sprat argues that *by nature* the *English* mind is framed to be sovereign in the empire of reason: "the general constitution of the minds of the English . . . [is such that England] may justly lay claim to be Head of a *Philosophical League* above all other Countries of Europe. . . . If there can be a true character given of the *Universal Temper* of any Nation: then certainly this must be ascrib'd to our Countrymen: that they love to *deliver their Minds* [ital. mine] with a sound simplicity."[13] As we observed in examining the logic and language of Restoration zero point, the new discourse of modernism was the natural philosophers' instrument for making what they considered to be transparent records, "histories of Nature." We can see from this observation of Sprat that the source from which sound, simple mimetic discourse, the analytico-referential discourse of modernism, is "delivered" is the human mind. However, we can also see here the subtle operation by which seemingly unbiased and transparent mimetic discourse becomes the discourse of nationalism. The "English Mind" is easily translatable into "England" and the "rational sense," its core, into London:

> But it is *London* alone that enjoys most of the others [cities' and nations'] advantages, without their inconveniencies. It is the head of a mighty *Empire,* the greatest that ever commanded the *Ocean;* It is compos'd of *Gentlemen,* as well as *Traders;* It has a large intercourse with all the *Earth;* It is as the *Poets* describe their *House of Fame,* a City, where all the noises and business in the World do meet: and therefore this honour is justly due to it, to be the *constant* place of *residence* for that Knowledg, which is to be made up of the Reports, and Intelligence of all Countreys.[14]

London has become a central nexus of all discourses, a seat of knowledge for that body, the world, as human reason is the seat of truth in the human self. In a consequent conversion, the delivery and extension of the English mind in writing (particularly literary or literary-critical writing) comes to be considered a patriotic activity that reflects and gives glory to the English mind, and, by extension, the English nation. Charles Gildon in the "Epistle Dedicatory" to his collection, *Miscellaneous Letters, and Essays on Several Subjects, Philosophical, Moral, Historical by Several Gentlemen and Ladies* (1694), says that the critical essays he has collected exist for "the Glory of the ENGLISH NATION," and that his patron, John Trenchard, must accept the essays and the modern poetry that they value above the works of ancient writers as he is a "TRUE ENGLISHMAN,"

> for the *Patriot's* Zeal ought to extend to the *Glory* as well as *Happyness* of his Country; so you must be *pleas'd* to shelter with your Protection, a Piece that aims at a Vindication of our known RIGHT and HONOUR, which are impiously invaded, and as *weakly,* as *ignobly* betray'd to a *Foreign People* [the Ancients] by a *bigotted* Veneration for a former Age. But *Poetry,* Sir, will appear from the following *Essays,* to be a Prize we ought no more to surrender to *Foreign* Nations than our *Courage* or *Liberty.* For *Greece* and *Rome,* who have given us the noblest Examples of the Latter, have been most famous for the Former. And as we are not inferior to either of those *Commonwealths,* in the Honor of Arms, or the Wisdom of our Laws, so I can never yield them the precedence in *Poetry.*[15]

Extending further and further outward from the discursively central self, "natural reason" and its mediating semiotic system, the discourse of modernism, strive to possess, and consolidate empire of, the world: "This is truly to command the world; to rank all the *varieties* and *degrees* of things, so orderly upon one another; that standing on the top of them we may perfectly behold all that are below, and make them all serviceable to the quiet, and peace, and plenty of Man's life."[16]

At the very historical moment when the deconstructionist thrust of Restoration zero point was erasing the "I" and shattering any possibility of a univalent perspective, any gaze of a single "eye," the constructionist new epistemology was reformulating the idea of self and making its core, "natural reason," the central switchboard of all social discourses. Radiating out from that discursive center a vast network of ordered and ordering discourses were redesigning reality and reconstructing the human world. For example, religion is no longer conceived either as the soul's mystical longing for transcendence and union with God, nor as "the good old Cause" for which to fight and die; rather "*Religion* is exalted *Reason* . . . it dwelleth in the upper Region of the *Mind,* where there are fewest *Clouds* or *Mists* to darken or offend it."[17] Money, as we heard from Davenant, is not filthy lucre, the food and fuel of cupiditas; it is the lifeblood of the nation. Virtue is learnable good manners and good, socially approved morals. But, most important for the future, power is not exercised by force but veiled by, and also established and maintained by, the ordering discourses of "natural reason" imposed in the name of "civilization" and "progress." A White Paper presented to the Board of Trade of 1696 strongly admonishes that "Governors [of colonies] should have more of the breeding of Merchants than Soldiers."[18]

When Self becomes discursively central, satire becomes Horatian, mimetic, and binary. No longer an instrument for exploding all whimsies of order, erasing all concepts of subjectivity, exploring the limits of language, and adumbrating the abyss, satire becomes a single voice issuing from, and reinforcing the validity of, the deepest self. It becomes a careful delineator of boundaries, a nice weigher of moral judgments, and a sharp instrument for discriminating not just "right" from "wrong," but also "us" from "them" and "English" from "Other."

William Wollaston's influential critical preface to *The Design of Part of the Book of Ecclesiastes . . . Represented in an English Poem* (1691) looks at Roman satire through the lens of the new modern paradigms. Wollaston prefers Horace above all other satirists because he is rational, serious, and logically argumentative: "For his [Horace's] thoughts are generally rational and yet modified with a sort of newness and delicacy almost proper to himself. And in this he excels Juvenal and all the World beside."[19] The shift from Juvenal to Horace as the favored model in satire, which we have ascribed to the unaccountable birth of a new "amiable humor" and dated from the eighteenth century, is rather a product of the new thinking of Restoration zero point—and is especially consequent upon the call for a transparent mimetic discourse and the new discursive centrality of "I," the rational knowing subject. As Raman Selden says, the hallmark characteristic of Horatian satire is "the apparently effortless and spontaneous presentation of the satirist's *inner* life, a quality not usually associated with classical poetry" (ital. mine).[20] At the center of an Horatian satire is a single "richly autobiographical narrative voice" which issues from that center in a clear logically argumentative style that both mirrors the self from which it issues—Selden says that "the plain style satire [of Horace] is the mirror of self"[21]—and orders the moral world around it. Wollaston prizes Horace's discourse because he finds it "true" to reason and experience: "tho' *Horace* hath a very familiar and pleasing Air, yet his discourses are for the most part true, and consequently different from that . . . that minds *jest* more than truth, and considers men rather as *risible* than *rational*."[22] We must remember that Horace first called his poems "sermones"—that is "conversations." Only in his second book of satires does he call them "saturae" and does he lay down the rules for the composition of what has become for him a genre with a distinct profile. (Juvenal called *his* satire "farrago," which, as we have seen in chapter 3, it indeed is.)

It was precisely the calm, serious narrative voice, issuing from a single, central, recognizable persona that made Horace so attractive to the new thinkers of the Restoration. Narrative is prized by them whether in experimental science or in art because logically ordered narrative does not call attention to itself as language, but most closely approaches the illusion of transparency. "The most innocent, graceful and *universal* Discourse," Fairfax says, "is telling Stories, and is Modern rather than Ancient."[23]

Wollaston, who in imitation of Horace sets down rules of composition in his Preface, sees as primary requirements that satire must be true, logically ordered, and clear. "As to the *matter* of Satyr," he says, "it should consist of *Arguments* against something, that is vicious or unreasonable."[24] Satire *must* discriminate between reason and unreason. Moreover, the argumentative lines of a satire must be ordered and ordering, and must be immediately intelligible to the ordinary, commonsensical reader: "The arguments must be *intelligible;* else the end of Satyr [moral reformation] is defeated. To this purpose they [the arguments] should all look the same way and be directed to the proof of some one thing, without . . . intermixture and confusion of subjects."[25]

In the new conception satires must be what Umberto Eco designates as "closed texts," texts which have as their primary aim "eliciting a sort of 'obedient' cooperation" from the reader. They must "have in mind an average addressee referred to a given social context. . . . [And must] obsessively aim at a precise response on the part of more or less precise *empirical* readers."[26] Therefore just as a satire must not call attention to its language, in Wollaston's view, neither must it call attention to its learning lest the "obedient" reader be distracted from the reformational effects of its narrative argument: "They should be free from . . . needless ostentation of learning because . . . [discourses that are learned work] not so much to benefit or delight a Reader, as to lose and perplex him."[27] As a "closed text" the newly conceived satire, then, "chooses"—or, more precisely, *constructs*—its Model Reader "in the same way as an advertisement chooses its possible audience."[28]

The new kind of satire need not—indeed, most often *should* not—be funny: "Some crimes ought not to be medled with but seriously . . . it would be trifling and levity to pretend to ridicule, or correct them that way . . . *and he might seem to be in a disposition to commit the same, who could be merry under the sense of them*" (ital. mine).[29] The new satire establishes a firm *bond* between the "author"—that "richly autobiographical narrative voice" of the discursively central "I"—and the "obedient" reader and 1) discriminates between them—both men of "rational sense"—and those "others," who commit the acts of vice and folly against which the satire argues, and 2) by the narrative logic of its argumentative discourse makes the "obedient" reader give himself to the direction of the text and thereby leads him to "right" judgment. Dacier, Dryden tells us, prizes Horace because,

> In these Two Books of Satire, 'tis the business of *Horace* to instruct us how to combat our Vices, to regulate our Passions, to follow Nature, to give Bounds to our desires, to Distinguish betwixt Truth and Falsehood, and betwixt our *Conceptions of Things and Things themselves* [ital. mine]; To come back from our predicate Opinions, to understand exactly the Principles and Motives of all our Actions; and to avoid the Ridicule, into which all men necessarily fall, who are Intoxicated with those Notions *which they have received from their Masters; and which they obstinately retain, without examining whether or no they are founded in right Reason*. [ital. mine][30]

Dacier might be Boyle, Sprat, or Locke in assessing the merits of Horace. What he values in Horace's closed-text satire is the regulatory function of its ordered and ordering discourse, which leads the Model Reader to exercise "right Reason," to discriminate virtue from vice, and, with the narrator, to derive understanding from experience. In the new conception satire regulates and reforms its readers by its own simplicity, logicality, and "reasonable" argumentation. The straight path of its narrative leads the obedient reader to shape himself to its own carefully restrained and ordered contours; rationally ordered, it makes its reader rationally ordered. The new satire is *prescriptive,* as all closed texts are, and if its reader chooses not to follow the prescription then s/he deserves to be morally sick: "They who endeavor not to correct themselves, according to so exact a Model; are just like the Patients, who have open before them a Book of Admirable Receipts, for their Deseases, and please themselves with reading it, without Comprehending the Nature of the Remedies, or how to apply them to their Cure."[31]

Because there is no place in the new, closed-text satire for the reader to exercise the continuous interpretive acts that an open-text, deconstructive satire demands, wit, and especially that wit that depends upon highly metaphoric wordplay, linguistic combat, heteroglossic voices, or ironic intertextual allusion is unacceptable. Wit is suspect because it destabilizes the central core of self, "natural reason"; "It has . . . no place in the Works where severe Knowledge and Judgment are chiefly exercis'd; those superior Productions of the Understanding must be express'd in a clear strong manner without intervening Strains of Wit."[32] By extension, wit also threatens that enlarged entity patterned on the self, the Nation. Wit is *un-English*—"Nor does it [wit] always agree well with the Temper of our *Nation;* which as it has a greater corage than to suffer *derision,* so it has a firmer *virtu* than to be wholly taken up about deriding of others."[33] And, finally, wit threatens the ordered and ordering discourses that emanate from the discursively central self because "it proceeds from the observation of the *deformity* of things; . . . there is a nobler and more masculine pleasure, which is rais'd from beholding their *Order* and *Beauty*."[34] Wit and raillery *are* acceptable only when they can be harnessed to the service of rationalistic, ordering discourse and put to the work of moral reformation and a social cohesion born out of conformity. Addison, looking backward upon the intentions and achievements of *The Spectator* and *The Tatler* says, "They endeavored to make mirth instructive," and goes on to discuss the social usefulness of rightly channeled wit:

> Such productions of wit and humour, as have a tendency to expose vice and folly, furnish useful diversions to all kinds of readers. The good or prudent man may, by these means, be diverted without prejudice to his discretion, or morality. Raillery, *under such regulations* [ital. mine] unbends the mind from serious studies and severer contemplations without throwing it off its *proper bias*. It serves the same design that is *promoted by Authors* of a graver turn, and only does

it in another manner. It also awakens *reflection* in those who are not indifferent in the cause of virtue or knowledge.[35]

The "regulation" exercised by the new, seemingly transparent, ordering discourse of satire, of necessity, produced the *binary* conceptual design that satire was to have from the Restoration onward and which in the twentieth century we would come to believe was a *generic* necessity in all satire. We will recall from chapter 2 that Paul de Man defines two kinds of irony which I have associated respectively with backward-looking Restoration *deconstructive* satire and forward-looking Restoration *constructive,* and eighteenth-century satire. To recapitulate de Man's distinction, whereas both ironies arise out of a perception of difference, the first, which I have argued is the irony employed in Restoration deconstructive satire, "transforms the *self* out of the empirical world into a world constituted out of and in language." That dislocated self thereby "exists only in the form of a language that asserts knowledge of . . . [its own] inauthenticity" and "before long the entire texture of the self is unravelled."[36]

We have followed the operation of this kind of irony in examining the "No-I"/"No-eye" deconstructive satire of Restoration zero point. The second irony de Man discriminates is basic to the "I"-centered satire we are discussing here. In the new Restoration satire, which is the foundation of eighteenth-century satire, difference is *intersubjective.* Irony occurs "in terms of the superiority of one subject over another, with all the implications of will to power, of violence, and possession which come into play when a person is laughing at someone else—including the will to educate and improve."[37]

As Selden argues, "The most striking difference between the satires of this period [the Restoration-eighteenth century] and that of the Elizabethan and Jacobean periods lies in the shift from the attack on general human types to the castigation of particular people in contemporary historical situations."[38] The *targets* of the new satire are "real people" not rhetorical tropes or figures that bubble to the surface of a self-combative, self-reflexive turbulent language. Moreover, the gaze that the new satire focuses upon these "real" satiric targets is the directed eyebeam of "good" and "prudent men"—the readers, who are cohorts of the rational, discursively central narrator-persona. What Dacier says of Horace applies generally to the new, constructive satires and theories of satire of the Restoration that, sometimes consciously and sometimes unconsciously, took Horace as their model: "In a Word [Horace] endeavors to make us happy to our selves, agreeable, and faithful to our Friends, and discreet, serviceable, and well bred in relation to those with whom we are oblig'd to live and converse."[39] The new ordered and ordering language of satire establishes a bond of trust between the discursively central I-narrator, modernism's knowing subject, and the "obedient" Model Reader and carefully discriminates the narrator + reader "us" from "them," the foolish or vicious "others" at whom the "reader" and the "author" gaze through the telescope of mediating discourse.

II. Ordered and Ordering: The New Theory of Satire

In the *Discourse Concerning the Original and Progress of Satire* Dryden says, "we should make *Horace* our Minister of State in Satire and *Juvenal* of our private pleasures."[40] That comment reflects not only the nature of the turn that occurred in our period from Juvenal to Horace as the favored model, but also the primary critical intention of Dryden's *Discourse* itself, which was 1) to reconstruct the generic profile of satire in line with new modern thinking, and 2) to project upon that new generic model a *conceptual* design for satire that has shaped our understanding of the genre for three hundred years. Paradoxically, although the *Discourse* is the critical preface to a collection of translations of Juvenal and Persius, and although Juvenal is Dryden's personal favorite among the ancient satirists, nevertheless the ideal model that the essay proposes for "how a Modern satire should be made"[41] is Horatian (at least as Horace was understood in 1693)—that is, rational, coherent, binary, ordered and ordering, upholding and promoting public virtue.

I observed earlier that twentieth-century canon makers would never have named "the Augustan Age" the "Age of Rochester, Pope, and Swift" or the "Age of Wycherley, Pope, and Swift," even though both Rochester and Wycherley were much more highly valued as satirists by their contemporaries than Dryden was. (Dryden himself refers to Wycherley twice in the *Discourse* with affection and admiration.) Inclusion of Dryden in the category occurs because the *Discourse*, a seminal critical treatise, stands at the threshold of the new satire that we have come to name "Augustan" and have come to believe reached its height of perfection in the eighteenth century. The *evolutionary* view that marks the "progress" (and it is significant that Dryden uses that word in his title) of *English* satire from its birth in Dryden to its zenith in Pope—dropping Renaissance English satire altogether, and reckoning Restoration deconstructive satires as crude and primitive toddler steps toward the perfected form—is, however, not a twentieth-century but an eighteenth-century invention. Walter Harte's critical verse essay, *An Essay on Satire* (1730), envisions Dryden as rising from a sea of darkest "Night" to bring in the birth of true satire:

> Great *Dryden* rose, and steer'd by Nature's light
> Two glimmering Orbs he just observ'd from far,
> The Ocean wide, and dubious either Star,
> *Donne* teem'd with Wit, but all was maim'd and bruis'd,
> The periods endless, and the sense confus'd;
> *Oldham* rush'd on, impetuous, and Sublime,
> But lame in Language, Harmony and Rhyme;
> These (with new Graces) vig'rous nature join'd
> In one, and center'd 'em in *Dryden's* mind.[42]

Nature, the ordered orderer, created Dryden the satirist from the chaotic raw materials of his predecessors. Harte praises Dryden's satire as it is measured, regular, and clear, and as it is a sacred instrument for discriminating the virtuous orderly from the foolish and vicious disorderly:

> How full thy verse? Thy meaning how severe?
> How dark thy theme? Yet made exactly clear.
> Not mortal is thy accent, nor thy rage
> Yet mercy softens, or contrasts each Page.
> Dread Bard! instruct us to revere thy rules,
> And hate like thee, all Rebels, and all Fools.[43]

However, Nature's movement, since it is considered to be *progressive* as well as orderly, has not quite reached perfection with Dryden. Harte links Dryden, through Garth, to Pope—

> dying Dryden breath'd, O Garth . . .
> thy [Garth's] pious hand repos'd his head . . .
> Ev'n *Pope* himself (who sees no Virtue bleed
> But bears th'affliction) envies thee thy deed[44]

—for Pope is the apex toward which the whole tradition, from Rome to Italy, to France, to England, has been steadily climbing.

> O Pope! Instructor of my studious days . . .
> Thou taught'st old Satire nobler fruits to bear,
> And check'd her License with a moral Care;
> Thou gav'st the Thought new beauties not its own,
> And touch'd the Verse with Graces yet unknown.
> Each lawless branch thy level eye survey'd
> And still corrected Nature as she stray'd:
> Warm'd Boileau's Sense with *Britain's* genuine Fire,
> And added Softness to *Tassone's* Lyre.[45]

In examining the new conceptions of logic and language that came into being in the constructive thrust of Restoration zero point, we observed that the new logicians and scientists conceived the course of knowledge to be progressive and cumulative and saw mimetic discourse as their lifeline to the future. This conception came to permeate all areas of thought, and, by the eighteenth century, poetry, like science and "natural philosophy," was thought to be a *developing* discipline. As a derivation, I think, from the preference for narrative as the most reliable true-to-experience form of discourse, linear conceptions of "progress" and "refinement" come to dominate thinking about literature, with the consequence that the idea of an upwardly evolving "tradition" in poetry emerged. It was Dryden who inaugurated this way of thinking about satire in the *Discourse concerning the Original and Progress of Satire:* "And thus, I have given the History of Satire, and deriv'd it as far from *Ennius,* to your Lordship [Dorset]; that is from its first Rudiments of Barbarity, to its last Polishing and Perfection."[46] By extension Dryden's "History of Satire" also inaugurates a "history" of critical analysis of satire and produces a prescriptive definition of what a poem *must* be, and *must* effect, in order to *be* satire. Dryden set a foundation mold upon which we build to this day. The *conceptual* design of satire, he says must be binary: "In general, all Virtues are every where to be prais'd, and recommended to Practice; and all Vice to be reprehended and made either Odious or Ridiculous; *or else there is a Fundamental Error in the Whole Design*" (p.81; ital. mine). So basic to his thinking is this binary conceptual design that he uses it as a measure throughout the essay to assess the worth of each of the satirists he considers. In Dryden's (*new*) view the sole purpose of satire is moral instruction and reformation: "Satire is of the nature of Moral Philosophy; as being instructive: He therefore who instructs most Usefully, will carry the palm" (p.55). Useful instruction, of course, depends upon a careful discrimination between virtue and vice and a correspondingly careful measure of praise and blame: "For amongst the *Romans* it [satire] was not only us'd for those Discourses which decry'd Vice, or expos'd Folly; but for others also, where Virtue was recommended" (p.48). Conceptually binary, satire to be morally effective must also be ordered so that it may *impose* order, and it is for this reason that although he loves Juvenal, Dryden often finds him unreliable, and, in one instance, truly faulty. Juvenal, Dryden says, is not always as useful as Horace because he praises virtue only by indirection, while Horace *actively instills* virtue in the reader: "*Juvenal* Exhorts to particular Virtues as they are oppos'd to those Vices against which he declaims: But *Horace* laughs to shame, all Follies and insinuates Virtue, rather by familiar Examples, than by the severity of Precepts" (p.63).

In the *Sixth Satire,* Dryden argues, Juvenal loses all claim to being a moral poet precisely because he does not strongly or actively enough promote virtue:"there is a latent Admonition to avoid Ill Women. . . . But this, tho' the Wittiest of all his Satires, has yet the least of Truth or Instruction in it. He has run himself into his old declamatory way, and almost forgotten, that he was now setting up for a Moral Poet" (p.80). What is most interesting about this particular point of comparison between Juvenal and Horace is that Dryden, quite unconsciously and against the grain of his own preference for "wit," is expressing his *age's* and not his *own* commitment to seemingly transparent, mimetic discourse. Horace is a better teacher than Juvenal because he "insinuates" virtue by using examples familiar in experience (almost novelistically); Juvenal is at fault when his declamatory language calls attention to itself and loses itself in the destabilizing play of wit: "[Juvenal's] Sentences [old logic's *sententiae*] are truly shining and instructive: But they are sprinkl'd here and there. *Horace* is teaching us in every line, and is perpetually Moral; he had found out the skill of *Virgil,* to hide his Sentences: To give you the Virtue of them without shewing them . . . Which is the Ostentation of a Poet, and not his Art: And this *Petronius* charges . . . as a Vice of Writing . . . *Ne Sententiae extra Corpus Orationis* [Sententiae, or witty tropes, should not stand out from the body of the text]" (p.62). Wit-play, and even rhyme-play, as Dryden says in criticizing Butler, debases the "Dignity of Style" and is therefore "not so proper for Manly Satire, for it turns Earnest too much to Jest" (p.81).

In short, Dryden must deny his own preference, and find Horace a superior teacher to Juvenal, for *discursive* reasons. It is because Horace's discourse is closer to experience, is regular as reason and nature are supposed to be regular, that his satire is more obvious in its effects and is therefore a better instrument for moral instruction:"It must be granted by the favorers of *Juvenal,* that *Horace* is the more Copious, and Profitable in his *Instructions of Humane Life*" (p.61). Indeed, Horace is the very answer to the new natural philosophers' call for a discourse that would bring ethics out of the Schools and, being "true" to experience, would be practically instructive (cf. Boyle's remarks on ethics, quoted in chapter 1). Horace's ordered discourse *creates* ordered lives, lays down "rules" of behavior, and regulates even communication itself: "granting that the Counsels which they [Juvenal and Horace] give, are equally good for Moral Use; *Horace,* who gives the most various Advice, and most applicable to all Occasions, which can occur to us in the course of our Lives; as including in his Discourses, not only the *Rules of Morality,* but also of *Civil* Conversation" (p.61); Dryden, then, whose ostensible project in the essay is to prepare his patron, Dorset, for a collection of satires by Juvenal and Persius, is constrained by the new *episteme* of modernism—which by the 1690s has become the dominant episteme—to construct his pattern of "how a Modern satire shou'd be made" on the discursive regularity and binary conceptual design of Horace, whose aim in satire was, Dryden says, "to correct the Vices and Follies of his Time, and to give Rules for a Happy and Virtuous Life" (p.59).

The principle requirement in "designing . . . a perfect satire," according to Dryden, is unity: "it ought to treat of one Subject; to be confin'd to one particular Theme; or at least to one principally" (p.78). The underlying reasons for this emphasis on unity are interesting, for they make us aware that in the aesthetics to which the new epistemology of modernism gives rise a poem is a single coherent entity projected from the coherently ordered "mind" of the discursively central "I"-narrator upon the "minds" of Model Readers, who are themselves "Persons of Understanding and Good Sense" (p.87), and are therefore amenable to rational control. The "I" satirist trope is shaped by discourse as a "good man" speaking from his "inner self" and "using words to communicate strongly felt attitudes";[47] from that inner arena, ordered *lines of thought* are projected outward to impose upon the "obedient" reader an ordered, easily comprehensible design for living: "Under this Unity of Theme, or Subject, is another Rule for perfecting the Design of true Satire. The Poet is bound, and that *ex officio,* to give the Reader some one Precept of Moral Virtue; and to caution him against some one particular Vice or Folly" (p.80). The unity and regularity of the new satire, then, expresses the univalent, coherent "reason" of the poet and is also the vehicle by means of which regularity and coherence are projected upon the "mind" of the reader to shape that "mind" and thereby morally regulate it. Dryden says the reason for Aristotle's judgment of tragedy as the most "Perfect Work of Poetry" is that tragedy is the most closed, self-consistent, and unified form, "Being exactly Proportion'd . . . and Uniform in all its Parts. The Mind is more Capable of Comprehending the whole Beauty of it without distraction" (pp.26-27). So must it be with satire, he says.

Among the three giants of Ancient satire, Dryden gives the prize for unity to Persius because his "mind," itself regulated by his Stoic philosophy, is whole: "Here is nothing propos'd but the quiet and tranquillity of Mind; Virtue lodg'd at home, and afterwards diffus'd in her general Effects, to the improvement and good of Humane Kind" (p.56). The movement here described from the "home" base of the coherent, tranquil mind of the narrator-poet "Persius" to the public arena is precisely the movement we observed at the beginning of this chapter—from the discursively central "I" through the telescope of discourse to possession and/or construction of "reality." The seemingly autobiographical "voice" which is its discursive center makes Persius's satire "true" and effective because it appears to the reader to issue from an inner self. Therefore, it not only authenticates the persona "Persius" but, by doing so, validates the truth of his utterance: "*Persius* is every where the same. . . . What he has learnt, he teaches vehemently; and what he teaches that he Practices himself. There is a spirit of sincerity in all he says: You may easily discern that he is in earnest, and is persuaded of that Truth he inculcates" (pp.56-57). How do we know that "Persius" is in earnest? How can we tell that he practices in his own life the morality he teaches? Because seen from the new modernist perspective the discourse of Persius's satire convinces the reader that it issues from a self, which has interiority and psychological depth, and that the satire itself is the direct, mimetically accurate delivery of that self's "mind." Dryden believes that Persius excels even Horace in this respect. The uniformity of his discourse creates the impression of uniformity in thought; in comparison, Horace's "sincerity" is suspect because he is "commonly in jest, and laughs while he instructs" (p.57). We can appreciate the extent to which Dryden is responding to the new episteme in making these judgments when we recall Sprat's argument, citied earlier in this chapter, that England is entitled to sovereignty in the empire of Reason because Englishmen by nature deliver their minds with simplicity and sincerity. Persius's teaching, in Dryden's opinion, "might be taught from Pulpits." Issuing from the "deepest self" the univocal voice of satire becomes a regulatory public discourse. In the opening pages of the *Discourse,* which are the most obviously dedicatory, Dryden favorably compares the role of the satirist with Dorset's in his capacity of public censor: "As Lord Chamberlain, I know, you [Dorset] are absolute by your Office, in all that belongs to the Decency and Good Manners of the Stage. You can banish from thence Scurrility and Profaness, and restrain the licentious insolents of Poets and their Actors, in all things that *shock the Public Quiet, or the Reputation of Private Persons under the notion of Humour*" (pp.9-10; ital. mine). Of course, the very idea that "the successful satirist is a public figure, either praised and rewarded by the political standard bearers of his society . . . or neglected by them to society's discredit"[48] is a rhetorical figuration, a strategy of the text in the new modern satire and modern readings of satire in exactly the same way as the "sharp-fanged satyr" is a textual strategy in Renaissance satire.

What finally loses Persius the palm in Dryden's estimation is his "scaborous and hobbling" verse and his "crabbed style." Dryden quotes Barten Holiday, his predecessor in translating Juvenal and Persius, who said, "in *Persius* the difficulty is to find a Meaning; in *Juvenal,* to chuse a meaning" (p.73). Persius's "Figures are generally too bold and daring; and his Tropes, particularly his Metaphors, insufferably strain'd" (p.51). There are puzzling contradictions in Dryden's judgment of the stylistic excellence of the three major Ancient satirists. In his 1683 elegy on Oldham Dryden upheld the old Renaissance/Restoration deconstructive conception of stylistic decorum and argued that satire demands a harsh, irregular style. We might, of course, explain the change of attitude simply as Dryden's unconscious response to the general move from linguistically self-reflexive to mimetic discourse that we have been tracing here—and surely that shift explains the change to some degree. However, if that were the sole explanation Dryden should admire the "urbanity" and "good manners" of the Horatian style, as he so clearly admires Horace's binary structure and narrative regularity. He does not; he finds the Horatian style "almost insipid" and prefers the "Wit" and "Salt" of Juvenal and his Restoration disciple, Wycherley: "*Juvenal* is of a more vigorous and Masculine Wit, he gives me as much Pleasure as I can bear; . . . His Spleen is rais'd and he raises mine. . . . He drives his Reader along with him; and when he is at the end of his way, I willingly stop with him; If he went another Stage, it wou'd be too far . . . and turn Delight into Fatigue. . . . If a Fault can justly be found in him; 'tis that he is sometimes too luxuriant, too redundant; says more than he needs, like my friend the *Plain Dealer,* but never more than pleases" (p.63).

We saw in chapter 3 that the self-reflexive, self-deconstructive style of Juvenal and Wycherley is the very antithesis of constructive mimetic discourse. Is it the case, then, that Dryden's delight in Juvenal and his conviction that Juvenal was "a Greater Poet" than Horace is merely a matter of personal preference, as Dryden claims it is? I think not. Dryden's exaltation of Juvenal as the greater poet is part of his plan to elevate the genre, satire, to make it a heroic mode, a subspecies of epic. Dryden quite deliberately ignores the manner in which the heroic style actually *operates* in Juvenal. As we have noted earlier, heroic epic style in Juvenal's satire exists *to collide with* low style, to create a destabilizing heteroglossia, and to produce in its self-deconstructing discursive turbulence the kind of irony that "transforms the self out of the empirical world into a world constituted out of and in language." Deliberately overlooking that irony, Dryden ascribes to Juvenal's style the power and effect which the pure, uncontextualized heroic style was thought to have, the power "to raise the Soul from this terrene of life": "[Juvenal's] Thoughts are . . . much more Elevated [than Horace's]; His Expressions are Sonorous and more Noble; his Verse more numerous, and his Words are suitable to his Thoughts; sublime and lofty. All these contribute to the Pleasure of the Reader, and the greater the Soul of him who Reads his Transports are the Greater" (p.64). Dryden's *Discourse* lifted satire out of the mouth of the maddened, snarling Juvenalian satyr-satirist and placed it at the top of the Aristotelian hit parade as a species of epic for ever after.

By the time that Harte writes his *Essay on Satire* in 1730 Dryden's ideas about satire have achieved the unquestioned status and authority of received truth. Satire is a heroic form—

> As Cynthia's *Orb* excels the gems of night;
> So *Epic Satire* shines distinctly bright.[49]

different from epic only in scope:

> True Epic's a vast World, and this a small.[50]

Its most salient feature is unity:

> As *Unities* in Epick works appear
> So must they shine in full distinction here . . .
> One *Harmony* must first with last unite;
> As all true Paintings have their *Place* and *Light*.[51]

The instrument by which such unity is achieved is narrative discourse— "*Fiction* and *Fable* are the Sense and Soul"—that veils its linguistic operation by weaving its effects into the seamless discursive fabric of the whole. "*Similies*" in satire must not call attention to their metaphoric nature, but must be "one flash of momentary Light" because satire's language must be entirely subordinate to its formal regularity. "The Moral must be clear and understood" and therefore style must be "dignify'd" but transparent, for "Sense subsists distinct from phrase or sound." The discriminating order that satire expresses and imposes is immutable Providential order,

> Hence Rules, and Truth, and Order, Dunces strike
> Of Arts, and Virtues, enemies alike.[52]

Finally, in its aesthetic function the aim of epic satire is to exalt the soul, while its moral function is to regulate our thoughts, our feelings, and, most especially, our behavior:

> T'Exalt the Soul, or make the Heart sincere
> To arm our Lives with honesty severe . . .
> To raise the fal'n, to hear the sufferer's cries
> To sanctify the virtues of the wise

> Old Satire rose from Probity of Mind,
> The noblest Ethics to reform mankind.[53]

In clear imitation of Dryden, Harte also provides a capsule history of
satire, which is interesting in revealing how drastically *respectable*—and bourgeois respectable at that—satire has become by 1730. In 1693 Dryden
could at least discuss Petronius's satire objectively (most often admiringly)
and with equanimity. Harte is unable to look squarely at a satire so obscene. He turns his glance instead at what he thinks was the target of
Petronius's satire—and gives a broad hint of what puts Petronius beyond
the pale by conflating his image with that of the titillatingly scandalous
wicked Earl of bad King Charles's days:

> The Vice and Luxury Petronius drew,
> In *Nero* meet: th'imperial point of view:
> The Roman *Wilmot,* that could Vice Chastize,
> Pleas'd the mad King he serv'd, to satirize.[54]

No more can Harte bring himself to mention Juvenal by name; he iden-
tifies him by dropping him, nameless, into the right chronological slot and
labelling him with a close paraphrase of Dryden's description of Juvenal's
style,

> What honest Heart could bear *Domitian's* age?
> See his strong Sense, and *Numbers Masculine*
> *His Soul is Kindled, and he Kindles mine:*
> Scornful of Vice, and fearless of Offence,
> He flows a Torrent of impetuous Sense. [ital. mine][55]

By the eighteenth century it is commonly assumed that the pinnacle in
the "progress" of satire has been reached. Perfection lies in the Horatian,
institution-upholding satire of Alexander Pope; and the canonical "tradition" and "progress" of satire is forever set in stone.

III. Satiric Discourse and the Sacred Nation

Theoretically Dryden reconciles the primary necessity for unity in a satire
and its binary conceptual design by constructing his model for "modern
satire" as a double walk: "As in a Play of the English Fashion, which we call
a *Tragicomedy,* there is to be but one main Design; and tho' there be an
Under-plot, or Second Walk of Comical Characters and Adventures, yet
they are subservient to the Chief Fable, carry'd along under it, and helping
to it."[56] He cites his own *Absalom and Achitophel* as a particularly fine mod-

ern achievement in this style. This poem, which rightly called is not a mock-epic but an *epic satire,* achieves in practice what Dryden prescribes in the *Discourse* in theory. Every single element in the poem—narrative, style, figure, allusion—delineates a binary form that is *heroic* in its "main design" and simultaneously is threatened by chaos and fragmentation from its "second walk" below—but really, of course, is conceptually buttressed by that under walk.

There have been many explanations offered of why Dryden chose the Biblical account of David and Absalom in which to set his narrative— from the sexual prowess associated with the two kings to the closely parallel examples of filial ingratitude in the two sons. In my view, setting the reign of Charles II in the context of the history of the Davidic kingdom was Dryden's way of constructing an essentially modern vision of "the Nation" that, paradoxically, looks backward for its governing metaphor yet looks forward in its choice of discursive strategies to naturalize that metaphor. In its conception of nationhood *Absalom and Achitophel's* is a cusp view. Its backward glance conjoins king-father-Providential/salvation history; its forward glance sets dichotomy between self and nation, rule and power, community and state.

As we have seen, the new modernism constructs an idea of nation that is an enlargement of the discursively central self and conceives of nation as a coherent body, as self is a coherent entity. That very strategy, however, contains an unresolveable contradiction. If the locus of reality and truth is the inner human self and not some metaphysical *discordia concors* wherein each self's value and authenticity is determined by its harmonious interrelation with all other creatures, then whose individual "truth" is the truth? If the determining fountainhead of reality is not God, or God in his vicars, king or pope, but rather is a projection from each human self, then what is to prevent "reality" from exploding into atomistic chaos?

It is to the Renaissance model of nation—that is, crown = nation—that Dryden looks for his governing metaphor, and to a modern conception of narrative that he looks in designing his ordered and ordering, heroic "main design."[57] As Richard Helgerson tells us,

> to the extent that the state was almost indistinguishably identified in this period [the Renaissance] with the crown ... the addition [of the concept "state" to the idea "monarchy"] seems inappropriate. State/nation, court/country, king/people, sovereign/subjects—if these pairs cannot be neatly mapped onto one another, neither can they be sharply distinguished. In each the left-hand term represents the governing order; the right-hand term that which is governed. And in each the right-hand term contains a multiplicity of interests and energies that escapes the simple subordination suggested by such binary couplings.[58]

It is the indistinguishable identity of state with crown that Dryden attempts to resurrect in making the equation of Charles II with David and England with the Davidic kingdom. David, his harp held in his left hand and the three fingers of his right hand poised above its strings, signifying both the unmistakable gesture of monarchy and also the sign of direct communication with God (see, for instance, the emblematic gesture of the Infant Christ), is the ultimate figural representation of the king as God's anointed. It can be found in psalter illuminations, emblem books, Biblical illustrations, and paintings from the eleventh century through the seventeenth. Moreover, the line of the Davidic kingdom, its regular unbroken succession, is ordained by God because the Messiah is destined to come from the House of David. The regularity of the main design of *Absalom and Achitophel,* then, is not only an expression of the new conception of unity and order in satire, but it also functions metaphorically as an emblem of the Providential order in monarchic succession. On the other hand, the "multiplicity of interests and energies" which, as Helgerson says, were veiled in the Renaissance conception, are nakedly apparent to a generation tutored by Hobbes. Dryden casts the chaotic forces in resistance to the Providentially determined main design as his second walk: "Less concerned with community and national particularity than with rule and an abstract system of order, *Leviathan* belongs not to the discourse of the nation but to the discourse of the state."[59] The heroic main design of *Absalom and Achitophel* makes the "nation" natural and eternal. The lower walk exposes and castigates the irrational, chaotic, self-interested forces of the future that are writing England into a "state." The forces in opposition in the conceptual design of the poem are political virtue and vice (Dryden's "one Subject only") but they are also heroic and antiheroic, natural and unnatural, cohesive and fragmented, discursively constructive and discursively deconstructive.

The first line of the poem sets a dichotomy between piety, which is associated with natural religion, and priest-craft, which is associated with man-made factionalism, the instrument of political subversion and the mask of demonic self-interest. That initial dichotomy propels the whole conceptual design of the poem. The kingship of Charles-David is ordained by the immutable order of nature; by extension lawful monarchic succession is inherent as the permanence-in-mutability order of nature. Moreover, monarchic succession is a tradition in *law* that follows a pattern in nature, and therefore, being the indissoluble union of law (abstract bond or oath) and nature, monarchic succession is *sacramental*. Monmouth, born *outside* of the sacramental order of marriage, is by nature princely but not by law. Government of the "nation" depends for its order and stability on the absolute union of nature with law.

While David-Charles is *naturally* king, and Absalom, his son, is by nature heroic, "His youthful image . . . renewed," composed of "angel's mettle," "Graceful in every motion," and revealing "paradise" in his face. Achitophel, the satanic adversary of God's anointed, is *de*formed, and is the deforming center of chaos. He embodies, as well as leading, the "multiplicity of interests and energies" that threaten the nation, for he is all chaotic energy, "turbulent of wit . . . Restless, unfixed in principles and place," "for calm unfit,"

> A fiery soul, which, working out its way
> Fretted the pigmy body to decay
> And o'er-informed the tenement of clay. [156-158][60]

As order begets order, so also Achitophel, the center of chaos, can produce only chaos, even in the realm of nature,

> a son
> Got, while his soul did huddled notions try,
> And born a shapeless lump like anarchy. [170-172]

The lawful-natural entity, the nation, over which the father-king presides had its origin in immemorial prehistory, and the rightful king's entitlement to reign is "a successive title, long and dark / Drawn from the moldy rolls of Noah's ark." In addition, the king himself embodies all the ordered and ordering virtues; he is

> Good, gracious, just, observant of the laws . . .
> Mild, easy, humble, studious of the good
> Inclined to mercy, and averse from blood. [319-326]

His successor too is possessed particularly of the orderly virtues. He is "severe and wise," and his most salient characteristics—"courage," "truth," "loyalty," "mercy"—are conspicuously regular. The king would prefer to exercise his power only to "save" and never to punish. He is forced by death-dealing rebellion to exercise justice by the sword. Only after "long revolving in his careful breast / The event of things"—that is, looking *inward* to the seat of truth—does he make his case for bringing the law to bear upon the disorderly. His argument, which is, of course, the "argument" that this new-style, well made satire is bringing to closure, is made in smooth, balanced, eminently reasonable and logical discourse:

> For gods and godlike kings, their care express,
> Still to defend their servants in distress,
> O that my power to saving were confined:

Why am I forced, like Heaven, against my mind
To make examples of another kind?
Must I at length the sword of justice draw?
O curst effects of necessary law! . . .
Law they require, let Law then show her face;
They could not be content to look on Grace. [997–1,007]

The style here is elevated epic style, the measured pronouncement of a god-like king. The argument moves in turns so smooth that they are Virgilian rather than merely Horatian (though in the *Discourse* Dryden says that Horace learned "the skill to hide his Sentence" from Virgil). Similies and allusions are so smoothly woven into the linear progression of the argument that they never reveal their linguistic, metaphoric operation. Like the orderly line of succession that the main design of the poem upholds and asserts, satiric discourse constructs an unbroken, linear, logically successive "argument."

In direct opposition to the main design, and upholding it by indirection, is the deconstructive satiric under walk. Achitophel, the adversary, associated as we have seen with restless, chaotic movement and wit so destabilizing that it is almost indistinguishable from madness, leads a turbulent horde of fragmented and fragmenting factions that "work up to foam, and threat the government." Even the best-intentioned of the rebels, "not wicked but seduced by impious arts," by refusing to be subsumed into the coherent whole, the nation, "crack'd the government." Any deviation by a part from congruence, however harmless in intention, threatens the self-consistent entity, the whole nation. The greater number of the rebels "run popularly mad." So atomized are they, each splinter group impelled by its own self-interest, that they cannot constitute wholeness of any kind. They are a turbulent energy, not just formless, but counter-formal

’Gainst form and order they their power employ
Nothing to build, and all things to destroy. [529–530]

The greatest threat that rebellious, mindless energy presents to the unified, orderly kingdom is that it might reveal the Hobbesian underside of its smooth and seamless surface and show that indeed, "All Empire is no more than power," as Achitophel puts it. It would thereby unmask "the nation," with its claim to natural origin and eternal presence, and reveal "the state" with all its terror and coercion lurking behind that benevolent aspect.

When, after announcing that the nameless monster, the mob, "a whole Hydra . . . of sprouting heads," is too formless and numerous to "score," the poem begins to catalogue the chief rebels in a perfect concordance of style with sense. Deconstructive satiric discourse erupts and breaks through the constructive, progressive narrative line. The satiric portraits of the under walk are separate set pieces: chunks that, like ice floes, break the narrative flow. Not only are they separate from one another but, unlike the logical progression of the main design, they are not causally related. Zimri, Shimei, Corah do not follow from one another logically; they could exist in any other order. The portraits exist in isolation from one another as the factions, or even the self-interested isolates that comprise the Hydra-headed crowd, do; each entity is a separate, randomly moving atom. Verse lines themselves are atomized, and words collide with words as they do in a deconstructive satire like "A Ramble in St. James's Park" or in the Bayes's dance confusion of *The Plain Dealer's* Whitehall. Zimri,

> A man so various, that he seemed to be
> Not one, but all mankind's epitome. [545-546]

is not a "self" but a kaleidoscope of splintered fragments. The portrait sounds the staccato beat of isolated words in combat:

> [Zimri] . . . in course of one revolving moon,
> Was chymist, fiddler, statesman, and buffoon:
> Then all for women, painting, rhyming, drinking,
> Besides ten thousand freaks that died in thinking.
> Blest madman . . . [549-553]

The whole structural design of the poem consists in 1) the unified, regular narrative line, the new satiric discourse that shapes the "main design" of *Absalom and Achitophel* and 2) the old-style satiric deconstructive discourse at work in the under walk, the chaos that "foams up" and threatens order. However, both stylistically *and* conceptually, the main design embraces and finally constrains the under walk. The main design takes that blessed wholeness, the kingdom-nation, from the "pious times" of its innocent infancy to the final, carefully reasoned and rationally measured Last Judgment of the father-king (to which *the* Father-King-Judge nods assent), in which reasoned judgment executes discriminating justice, restores order, and renews time:

> Henceforth a series of new time began,
> The mighty years in long succession ran:
> Once more the god-like David was restored,
> And willing nations knew their lawful lord. [1,028-1,031]

Just like an epic in its heroic narrative, this epic satire tells the history-in-eternity of the eternal kingdom. The most elevated of all genres praises the virtuous king and his virtuous, willing subjects in the constructive mode of the new satire. The downward angle of the poem's binary conceptual design exposes and castigates the vicious and irrational deviants, who, by resisting subordination to the rightful, natural order, threaten the stability of the whole.

Although *Absalom and Achitophel* looks to the past for its governing metaphor, the medieval/Renaissance emblem of David that makes the nation and the crown identical, the conceptual design in satire and the discourse in which that design is realized are determined by the new episteme of modernism. That new ordered and ordering discourse and the carefully discriminatory binary conceptual design it produces as much construct the new conception of the nation in this poem as it does in the prosaic description of an economist like Charles Davenant writing a treatise on trade: "In these sorts of Speculations [about what constitutes the Nation] not only the Quantity but Quality of the Inhabitants must be duly ponder'd . . . It must be distinguish'd who by their Arts, Labour, or Industry are increasing, and who by their Expence, Poverty, or Sloth are decreasing the Kingdom's Wealth."[61]

IV. The "Other" End of the Telescope

the critic of texts ought to be investigating the system of discourse by which the "world" is divided, administered, plundered, by which humanity is thrust into pigeonholes, by which "we" are human and "they" are not, and so forth.

Edward Said

Edward Said has said that "the imaginative examination of things Oriental was based more or less exclusively upon a sovereign Western consciousness out of whose unchallenged centrality an Oriental world emerged, first according to general ideas about who or what was an Oriental, then according to a detailed logic governed not simply by empirical reality but by a battery of desires, repressions, investments, and projections."[62] The distance between Point A ("first according to general ideas . . . etc.") and Point B ("then . . . not simply by empirical reality . . . etc.") is in England a distance of roughly a hundred years, from the end of the sixteenth century to the end of the seventeenth century: a short moment of time, perhaps, but one containing a radical turn in consciousness and a restructuring of "reality." The distance marks the difference between "seeing" an Oriental city as a dazzling multicultural center of wealth and freedom—"hither resort Jews, Tartarians, Persians, Armenians, Egyptians, Indians, and many sorts of Christians; and enjoy freedom of their consciences and bring thither many rich merchandizes"[63]—and seeing that *same* city as a filthy, alien, threatening wilderness—"we durst not go to any house in the town for fear of lice, of which cattle the Turks have great store";[64] a wilderness *through which* an Englishman can make his way only with trepidation— "Captain Harman and myself were placed in the front, the two janizaries only going before us: and all the rest of the gentlemen (of which at least forty came to meet us) came aloof off behind, to signify we were strangers."[65] A wilderness *in which* he can survive only by consolidating himself immediately with other Europeans—"I went about (as is the custom of the place) to each Frank's [European's] house and chamber in particular to give them thanks for their yesterday's welcoming us to the town."[66] A wilderness in which an Englishman can *endure* only by creating an island of safety and security upon the seemingly unpeopled landscape, a little bit of England: "This morning early (as it is the custom all summer long) at least forty of the English, with his worship the Consul, rode out of the city about four miles to ... a fine valley by a riverside, to recreate themselves. Where a princely tent was pitched: and we had several pastimes and sports ... and then a noble dinner brought thither, with great plenty of all sorts of wines, punch, and lemonade and at 6 we return all home in good order, but soundly tired and weary."[67] The "natives"—indeed the whole polyglot population that so impressed the sixteenth-century merchant-traveler— have become invisible except as they are of *use,* as servants or guides.

The distance from the end of the sixteenth to the end of the seventeenth century also marks the difference between seeing the "Other" as different in external appearance but recognizably human and seeing that same "Other" through the distorting lens of xenophobic fear and loathing. To the sixteenth-century traveler the difference between English and Other is interesting and can even sometimes provide a self-reflexive critical glance. In 1579 Thomas Stevens describes the Indians of Goa in a letter to his father: "The people be tawny, but not disfigured. .... They that be not of reputation—or at least the most part—go naked saving an apron of a span long and as much in breadth before them, and a lace two fingers broad before them girded about with a string, and no more. And thus they think themselves as well as we with all our trimming."[68]

John Eldred finds Arabians familiar by their resemblance to English Gypsies, and his description of Arabian women is objective and discursively neutral: "[The Arabians'] hair, apparel and colour are altogether like those vagabond Egyptians which here to fore have gone about in England. Their women all without exception wear a great round ring in one of their nostrils, of gold, silver, or iron according to their ability, and about their arms and smalls of their legs they have hoops of gold, silver, or iron."[69] In contrast, Henry Teonge, writing almost exactly a hundred years later,

cannot keep out of his discourse the sexual fear and loathing induced in
him by the appearance of a group of Arabian women who have come out
of their poor village to offer him food and drink. "The chief lady of the
town," he says, mocking her poverty,

> was tall and very slender, very swarthy of complexion and very thin-faced, as
> they all generally; having nothing on but a thin loose garment, a kind of girdle
> about her middle and the garment open before. She had a ring in her left
> nostril, which hung down beneath her nether lip; at each ear a round globe as
> big as a tennis ball, shining like gold and hanging ... almost as low as her breast,
> *which you could easily see and loathe them for their ugly yellowish colour* [ital. mine],
> She had also gold chains about her wrists and the smalls of her naked legs. Her
> nails of her fingers were coloured almost red, and her lips coloured as blue as
> indigo; and so also were her belly from the navel to her hams, painted with
> blue like branches of trees or strawberry leaves. *Nor was she cautious, but rather
> ambitious to show you this* [ital. mine]....The rest of the women were all alike for
> their painting in all places, but far fouler.[70]

The telescopic discourse of modernism is sharply focused, mimetic, and
scrupulously detailed, but it also distances the "Other" and makes the other
an "It." The "battery of desires, repressions, investments, projections" through
which the discourse must pass in its movement from the inner Self to
projection upon the world makes it delineate an impassable boundary
between English and Other, human and subhuman.

In the seventeenth century, "Europe becomes conscious of itself, writes
its own description and understands itself increasingly as the guiding principle of a planetary process, no longer simply as a region of the world."[71]
Europe's writing itself, of necessity, depended upon writing the other-
than-itself and, as Said has shown us, "the Orient" is "one of [Europe's]
deepest and most recurring images of the Other."[72]

Said goes on to argue that "without understanding Orientalism as a
discourse one cannot possibly understand the enormously systematic
discipline by which European culture was able to manage—and even
produce—the Orient politically, scientifically, and imaginatively in the
post-Enlightenment period."[73] It is my contention that in England the
discourse "orientalism" is a product of the Restoration's new discourse
of modernism.

At Restoration zero point a change occurred in representation of the
Oriental that follows with remarkable accuracy the shift from metaphoric
to mimetic discourse with which we have been concerned. In literary
terms the shift might be said to be from emblematic to novelistic representation. In the sixteenth century and into the early Restoration period

(the 1660s and 1670s) the Oriental appears almost exclusively in romance and in heroic drama, modes that were the high heroic, or epic genres of their time:

> Epic discourse is a discourse handed down by tradition. By its very nature the epic world . . . is inaccessible to personal experience and does not permit an individual, personal point of view or evaluation. One cannot glimpse it, grope for it, touch it; one cannot look at it from just any point of view; it is impossible to experience it, analyze it . . . penetrate into its core. . . . the important thing is not the factual sources of the epic, not the content of its historical events . . . the important thing is this formal constitutive characteristic of the epic as a genre . . . its reliance on *impersonal* and sacrosanct tradition.[74]

In the high heroic modes of the late sixteenth century and early Restoration period Orientals are emblematic figures; indeed, *all* characters are allegorical figures rather than mimetic representations. Such emblematic figures are the products of the old medieval/Renaissance discourse of patterning, the very antithesis of the new mimetic discourse which conceives of language as secondary to, and dependent on, the material actual. As we have seen, the discourse of modernism was designed to produce transparent "Histories of Nature." And, as de Man has argued, allegory, which is the basis of all medieval and Renaissance representation, "is at the furthest remove from historiography. The 'realism' that appeals to us in the details of medieval art is a calligraphy rather than a mimesis, a technical device to insure that the emblem will be correctly identified and decoded, not an appeal to the . . . pleasures of mimesis."[75]

As I have argued extensively elsewhere,[76] until the Restoration zero-point turn to mimetic discourse, in the high heroic modes, particularly romance and drama, characters can best be understood as emblematic figurations, typological counters whose meaning is iconographic and whose function is determined by the positions they occupy in relation to one another within whatever pattern of discourse constitutes the rhetorical design of the text—whether the mounting dialectical pattern of a heroic drama of the 1660s, or the more complex, more medieval (and consequently more obviously allegorical) system of signs that comprises a sixteenth-century drama like *Tamberlaine* or romance like *The Faerie Queene*. That is to say, until the late seventeenth century "characters," especially in the drama, are not imitative of persons, like ourselves assumed to have interiority and psychology, but are rather delineations of ideas. As Richard Flecknoe defines the distinction in 1658, characters "differ from Portracts [painted portraits] in that they are onely Pictures of the Mind, abstracting from the Body."[77] In the drama before the 1690s a character is a sign, the name of an idea; a text is the organization of a pattern of such signs, or emblematic figures, "whose function is to guarantee ideal convertability between the celestial and the terrestrial."[78]

In the earlier English high heroic modes particularly there are neither characters in the modern sense, nor naturalistic dialogue, that is, imitation of conversation. Rather, the medieval/Renaissance discourse of patterning figures moving systems of ideational relationship which reveal to the spectator or reader systematic interaction among *Ideas*—exactly as is the case in pre-modern logic and dialectic. As we have seen, in the sixteenth century and into the early Restoration period the human mind is thought both to reflect, and also to participate in, linguistic systems—mental and metaphysical—which the discursive pattern of a logical argument, or a literary text, sets. Within a poetic text characters are *ideas* of the passions as in logic words are characters of ideas in the mind and in eternity. As Theophilus Gale puts the matter in 1669, "*Names* are imitates . . . *There are in Speech certain Symbols or notices of the Soul's passions* . . . as in the *Mind* there is a certain *Idea* of things; so likewise in *Oration*."[79]

In the emblematic representational mode of the early period the Oriental was a figure of heroic greatness; whether good or evil the figure of the Oriental was a sign of uncontainable spirit and uncontestable valor. In *Tamberlaine,* for instance, the protagonist is a sign of uncontrollable energy—linguistic as well as martial. In *The Merchant of Venice* the Prince of Morocco is even more obviously a type of the Herculean hero, different from the European, but by his very difference elevated to almost godlike stature:

> Mislike me not for my complexion,
> The shadowed livery of the burnish'd sun,
> To whom I am a neighbour, and near bred.
> [*The Merchant of Venice* II,i,1-3]

For Shakespeare, his forebears, and his contemporaries, the figure of an Oriental, as well as an Oriental context, signalled the "distanced zone" of the high genres, the metaphorical and metaphysical realm of romance:

> by this scimitar
> That slew the Sophy, and a Persian prince,
> That won three fields of Sultan Solyman,
> I would o'erstare the sternest eyes that look:
> Outbrave the heart most daring on the earth:
> Pluck the young sucking cubs from the she-bear,
> Yea, mock the lion when a roars for prey
> To win thee lady. [II,i, 24-31]

The emblematic figuration that instantly signifies Oriental as high heroic lasted into the early decades of the Restoration period. The heroic drama, the most prevalent of high heroic modes in the 1660s and 1670s, is dominated by Oriental settings, characters, and motifs, as even the most superficial glance will affirm: consider, *The Conquest of Granada, The Empress of Morocco, Abdelazer, Aureng-Zebe, Ibrahim the Illustrious Bassa, Tyrranick Love* (which concerns the martyrdom of Saint Catherine of Alexandria). Characters in these plays are positions on a rhetorical grid; like pre-modern logic's "places," they are entirely *in* language and *of* language. As in sixteenth-century logic and rhetoric, here words and character-emblem tropes *are* ideas. In the generic pattern of the heroic drama these word-ideas shape a dialectical progression of mounting definition that moves toward the refinement of some overarching idea, like *gloire* or heroic love. For example, in *Aureng-Zebe,* Aureng-Zebe figures prophetic passion, Arimant heroic passion, the Emperor worldly passion, and Nourmahal Hobbesian passion, or raw power. The villain of *Tyrannick Love,* Maximin, though he is the villain of the piece, nevertheless is heroic. He is an emblem of the highest power attainable within the earthly sphere. Saint Catherine is greater than he only because her spirit is capable of breaking through all earthly boundaries. In pre-modern coding, then, Orientals are heightened "Characters of Valour" and "Ideas of Greatness." A text in an Oriental setting is a concatenation of "Images . . . rais'd above the Life" designed to transport the minds of the audience to celestial truth.[80]

How did we come, then, from thinking of "Characters in Plays [as] being representations of the Vertues or Vices, Passions or Affectations of Mankind, the Ideas of these," that Thomas Shadwell called them in 1671,[81] to the reverse position of thinking the whole of a play an outward projection of the innermost being of its principal character, as Shaftesbury in 1711 thought *Hamlet* to be, "a Series of deep Reflections, drawn from one Mouth, upon the Subject of one single Accident and Calamity, naturally fitted to move Horror and Compassion. It may be properly said of this Play, if I mistake not, that it has ONE *Character or Principal Part.*"[82] And what, furthermore, did the change in representation mean for the discourse of Orientalism?

We have been aware for some time that in the last decade of the seventeenth century drama became "novelistic." And among the literary genres the novel is unquestionably the child of the new epistemology which was in the process of construction at Restoration zero point and the new analytico-referential discourse to which it gave rise. As Bergonzi tells us, "the ideology that sustained the novel for the first two centuries of its existence [was] its belief in unmediated experience, in originality and in-

dividuality and progress."[83] When the discourse of modernism invaded
the high heroic genres it broke the boundaries of traditional, sacrosanct
epic discourse and shattered the possibility of typological figuration: "In
the high genres all authority and privilege, all lofty significance and gran-
deur abandon the zone of familiar contact for the distanced plane . . . the
style of the hero's speech and the style of speech about him. . . . The novel,
however, is associated with the eternally living element of unofficial language and unofficial thought."[84]

An interesting case of novelization of a heroic drama and the effect of
that novelization upon the figuration of Orientals is presented to us by
Dryden's play *Don Sebastian* (1690). The play is, or, more precisely, has
been thought to be, a heroic drama, but it is vastly different from the
heroic drama of the 1660s, which exist under the representational codes
of pre-modern emblematic figuration. The ways that it differs from its
predecessors on the other side of the zero-point divide can illuminate the
transformation in consciousness that the discourse of modernism produced. Earl Miner, the editor of the California edition of the play says,
"The major difference felt between Dryden's version of the story and that
of the anonymous romance *Don Sebastian* is the force of Dryden's characterization. His Sebastian and Almeyda possess greater vitality, are more
'real.' This is not to say that Dryden's hero possesses any greater historical
accuracy than the hero of romance. . . . It was instead the world of idealized heroism that Dryden transformed into tragedy."[85] In saying that the
characters in *Don Sebastian* are more "real" than the characters in the romance, the modern commentator reveals the extent to which the discourse of modernism has shaped our own twentieth-century imagination.
Dryden's audience, on the contrary, complained that the characters in this
play were *un*real, "unnatural." That, of course, is because the horizon of
expectation in an audience of 1690 would have led them to expect the
closed, emblematic, typological figures of the earlier representational mode
in a heroic drama set in the Orient. Dryden answers their objections by
referring them to the great philosopher of the Self, Montaigne: "A more
ignorant sort of Creatures maintain that the Character of *Dorax,* is not
only unnatural but inconsistent with it self; let them read the play and
think again, and if yet they are not satisfied, cast their eyes on that Chapter
of the wise *Montaigne* which is intitl'd *de l'Inconstance des actions humaines.*"[86]
Dryden is thinking of those passages wherein Montaigne discusses his
exploration of the "corners" of his inner self and expresses his delight in
"rolling around" in them.

Dryden was aware that his problem in writing the play was to present
within the confines of a traditional heroic form a complexity of character,

variety of detail, and irregularity of language, in short, a "realism," that strained the limits of heroic drama: "Whether it happen'd through long disuse of Writing, that I forgot the usual compass of a Play, or that by crowding it with Characters and Incidents, I put upon my self a necessity of lengthening the main Action, I know not."[87] What he has written, he says, is more suitable for the study than for the stage, for "there is a vast difference betwixt a publick entertainment on the Theater, and a private reading in the Closet: In the first we are confin'd to time . . . in the last every Reader is judge of his own convenience; he can take up the book and lay it down at his pleasure and find those beauties of propriety in thought and writing which escaped him in the tumult of representing."[88] What Dryden is saying, in effect, is that what he has written is more nearly a novel than a play. A play is always a *show* of meaning, inevitably emblematic since it produces its effects by signs. The novel, on the other hand, not only allows its narrator, the discursively central "I," to "deliver his mind" to the reader seemingly without the encumbrance of generic and linguistic shackles, but it also creates a space, a terrain in which "writer" and "reader" meet and an environment which they mutually "inhabit." It is for that reason that the novel is so suited to the aims of the new discourse and the new conception of writing.

It is the new discourse of modernism that impels Dryden toward a new methodology of characterization. Characters must come to simulate actual persons when discourse is conceived as issuing from some interior center of the self. Whereas in the 1670s Dryden had argued the priority of *design,* or "fable," before figures, or "persons" in the construction of a drama, in the Preface to *Don Sebastian* he clearly indicates that the action of a play must arise out of the inner motivation of its characters. He says that the cuts which Betterton had to make in order to make *Don Sebastian* playable caused "some part of the action from being percipitated and coming on without due preparation, which is requir'd to all great events: as in particular, that of raising the Mobile . . . which a Man of Benducar's cool Character could not *naturally* attempt, without taking those precautions which he *foresaw* wou'd be necessary to render his design successful" (ital. mine).[89] The aim of the new representational mode is to create for us, as the novel does, the illusion that we are experiencing the events enacted or described as we experience events in life. Moreover, just as in a novel, we must be given the illusion of exploring behind the surface of the text to the inner arena of the characters—Benducar's coolness and what he "foresaw." Whereas in the heroic drama of the 1660s characters figure positions on a rhetorical scale, in the new novelistic drama of the 1690s, when the discourse of modernism is in full ascendance, character is person and character is primary. Action moves to the pace of the characters' "inner thoughts" and unspoken "motives" and "desires." In drama too "I" has become discursively central.

The setting of *Don Sebastian* too is novelistic, far more detailed than the wash-tint, never-never land where sixties' heroic figures declaim. Dryden drew the crowded characters and detailed incidents that he knew strained dramatic form from contemporary travel accounts. Earl Miner says that "No one book contains the wealth of detail found in *Don Sebastian* concerning what was then referred to as Barbary or the Moors."[90] What is interesting, however, is that all the travel books—or at least all that I have read—contain the *same* details, and, more significantly still, repeatedly describe the *same* Oriental qualities, customs, and behaviors. Two obvious sources from which Dryden drew are John Ogilby's *Africa* (1670) and *The Travels of Monsieur de Thenevot into the Levant* (1686). Of the latter Miner says, "Thenevot was a careful observer, although, like his fellow travel-writers, he took more from books than from observation. . . . What he has to say, however, on Turkish women . . . provides perhaps the closest analogue to Dryden's details."[91] What Thenevot has to say about Turkish women, however, is exactly what Henry Teonge has to say about them in 1675 and what Lady Mary Whortley Montagu (though with admiration rather than scorn) will be saying about them twenty-seven years later: that they are sexually voracious. The "observation" that Oriental women find European men, even their slaves, irresistibly attractive (presumably because they are not circumcised) is formulaic in the travel accounts of the late seventeenth century. Indeed, the story of the Oriental woman who lures a European man into her garden (Oh, those passion palace Oriental gardens! They are everywhere!) to use him sexually is already a good ol' boys' locker-room story when Henry Teonge retells it in 1675:

> Not above half a year before I came hither, came a noble Englishman, who must be nameless; he had not been many weeks in town; but by his walking about to see the city, he was taken notice of by one of the chief Turks' ladies of the city, who sent a Turk to him to acquaint him that his lady, a person of great quality did desire his company . . . and withal she would have no denial. The gentleman consults with the Consul, who in short told him he must go or expect to be stabbed the next time he went out. Seeing no remedy, he goes with the Turk, who brings him by back-ways into a stately house, and there to a beautiful lady, who entertained him above what was promised; and with her he stayed three nights, and with a great gratuity.

The lady sends for the Englishman a second time, and again he stays three nights. A third time she sends for him (the fairy-tale repetition of threes might in itself make us suspicious), and "the third night she told him her husband was unexpectedly come home, but bade him not to trouble himself at all, for that he should be secure as ever he was before, and that she would lie with him that night also: which she performed accordingly, and the gentleman returned safe and well rewarded." The Englishman becomes uneasy, however, at the thought of being caught by the husband, and, knowing that as long as he stays in the city, the lust-driven lady will never be able to leave him alone, he leaves, "whose departure was much lamented by the lady, as was after known to the Consul, by the Turk which used to come for him; *and this shows they love the English.*"[92] So much for the empirical reality and accuracy to experience of the travel accounts and the "realism" of Dryden's novelistic drama. The details of Moorish life recorded by the travel writers' supposedly transparent "histories" of experience, in fact give evidence of the fears and desires that the English "mind," secure in the belief that it is the universal human standard, projects upon the Oriental "Other."

In *Don Sebastian* the sexual licentiousness of the Oriental woman and her lustful desire for her European slave become the subject of racy satiric play in the low-plot antics of the Mufti's wife, Joyama, in her pursuit of Antonio, her European slave. More significantly however, satiric allusions to female sexuality and naturalistic comic discourse invade the high plot and break the "exclusive beauty, crystal clarity and artistic completedness" of those figures that had traditionally been found in the distanced zone of the heroic genres.[93] For example, consider the figure of Almeyda. In the rhetorical fabric of a 1660s heroic drama Almeyda would be an ideational emblem of Perfect Beauty (as Saint Catherine is in *Tyrannick Love*) for which the perfect hero, Sebastian, and the imperfect hero of irregular greatness, Muley Moloch, contend. Almeyda is introduced to us in descriptions that break that figuration. We first hear of her from Dorax in language so obscene that it would be inconceivable in traditional heroic discourse:

> I hope she dy'd in her own Female calling,
> Choak'd up with Man, and gorg'd with Circumcision. [I,i,132-133]

Preparation for the heroine's first entrance extends upon this style, for it is rendered in a low-comic dialect that, while not savagely obscene as Dorax's lines are, is still inappropriate to a heroic figure in a heroic context. Moreover, the language is inappropriate to the scene as well as to the figuration of a heroic queen. Muley Moloch is preparing a ritual sacrifice of Christians to celebrate his victory. Neither so serious an event nor the occasion of the first appearance of the heroic protagonists would be treated comically in the traditional heroic genres. The Mufti has told Mustapha, the captain of the guards, that he should hold back Sebastian and Almeyda from deliverance into the hands of Muley Moloch, bribing him with the promise of Heaven. The low-comic language of Mustapha, as he betrays the Mufti to the emperor, is not only generically inconsistent, it is gratuitous, necessary neither to the action nor to the characterization:

> **Mustapha** Your Majesty may lay your Soul on't: but for my part, though I am a plain Fellow, yet I scorn to be trick'd into Paradice. I wou'd he [the Mufti] shou'd know it. The troth on't is, an't like you, His reverence bought of me the flower of all the Market: these—these are but Dogs meat to 'em, and a round price he pay'd me too I'll say that for him: but not enough for me to venture my neck for. . . . there was a dainty Virgin (*Virgin* said I! but I won't be too positive of that neither) with a leering eye! he paid me down for her upon the nail a thousand golden *Sultanins;* . . . Now is it very likely he wou'd pay so dear for such a delicious Morsel, and give it away out of his own mouth; when it had such a farewel with it too? [I,i,217-23; 232-38]

This low-comic dialect is very far removed from formal, heroic discourse; it attempts to simulate ordinary conversation; it is decidedly not the rhetorical declamation appropriate to the heroic drama. Novelistic, familiar discourse serves a number of functions here. First, it shatters typological figuration. No ideal female figure in the earlier heroic drama or prose romance was ever called a "delicious Morsel" with a "roguish, leering eye" and dubious virginity. Clearly, the derogatory discourse of late seventeenth-century travel-book descriptions of Oriental women has overwhelmed pre-modern emblematic figuration of the heroic Oriental queen. Second, the passage exposes the Mufti as a greedy, lustful hypocrite. Once again, the discourse of travel-book accounts has overtaken the earlier discursive mode.

English attitudes toward Muslim religion as well as figurations and descriptions of Muslim holy men by themselves could trace the origins of the discourse of Orientalism. For example, in medieval representation "Mahomut" is a simple devil, an entirely allegorical figure. Elizabethan travelers (Eldred, Newbury, and Fitch in particular) show remarkable respect and admiration for Islamic holy men, and when they discuss theological differences between Christianity and Islam they do so seriously and, as far as possible, with objectivity. Furthermore, they are especially impressed, as we have seen, by the freedom of conscience afforded to all people in the Ottoman territories. Late seventeenth-century writers, on the other hand, degrade the religion of the East as superstition at best and at worst as the hypocrisy of scoundrels:

Mahomet was born . . . but of mean parentage; bred up to merchandise; but he soon left that trade, and accompanied himself with thieves, by means of which he got to himself a great number of men. . . . To maintain his repute among his soldiers, he pretended in his fits of the falling sickness (to which he was much addicted) to have conference with the Holy Ghost. Then he ordained a new religion. . . . He lived a very lascivious life; and was buried . . . at Mecca, in honour of whom there is built a stately temple, to which the Turks and Saracens from all parts go every year on pilgrimage (as they would have you believe and many of the poorer sort do believe so themselves); but the truth is, their going is for merchandizing . . . for all commodities that come from the East Indies.[94]

Dryden's play relegates the Mufti and his lustful wife, Joyama, to the low, comically satiric under walk of the play. However, unlike *Absalom and Achitophel, Don Sebastian* is not a binary satire; it does not have a heroic "main design" and a satiric under walk. Rather, levels of discourse are loosely woven; the style may switch from the sacrosanct, rhetorical heroic style to the low-comic dialect, to mimetic novelistic desciption—sometimes within a single speech—with the consequence that discourse becomes polyglossic. Low, familiar discourse or comically satiric discourse does not exist in combat with high, as in a deconstructive satire; rather, levels of discourse *mingle* to produce a layered textual fabric that simulates the zone of experience. Consequently, characterization ceases to be typological, and "heroic" characters descend from the distanced zone and become "familiar." The nearer to sight the character, and the stronger the illusion of a "deep" and "mysterious" inner arena in the character, the more threatening the Oriental. The details by which we decode an emblematic figure, however detailed they may be, are *surface* embellishments. We do not try to look *into* the "mind" of the Prince of Morocco, and twentieth-century critics' vain attempts to figure out why Tamberlaine does the things he does are simply evidence of their novel-conditioned misreading. We "have" the meaning of the emblematic figure as soon as we have recognized the typological code, the calligraphy in which it is figured. But a novelistic character cannot be read at a glance any more than a person whom we encounter in experience can be. If the character's "inner depths" are foreign, are related to a cultural setting that is alien to our own, we are threatened by him. To lessen that threat writing diminishes the character, makes him clownish, ignorant, irrational, totally at the mercy of his appetites.

Said has said that "European culture gained in strength and identity by setting itself off against the Orient as a sort of surrogate and even underground self."[95] Once the heroic Oriental figure is secularized and novelized the Herculean Idea of Greatness he figured as an emblem is diminished into the irrational, appetitive, uncontrollable impulses within ourselves that we fear. The Oriental becomes the dark inside the self which the rational "man of sense" does not acknowledge.

The three characteristics of the Oriental most often mentioned in the travelers' accounts—and, therefore, one supposes, most threatening to the English—are all qualities which violate newly constructed bourgeois codes: unproductive laziness, sexual licentiousness, and resistance to control except by force. It is clear that European writers project upon the "Other" those qualities they most fear in themselves, impulses that are unamenable to rational control. Rauwolff, whose travels were collected by the Royal Society Fellow and distinguished naturalist, John Ray, ascribes to the Turks the very qualities that the new social thinkers of Restoration zero point most deplored in their own courtier wits:

> The *Turks* have also some very fine Manners and Customs, they are affable, they begin their Discourses (chiefly to Relations and Acquaintances) with a friendly Salutation and Kissing: but they are also lazy, and . . . love Idleness better than Labour, for you shall see them spend their whole Day in a Game of Chesse, and other Games, and playing their (Quiterns) Guitarhs . . . they walk about with them in the Streets . . . all day long, and so use themselves to Laziness and Leachery, and contaminate themselves with all sorts of terrible, and chiefly Sodomitical Sins, which by them (because both high and low are equally guilty thereof) are not at all punished.[96]

Rauwolff also believes that Orientals are ignorant because their knowledge is not useful, not New Scientific, not Western. They waste their time with poetry, especially heroic poetry: "in Liberal Arts and Sciences, such as we teach in our Countries, they are not Instructed, for they have not only none of these Learned Men, but esteem learning of these Sciences a Superfluity, and, loss of Time. They rather love old Rimes, and Ballads that speak of and commend the Mighty Deeds of their Ancient Emperours and Champions."[97]

All of the seventeenth-century travel writers are at once impressed and terrified by the absolute power of the Grand Seignor, his Bassas and Cadis. Though they despise such un-English arbitrary rule, it also fascinates them. Rule by ignorant, irrational power = Oriental, and rule by rational judgment and discourse = English in the equations they construct. Teonge describes a scene in which the English consul tries in vain to argue a case logically with the Cadi, who, sitting cross-legged on a raised dias, "with his Bugger-boy beside him sitting on a cushion," is utterly impervious to the Englishman's persuasion.[98] Miner and others believe that the raising of the mob in *Don Sebastian* reflects events in Dryden's own experience—Shaftesbury's rousing a crowd of thousands in 1679 for a Pope-Burning as a demonstration of his party's power.

While it is true that the political events of the day, and certainly the political atmosphere of Restoration London are reflected in this text, the raising of the mob also raises some interesting issues about the regulatory power of discourse itself. One of the most interesting comic interludes in the play is the Act IV contest between a brilliant rhetorician, the Mufti, and a plainspoken man of action, Mustapha, for control of the crowd. The Mufti uses all of the devices of classical rhetoric, and so effective is his language that his adversary, Mustapha, almost succumbs to the power of his persuasion—" 'Tis excellent fine matter indeed, Slave *Antonio*; Oh, he would move a Rock of Elephant!" (IV,iii,73-74). Mustapha, with the clown Antonio's help, however, throws off the enchantment of the Mufti's rhetoric. When it is his turn to address the crowd, he urges upon them the superiority of acts over words—"Believers, he only preach'd you up to it [rebellion and plunder]; but durst not lead you; he was but your Counsellor, but I was your Captain" (IV,iii,135-137). Mockery of classical rhetoric, so self-enclosed that it is ineffectual in the world of action and experience, would have appealed to a Sprat, a Locke, or a Boyle.

In his preface to Rauwolff's *A Collection of Curious Travels and Voyages,* John Ray says that his sole aim in publishing these accounts is "enlarging the Empire of Knowledge."[99] Curiously enough, Ray does not include any sixteenth-century voyages in any of his collections, though Hakluyt's extensive collection must have been known to him. Rather he restricts himself to accounts of his near contemporaries, and especially his fellow natural philosopher, Rauwolff. Late sixteenth-century English travellers to the East are full of admiration for everything they encounter. They marvel at the East's technological superiority—that is, highly sophisticated irrigation systems, pre-electricity methods of air conditioning houses, or the use of asbestos for cremation of the dead in India. They appreciate Eastern accomplishments in poetry, painting, manuscript illumination, and architecture (even the architecture of mosques). They are equally impressed with the cleanliness of Easterners (though some feel that all that bathing is probably unhealthy) and with the gentility of their manners. In direct contrast, late seventeenth-century/early eighteenth-century English travellers find Easterners dirty, ignorant, superstitious, and, as we have seen, invariably oversexed.

The same gardens and skillfully engineered method of irrigating them that filled the fifteenth- and sixteenth-century traveller with delight and awe are as accurately described by the seventeenth-century traveller but then, paradoxically, dismissed as inferior, though still too good for the brutes who own them:

It contains a large quadrangular plot of ground, divided into sixteen lesser squares, four in a row with walks between them. The walks are shaded with orange trees, of a large and spreading size. . . . Every one of these lesser squares in the garden was bordered with stone; and the stone-work were troughs very artistically contrived [to water each of the plants]. . . . Were this place under the supervision of an *English* gardner it is impossible anything could be more delightful. . . . [But] so little sense have the Turks of refin'd delights as these, being a people generally of the grossest apprehension, and knowing few other pleasures but such sensualities, as are equally common to both men and beasts.[100]

The religious diversity and freedom of conscience prevalent in an Oriental city that, as we have seen, the sixteenth-century traveller enthusiastically embraced is offensive to the Restoration Englishman. Henry Maundrell, making the pilgrimage to Jerusalem from Aleppo where he was chaplain to the English "factory," or trade embassy, is revolted by the way in which his Greek and Syrian fellow Christians (whom he never acknowledges as fellows) celebrate Holy Saturday:

They began their disorders by running around the Holy Sepulcher with all their might and swiftness, crying out as they went, Huia! Which signifies 'this is he' or 'this is it,' an expression by which they assert the verity of the Christian religion. And after they had by these vertiginous circulations and clamours turn'd their heads and inflam'd their madness, they began to act the most antic tricks and postures, in a thousand shapes of distraction. . . . In a word nothing can be imagin'd more rude or extravagant than what was enacted upon this occasion.[101]

Nothing could be further from English "natural reason," the newly conceived seat of religious sensibility, than this disorderly "madness." The further from English "mind" the further from the center of civilization, and, indeed, the further from humaness.

John Ray said that his aim in writing of his travels was to enlarge the empire of knowledge. Sprat declared that English mind was *by nature* sovereign of that empire. Under the dispensation of the new episteme ordered and ordering English "reason" discriminates the rational from the irrational, delineates the boundaries of civilization, and, finally, decides the borderlines of humanity. From the discursively central English "I" whole orders of thought radiate to design the world; the discourse of modernism becomes the discourse of empire, and the discourse of colonialism. English mind writes itself upon the whole world, and, as it names it, takes possession of it.

CONCLUSION

> They interfered with place,
> Time, people, lives, and so to bed.
> They died
> When it died. It had died before.
> It died
> Before they did. They did not know it. Race,
> Power, Trade, Fleet, a hundred regiments
> Postponed that final reckoning with pride,
> Which was expensive.
>
> Douglas Dunn, *Barbarians*

Lacan calls language "the world of words that creates the world of things."[1] This book has tried to show that the world of words was a world destroyed and a world reborn in the cataclysmic epistemological rupture that occurred in England in the Restoration period. The modern world of things—of trade, of empire, of technological invention, professionalism, and print culture—emerged out of that big bang. We ourselves, we twentieth-century people, were created by the explosion, with our linear logic, our conceptions of economic growth and productivity, with our discursive delineations, such as "the developing nations," "the Dow Jones Average," or the "Euro-dollar."

In my view, postmodernism signals the arrival in culture (at least in that culture that is designed by the English language) of yet another zero point. The ideas that language is mimetic, that "reality" is material, that the "self" is a natural entity, that Western hegemony is God-ordained, are collapsing under the weight of questions raised by the very epistemology that gave birth to them. For example, "the sovereign individual confronting the world,"[2] whose direct observation and mimetic discourse laid bare to view the natural operations of the universe, was himself laid waste by the very knowledge he acquired. Particle physics has made mockery of the eye that observed nature *and* the telescope through which it gazed. "Race," a distinction so readily apparent to the naked eye, has not only erased itself as a biological category but challenges the idea of categorization itself. The "natural" straitjacket, gender, has proven to be a "show," a semiotic performance.[3] If everybody's "natural reason" is sovereign, whose draws the lines of demarcation, whose charts the map? And how are we supposed to conceive of "nation" when every principality from "Queer Nation" to the ethnically purifying Serbs clamors for dominance and self-determination?

There is an uncanny, decade by decade resemblence between Restoration zero point and postmodern American zero point. The deconstructive 1960s with their ringing admonition to "tune in, turn on, drop out" of the false values and strangling social fictions of the establishment; the '80s, decade of overweening capitalistic greed and self-confidence; the new holy nationalism, conservatism, and racism emerging in the '90s—all seem a terrifying do-over.

However, most significant in terms of the discussion raised in this book, is that once again the discourses of zero point, and the "cultures" they design are contending for dominance. The deconstructive language of zero point—ostentatiously self-referential and self-reflexive—once more is exploring the power and the limitations of language, once again is pursuing itself *into* itself and into the abyss. The constructive discourse of postmodern zero point, on the other hand, is once again the discourse of nationalism and capitalism. And the most popular mode in literature is the biography and the memoir, forms most congenial to the discursively central "I," strong linguistic fortifications of the "self."

Dollimore has argued that "culture itself is not a unitary phenomenon; non-dominant elements interact with the dominant forms, sometimes coexisting with, or being absorbed or even destroyed by them, but also challenging, modifying or even displacing them."[4] It will be interesting to scholars in the future, perhaps, to trace the processes of historical change that are at work in our own end of the century zero point.

NOTES

Introduction

1. J.G.A. Pocock, *Virtue, Commerce and History,* Cambridge: Cambridge University Press, 1985, p. 13.

2. Dominick La Capra, *Rethinking Intellectual History: Texts, Contexts, Languages,* Ithaca: Cornell University Press, 1983, p. 17.

3. Hans Blumenberg, *The Legitimacy of the Modern Age,* tr. Robert M. Wallace, Cambridge, Mass.: MIT Press, 1983, p. 220.

4. Sandra Rudnick Luft, "The Legitimacy of Hans Blumenberg's Conception of Originary Activity," *Annals of Scholarship* 5 (fall, 1987), 3-36, p. 27.

5. Timothy J. Reiss, *The Discourse of Modernism,* Ithaca and London: Cornell University Press, 1982.

6. Karlis Racevskis, "Genealogical Critique: Michel Foucault," *Contemporary Literary Theory,* ed. D.G. Atkins and L. Morrow, Amherst, Mass.: University of Massachusetts Press, 1988, 229-245, p. 231. Quotations are of Racevskis's summary of Foucault.

7. Pocock, *Virtue, Commerce and History,* p. 29.

8. La Capra, *Rethinking Intellectual History,* p. 18.

9. Pocock, *Virtue, Commerce and History,* p. 29.

10. Pocock, *Virtue, Commerce and History,* p. 28.

11. Daniel Defoe, *Tour thro' the Whole Island of Great Britain,* 2 vols., London, 1722, I, 173-174.

12. Reiss, *The Discourse of Modernism.*

13. Gayatri Spivack, Translator's Preface, to Jacques Derrida, *Of Grammatology,* Baltimore: Johns Hopkins University Press, 1976, p. xvii.

14. Defoe, *An Essay upon Projects,* London, 1697, p. 8.

15. Anonymous, "A Discourse of London," 1578, included in the appendix of John Stow, *Survey of London,* 1747. I have chosen this passage because it seems to me to have been written by a "City man," a tradesman and even, perhaps, a Puritan. If that is the case, then the writer's sympathies in regard to commerce as well as religion would be very close to Defoe's. The passage, therefore, strikingly makes my case that the epistemology and discourse of a particular age—and *not* the sentiments of a person—determine what it is possible to write, to see, and to think in that age.

16. Zimbardo, "At Zero Point: Discourse, Politics, and Satire in Restoration England," *ELH* 59 (1992), 785-798.

17. Jonathan Dollimore, *Radical Tragedy: Religion, Ideology, and Power in the Drama of Shakespeare and his Contemporaries,* London: Wheatsheaf Press, 1989, p. 277, n. 12.

18. Steven Shapin, *A Social History of Truth,* Chicago: University of Chicago Press, 1994.

19. Luft, "Hans Blumenberg's Conception of Originary Activity," p. 20.

20. John Wilkins, *Toward a Real Character and a Philosophical Language,* London, 1668, p. 21.

21. Samuel Parker, *A Demonstration of the Divine Authority of the Law and Christian Religion,* London, 1681.

22. Robert Boyle, *Some Considerations Touching the Style of the H. Scriptures,* London: Herringman, 1661.

23. See David Trotter's important essay on this subject: "Wanton Expressions," *Spirit of Wit,* ed. Jeremy Treglown, Hamden, Conn.: Archon Books, 1982, 111-132.

24. Cf. particularly, Augustine, *de Magistro,* tr. Robert B. Russel, Fathers of the Church 59, Washington, D.C.: Catholic University of America, 1968. A good example that Augustine uses to illustrate the absence inherent in the sign is his playing with the word nihil: "instead of saying *nihil* signifies something which is nothing, shall we say that this word signifies a certain state of mind when failing to perceive a reality, the mind finds, or thinks it finds, that such a reality does not exist?" p. 10.

25. Gilbert Burnet, *Passages of the Life and Death of John, Earl of Rochester,* 1680, included in toto in *Rochester; the Critical Heritage,* ed. David Farley-Hills, London: Routledge and Kegan Paul, 1972, 47-92, p. 54.

26. Umberto Eco, *The Role of the Reader: Explorations in the Semiotics of Texts,* Bloomington: Indiana University Press, 1979, p. 52.

27. Shapin, *A Social History,* p. 16.

28. Tillotson, quoted in Richard Blackmore, *Essays upon Several Subjects,* London, 1712, p. 208.

29. Jacques Derrida, "Living on the Borderlines," *Deconstruction and Criticism,* ed. Harold Bloom et al., London: Routledge and Kegan Paul, 1979, 75-176, p. 84.

30. Hobbes, *Leviathan,* ed. A.B. Waller, Cambridge: Cambridge University Press, 1935, p. 254.

31. Edward Stillingfleet, *Works,* 2 vols., London, 1710, I, 227. The target of Stillingfleet's wrath is, of course, Rochester's *Satyr Against Reason and Mankind.* This excerpt is from a sermon that Stillingfleet preached before King Charles II.

32. Blackmore, "Essay on Wit," *Essays upon Several Subjects,* London, 1712, p. 191.

33. Blackmore, "Essay on Wit," p. 190.

34. John Buchanan-Brown, Introduction, *John Aubrey, Three Prose Works,* Fontwell, Sussex: Centaur Press, Ltd., 1972, p. xix.

35. Blackmore, "Essay on Wit," p. 214.

36. Blackmore, "Essay on Wit," p. 215.

37. Locke, quoted in Richard C. Boys, *Sir Richard Blackmore and the Wits,* New York: Octagon Books, p. 27.

38. Peter Laslett, "John Locke, the Great Coinage and the Origins of the Board of Trade," *John Locke: Problems and Perspectives,* ed. John W. Yolton, Cambridge: Cambridge University Press, 1969, 137-166, p. 137.

39. Laslett, "John Locke," p. 144.

40. Laslett, "John Locke," p. 144, fn. 1.

41. Laslett, "John Locke," p. 138.

42. John Locke, *An Essay Concerning Human Understanding,* ed. Peter Niddich, Oxford: Oxford University Press, 1975, p. 522.

43. Locke, "On Conduct," *Works,* 9 vols., London, 1794, II, 36-37.

44. Locke, *Works,* II, 361.

45. Locke, "To Stillingfleet," *Works,* III, 139.

46. Derrida, "Living on the Borderlines."

47. Howard Weinbrot, *Alexander Pope and the Tradition of Formal Verse Satire,* Princeton: Princeton University Press, 1982, p. xiii.

48. Shaftesbury, *Characteristics,* 1711, ed. John M. Robertson, reprint, Gloucester, Mass.: Peter Smith, 1963, I, 72.

49. Pocock, *Virtue, Commerce and History.*

50. Jonathan Culler, *The Pursuit of Signs,* Ithaca, N.Y.: Cornell University Press, 1981, p. 37.

51. Luft, "Hans Blumenberg's Conception of Originary Activity," p. 27.

52. Rochester, "Upon Nothing," *The Complete Poems of John Wilmot, Earl of Rochester,* ed. David M. Vieth, New Haven and London: Yale University Press, 1968, p. 119.

53. Barbara Everett, "The Sense of Nothing," *Spirit of Wit,* ed. Jeremy Treglown, Hamden, Conn.: Archon Books, 1982, 1-41, p. 32.

54. Ken Robinson, Introduction, *John Oldham, Selected Poems,* Bloodaxe Books, Plymouth and London: The Bowring Press, 1980, p. 8.

55. *The Works of the Right Honorable Earls of Rochester and Roscommon,* London, 1709, p. 13.

56. Keir Elam, *The Semiotics of Theater and Drama,* London and New York: Methuen, 1980, p. 9.

57. G. Douglas Atkins, *Reading Deconstruction/Deconstructive Reading,* Lexington: University Press of Kentucky, 1983, p. 22.

58. Raman Selden, *English Verse Satire, 1590-1765,* London: George Allen and Unwin, 1978, p. 93.

59. Peter Porter, "The Professional Amateur," *Spirit of Wit,* ed. Jeremy Treglown, Hamden, Conn.: Archon Books, 1982, 58-74, p. 72.

60. Roland Barthes, *The Pleasures of the Text,* tr. Richard Miller, New York: Hill and Wang, 1975, p. 40.

61. Umberto Eco, *The Role of the Reader,* p. 40.

62. Eco, "On the Possibility of Generating Aesthetic Messages in an Edenic Language," *The Role of the Reader,* pp. 101-102.

63. Shapin, *A Social History,* p. 16.

64. Derrida, "Living on the Borderlines," p. 84.

65. Augustine, *Confessions,* tr. Vernon J. Burke, The Fathers of the Church, Washington, D.C.: Catholic University Press, 1953, reprint, 1966, pp. 331-332.

66. Robert Boyle, "The Doctrine of Thinking," The Early Essays and Ethics of Robert Boyle, ed. John T. Harwood, Carbondale: Southern Illinois University Press, 1991, p. 184.

67. Reiss, *The Discourse of Modernism,* p. 31.

68. Edward Said, *Orientalism,* London: Peregrine Books, 1985, p. 8.

Chapter 1. *"From Words to Experimental Philosophy"*

1. Umberto Eco, "On the Possibility of Generating Aesthetic Messages in an Edenic Language," p. 91.

2. Eco, "Generating Aesthetic Messages," pp. 101-102.

3. Ralph Lever, *The Art of Reason* (1573), reprint, Menston, England: The Scholar Press Ltd., 1972, p. 139. Lever's book was preceded only by Thomas Wilson's *Rule of Reason* as a complete treatise on logic written in English.

4. Thomas Wilson, *Rule of Reason,* London, 1551, Sig B3r-B3v.

5. Abraham Fraunce, *Arcadian Rhetoricks,* ed. from the edition of 1588 by Ethel Seaton, Oxford: B. Blackwell, 1950. Thomas Wilson, *The Art of Rhetorique,* London, 1585.

6. Thomas Sprat, *History of the Royal Society,* a facsimile text [of the 1661 edition] with introduction, notes, and appendices by Jackson I. Cope and Harold M. Jones, St. Louis, Mo.: Washington University Studies, 1959, p. 27.

7. Sprat, *History of the Royal Society,* p. 484.

8. Sprat, *History of the Royal Society,* p. 54.

9. Sprat, *History of the Royal Society,* p. 111.

10. Sprat, *History of the Royal Society,* p. 116.

11. Stephen Hawes, *The Pastime of Pleasure* (1555), reprint, London: The Percy Society, 1845, p. 62.

12. Hawes, *The Pastime of Pleasure,* p. 37.

13. Wilson, *Rule of Reason,* Sig. B2r.

14. Hawes, *The Pastime of Pleasure,* p. 24.

15. Francis Clement, *The Petie Schole,* London, 1587, p. 11.

16. Ralph Lever, *The Art of Reason,* London, 1573, pp. 1, 65.

17. Augustine, *de Doctrina Christina,* tr. D. W. Robertson, Indianapolis, Ind.: Bobbs Merrill Co., 1958, p. 14.

18. Theophilus Gale, *The Court of the Gentiles,* 2 vols., London, 1669, I, 52.

19. Cf. Augustine, *de Magistro,* pp. 53-54.

20. Marcia Colish, *The Mirror of Language: A Study in the Medieval Theory of Knowledge,* New Haven, Conn.: Yale University Press, 1968, pp. 176-177.

21. R. Howard Bloch, *Etymologies and Genealogies: A Literary Anthropology of the French Middle Ages,* Chicago: University of Chicago Press, 1983, p. 157.

22. Peter Ramus, *DIALECTIQUE de Pierre de la Ramee,* Paris: Andre Wechel, 1555, p. 69, tr. and cited by Wilbur Samuel Howell, *Logic and Rhetoric in England,*

1500-1700, Princeton: Princeton University Press, 1956, p. 152. This book of Mr. Howell's, and his *Eighteenth-Century British Logic and Rhetoric*, Princeton: Princeton University Press, 1971, have been invaluable to me, as they must be to every scholar interested in the history of English logic and rhetoric. I am deeply grateful to have had these treasure-houses of exemplary scholarship to guide my investigations.

23. Robert Sanderson, *Logicae Artis Compendium*, Oxford, 1615, p. 23.

24. Samuel Smith, *Aditus ad Logicum*, London, 1627, Sig. A3r.

25. Howell, *Eighteenth-Century British Logic and Rhetoric*, pp. 5-6.

26. Wilson, *Rule of Reason*, London, 1590, Sig. J5v-J6r.

27. Thomas Grainger, *Syntagma Logicum, or the Divine Logic*, London, 1620, p. 32.

28. Howell, *Logic and Rhetoric in England, 1500-1700*, p. 233.

29. Ramus, *DIALECTIQUE de Pierre de la Ramee*, p. 118.

30. John Wynne, *An Abridgement of Mr. Locke's Essay Concerning Human Understanding*, London, 1696.

31. William Molyneux, *Familiar Letters Between Mr. Locke and Several of his Friends*, ed. John Wallis, London, 1708, pp. 16-17.

32. For the importance of Locke's contribution see Hans Arleff, *The Study of Language in England, 1780-1860*, Minneapolis: University of Minnesota Press, 1983, and *From Locke to Saussure*, Minneapolis: University of Minnesota Press, 1982.

33. Antoine Foclin, *La Rhetorique Francoise d'Antoine Foclin de Chauncy au Vermandois*, Paris: Andre Wechel, 1555, p. 1.

34. Robert Boyle, *Some Considerations Touching the Style of the H. Scriptures*, p. 126.

35. Abraham Cowley, "To the Royal Society," Preface to Thomas Sprat, *History of the Royal Society*, London, 1667.

36. Sprat, *History of the Royal Society*, 1661 ed., p. 111.

37. Sprat, *History of the Royal Society*, p. 112.

38. Cf. John Ray, *Catalogus plantarum Angliae*, London, 1677; John Ray, *The Ornithology of Francis Willughby*, London, 1678; and *Philosophical Letters between the late Mr. Ray and several of his ingenious correspondents . . . to which are added those of Francis Willughby*, London, 1718.

39. John Ray, *Observations Topographical, Moral, and Physiological*, London, 1673, p. 50.

40. Sprat, *History of the Royal Society*, pp. 90-91.

41. Boyle, *Style of the H. Scriptures*, pp. 32-33.

42. Boyle, *Style of the H. Scriptures*, pp. 164-165.

43. Boyle, *Style of the H. Scriptures*, pp. 34-35.

44. Sprat, *History of the Royal Society*, p. 113.

45. Sprat, *History of the Royal Society*, p. 97.

46. Locke, *Human Understanding*, p. 405.

47. Locke, *Human Understanding*, p. 104.

48. Jonathan Culler, *The Pursuit of Signs*, p. 48.

49. Locke, *Human Understanding*, p. 403.

50. Locke, *Human Understanding*, p. 415.

51. Locke, *Human Understanding*, p. 8.

52. Locke, "The Conduct of the Understanding in the Search of Truths" (1697), *Essays Moral, Economical, and Political collected by Lord Moon*, New York, 1825, p. 12.

53. Locke, "Conduct," p. 50.

54. Sprat, *History of the Royal Society,* pp. 89–90.

55. Boyle, *The Early Essays and Ethics,* p. 188.

56. Boyle, *Style of H. Scriptures,* pp. 116-117.

57. Sprat, *History of the Royal Society,* p. 116.

58. Karlis Racevskis, "Genealogical Critique: Michel Foucault," p. 234.

59. *The Ars Minor of Donatus,* University of Wisconsin Studies in Language and Literature, no. 11, Madison: University of Wisconsin Press, 1926, p. 16.

60. Chaucer, *The House of Fame, The Works of Geoffrey Chaucer,* 2nd ed., ed. F.N. Robinson, Cambridge, Mass.: Riverside Press, 1957, p. 289.

61. Baltassar Castiglione, *The Courtier,* tr. Sir Thomas Hoby, London, 1588, Sig. F3v.

62. Christopher Norris, *The Deconstructive Turn: Essays in the Rhetoric of Philosophy,* London: Methuen and Co., 1983, p. 3.

63. Norris, *The Deconstructive Turn,* p. 6.

64. David Foxon, *Libertine Literature in England, 1660-1745,* New Hyde Park, N.Y.: University Books, 1965, p. 10.

65. *The Whores Rhetorick, Calculated to the Meridian of London and Conformed to the Rules of Art,* London, 1683, p. 33. Subsequent references are to this edition and page references will be cited in the text.

66. "Epistle to the Reader," *The Whores Rhetorick,* Sig. A10.

67. Racevskis, "Genealogical Critique: Michel Foucault," p. 231.

Chapter 2. *The Semiotics of Restoration Deconstructive Satire*

This chapter has been published as an article in *Cutting Edges: Postmodern Critical Essays in 18th Century Satire,* Tennessee Studies in Literature 37, Knoxville: University of Tennessee Press, 1995.

1. Cf. David Vieth, *Attribution in Restoration Poetry,* New Haven, Conn.: Yale University Press, 1963; "Toward an Anti-Aristotlean Poetic: Rochester's *Satyr Against Mankind* and *Artemisia to Chloe,* with Notes on Swift's *Tale of a Tub* and *Gulliver's Travels," Language and Style* 5 (1972); and, most particularly, *The Moriae Encomium as a Model for Satire in Restoration Court Literature: Rochester and Others,* Los Angeles: The William Andrews Clark Memorial Library, 1988.

Dustin Griffin, *Satires against Man,* Berkeley and Los Angeles: University of California Press, 1973; and, more particularly, "Satiric Closure," *Genre* 18 (summer, 1985), 173-189. Kevin Cope, "The Conquest of Truth: Wycherley, Butler, Rochester, and Dryden," *Restoration* 10:1 (spring, 1986), 19-40. Barbara Everett, "The Sense of Nothing."

2. Selden, *English Verse Satire, 1590-1765,* p. 73.

3. Cope, "The Conquest of Truth," p. 31.

4. Racevskis, "Genealogical Critique: Michel Foucault," p. 234.

5. Everett Zimmerman, *Swift's Narrative Satire,* Ithaca, N.Y.: Cornell University Press, 1983, pp. 62-63.

6. Zimmerman, *Swift's Narrative Satire,* p. 87.

7. Claude Rawson, *Order from Confusion Sprung,* London: George Allen and Unwin, 1985, p. 7.

8. Derrida, "Living on the Borderlines," p. 84.

9. Gayatri Spivack, Translator's Preface, p. xii.

10. Spivack, Translator's Preface, p. xvii.

11. Derrida, *Writing and Difference,* tr. Alan Bass, Chicago: University of Chicago Press, 1978, p. 279.

12. Augustine, *de Doctrina,* p. 14.

13. Augustine, *The Teacher,* tr. Robert B. Russel, The Fathers of the Church, vol. 59, Washington D.C.: Catholic University of America Press, 1968, pp. 10-11.

14. Augustine, *Confessions,* pp. 331-332.

15. *de Magistro, The Philosophy of St. Augustine: Selected Readings and Commentaries,* ed. John A. Mourant, University Park: Pennsylvania State University Press, 1964, p. 192.

16. Derrida, *Positions,* tr. Alan Bass, Chicago: University of Chicago Press, 1981, p. 26.

17. Augustine, *Confessions,* pp. 343-344.

18. Hobbes, *Leviathan,* ed. Michael Oakeshott, Oxford: Oxford University Press, 1960, p. 11.

19. Rochester, "Love and Life: A Song," *The Works of John, Earl of Rochester,* London, 1714, p. 22.

20. Everett, "Sense of Nothing," p. 11.

21. Hobbes, *Leviathan,* ed. Oakeshott, p. 440.

22. Augustine, *de Magistro, The Philosophy of St. Augustine,* ed. Mourant, p. 33.

23. Howard R. Bloch, *Etymologies and Genealogies: A Literary Anthropology of the French Middle Ages,* Chicago: University of Chicago Press, 1983, p. 146.

24. Eco, *The Role of the Reader,* pp. 53-54.

25. Eco, *The Role of the Reader,* pp. 57-58. Eco here is describing the end of the twentieth century; I believe that his description is as valid for the end of the seventeenth century.

26. Everett, "Sense of Nothing," p. 11.

27. Paul de Man, "The Rhetoric of Temporality," *Interpretation: Theory and Practice,* ed. Charles S. Singleton, Baltimore: Johns Hopkins University Press, 1969, 173-209, pp. 195-196.

28. de Man, "Rhetoric of Temporality," p. 197.

29. See, for example, Arthur R. Huseboe, *Sir George Etherege,* Boston: G.K. Hall, 1987.

30. Willard Connelly, *Brawny Wycherley,* London: C. Scribner's Sons, 1930. Eugene McCarthy, *William Wycherley,* Athens: Ohio University Press, 1979, attributes Wycherley's whole personality to his relation with his father precisely because Daniel Wycherley was so litigious that court records provide a good deal of evidence about his life, while there is no data on his son's life until William reached the age of thirty, and precious little after that time beyond anecdotal evidence.

31. Griffin, *Satires against Man,* p. 60.

32. Earl Miner, "In Satire's Falling City," *The Satirist's Art,* ed. H.J. Jensen and M.R. Zirken, Bloomington: University of Indiana Press, 1972, p. 16.

33. Such widely different personalities as Marvell and Voltaire thought Rochester a great satirist and genius. Charles II thought Wycherley a satirist of such penetrating sense that he would be a fit tutor for kings, while most of his contemporaries, including Dryden, thought him the Restoration's Juvenal.

34. Michael Seidel, *Satiric Inheritance: Rabelais to Sterne,* Princeton: Princeton University Press, 1979, p. 21.

35. Quintillian, *Institutio Oratoria,* 10:1, 93, *The Institutio Oratoria of Quintllian,* tr. H.E. Butler, 4 vols. London: Heinemann; New York: Putnam and Sons, 1921-22.

36. Derrida, "Structure, Sign and Play," *The Languages of Criticism and the Sciences of Man: The Structuralist Controversy,* ed. R. Macksey and E. Donato, Baltimore: Johns Hopkins University Press, 1970, p. 249.

37. Gayatri Spivack, Translator's Preface, p. xii.

38. Keir Elam, *The Semiotics of Theatre and Drama,* London and New York: Methuen, 1980, p. 9.

39. Griffin, *Satire against Man,* p. 29.

40. Thomas E. Maresca, "*The Satyricon:* No Text, Context, Pretext." This is a chapter in a forthcoming book on allegory which the author has graciously allowed me to read in manuscript.

41. Rochester, "A Ramble in St. James's Park," *The Complete Poems of John Wilmot, Earl of Rochester,* ed. David M. Vieth, New Haven and London: Yale University Press, 1968. All subsequent references will be to this edition.

Chapter 3. No "I" and No "Eye"

1. Maynard Mack, "The Muse of Satire," *Studies in the Literature of the Augustan Age,* ed. R.C. Boys, Ann Arbor: University of Michigan Press, 1950, 219-232.

2. Samuel Johnson, "Dryden," *Lives of the English Poets,* ed. George Birbeck Hill, 3 vols., Oxford: Clarendon Press, 1905, I, 410.

3. Ian Donaldson, "Jonson and Anger," *English Satire and the Satiric Tradition,* ed. Claude Rawson, Oxford: Blackwell, 1984, 56-71, p. 68.

4. Ben Jonson, *Ben Jonson,* ed. C.H. Herford and P.E. Simpson, 2 vols., Oxford: Oxford University Press, 1925-52, I, 158.

5. Joseph Hall, *Vergidemiarum,* London, 1597, p. 99.

6. John Marston, *The Scourge of Villanie* (1599), reprint, New York: Barnes and Noble, 1966, p. 12.

7. Marston, *The Scourge of Villanie,* pp. 11-12.

8. Marston, *The Scourge of Villanie,* p. 10.

9. Jonson, "Epistle Dedicatory to the Universities of Oxford and Cambridge," prefixed to *Volpone,* 1607 edition, *Ben Jonson,* ed. C.H. Herford and P.E. Simpson, 2 vols., Oxford: Oxford University Press, 1925-52, I, 138.

10. Raman Selden, *English Verse Satire, 1590-1765,* p. 71.

11. Mary Claire Randolph, "The Medical Conception in English Renaissance Satiric Theory: Its Possible Relationships and Implications," *SP* 38 (1941), 125-57, p. 129. R.C. Elliot, *The Power of Satire,* Princeton: Princeton University Press, 1960, develops this theory more fully over more extensive historical ground.

12. John Oldham, "A Satyr upon a Woman," *John Oldham Selected Poems,* ed. Ken Robinson, Plymouth and London: Bloodaxe Books, The Bowering Press, 1980, p. 42.

13. G.R. Owst, *Literature and Pulpit in Medieval England,* 2nd ed., rev., Oxford: Basil Blackwell, 1961, p. 216. Owst was the earliest proponent of the "goliardic" school of thought on the origins of English satire; its most recent adherent is H.A. Mason, *Humanism and Poetry in the Early Tudor Period* (1959).

14. All references are to *The Complete Works of Chaucer,* ed. F.N. Robinson, Cambridge, Mass: Harvard University Press, 1933.

15. Marston, *The Scourge of Villanie,* p. 10.

16. This error was not corrected until 1605, by Isaac Casaubon.

17. Henry Puttenham, *The Arte of English Poesie* (1589), *Elizabethan Critical Essays,* ed. G. Smith, 2 vols., Oxford: Oxford University Press, 1909, II, 32.

18. Thomas Lodge, in *Elizabethan Critical Essays,* ed. G. Smith, 2 vols., Oxford: Oxford University Press, 1909, I, 80.

19. George Wither, "Vice's Executioner," *The Works of George Wither,* London, 1620.

20. Henry Peachum, *The Compleat Gentleman,* 3rd ed., London, 1622.

21. Thomas Shadwell, *Complete Works,* ed. Montague Summers, 5 vols., London: Nonesuch Press, 1927, V, 293.

22. Robert Gould, in Oldham, *Works,* 4 vols., IV, sig. B5v.

23. Dryden, "A Discourse Concerning the Original and Progress of Satire," *The Works of John Dryden,* vol. 4: *Poems, 1693-96,* ed. A.B. Chambers and William Frost, Berkeley, Los Angeles, and London: University of California Press, 1974, p. 76.

24. Weinbrot, *Alexander Pope and the Tradition of Formal Verse Satire,* p. xiii.

25. Selden, *English Verse Satire,* p. 40.

26. Marston, *The Scourge of Villanie,* p. 4.

27. Selden, *English Verse Satire,* p. 53.

28. C.S. Lewis, *English Literature in the Sixteenth Century,* OHEL, Oxford: Oxford University Press, 1954, pp. 469–470.

29. Ken Robinson, "The Art of Violence in Rochester's Satire," *English Satire and the Satiric Tradition,* ed. Claude Rawson, Oxford: Basil Blackwell, 1984, 93–108, p. 94.

30. Pope, *Imitations of Horace,* ed. John Butt, The Twickenham Edition of the Poems of Alexander Pope, 2nd ed., vol. 4, London and New Haven: Methuen and Yale University Press, 1953, Satire II,i,ll.212, 217.

31. Joseph Spence, *Observations, Anecdotes, and Characters of Books and Men, Pope and His Contemporaries,* ed. James Osbourn, Oxford: Clarendon Press, 1966, p. 473.

32. Tom Brown, *The Works of Mr. Thomas Brown,* 4 vols., London, 1760, I, 143.

33. Ken Robinson, *John Oldham, Selected Poems,* p. 16

34. John Oldham, Preface, *Some New Pieces,* London, 1681.

35. John Traugott, "A Tale of a Tub," *The Character of Swift's Satire,* ed. Claude Rawson, Newark: University of Delaware Press, 1983, 83–126, p. 101.

36. Ann Cline Kelly, *Swift and the English Language,* Philadelphia: University of Pennsylvania Press, 1988, p. 15.

37. Kelly, *Swift and the English Language,* p. 36.

38. For a discussion of textual matters in Oldham see the commentary to *The Poems of John Oldham,* ed. Harold Brooks with the collaboration of Raman Selden, Oxford: Clarendon Press, 1987. All references, unless otherwise indicated, are to this edition, and will be abbreviated as Brooks and Selden.

39. Aubrey, *Lives,* quoted by Brooks and Selden, Notes, p. 400.

40. Sharrock, quoted in Introduction to Brooks and Selden, p. xxvi.

41. Geoffrey S. Conway, Introduction, *The Odes of Pindar,* tr. Geoffrey S. Conway, London: J.M. Dent & Sons Ltd., 1972, p. xiii.

42. Selden, "Oldham, Pope, and Restoration Satire," *English Satire and the Satiric Tradition,* ed. Claude Rawson, Oxford: Basil Blackwell, 1984, 109-126, p. 117.

43. Conway, Introduction, *The Odes of Pindar,* pp. xii–xiii.

44. Conway, Intrduction, *The Odes of Pindar,* p. xiii.

45. Conway, Introduction, *The Odes of Pindar,* p. xix.

46. Cowley, *Poems,* London, 1714, pp. 195, 197.

47. Dio Cassius, XLVII.49 quoted by Bacon in *Advancement of Learning,* ed. F.G. Selby, 2 vols., New York, 1892-95, II,xxiii,46 and by Brooks and Selden, Notes, p. 402.

48. H.K. Miller, "The Paradoxical Encomium, with special reference to its vogue in England from 1600 to 1800," *Modern Philology* 53 (1956), 145-178.

49. See Brooks and Selden, footnote p. 403; Theopompus reclaimed the story in his history and thereby embalmed the name of Herostratus "like a fly in amber." Cf. Strabo XIV.22, Valerius Maximus, VII,14.5, and Allus Gellius II.6.

50. Cowley, *Essays,* London, 1714, p. 373.

51. Conway, Introduction, *The Odes of Pindar,* pp. xii–xiii.

52. Conway, Introduction, *The Odes of Pindar,* p. xxiv.

53. *Athenae Oxoniensis,* Oxford, 1691-1692, 4 vols., IV, 121.

54. Harold Fisch, "Character as Linguistic Sign," *NLH* 21 (1990), 593-606, p. 593.

55. Fisch, "Character as Linguistic Sign," p. 599.

56. Sarah Winkle, "Libertinism and Sexual Politics," *Spirit of Wit,* ed. Jeremy Treglown, Hamden, Conn.: Archon Books, 1982, 133-165, p. 135.

57. Dale Underwood, *Etherege and the Seventeenth Century Comedy of Manners,* New Haven: Yale University Press, 1957, see chapter I, "The Fertile Ground," p. 26.

58. Underwood, *Etherege and the Seventeenth Century,* p. 14

59. Underwood, *Etherege and the Seventeenth Century,* p. 23.

60. Underwood, *Etherege and the Seventeenth Century,* p. 19.

61. Underwood, *Etherege and the Seventeenth Century,* p. 24.

62. Dryden, Preface to *The State of Innocence, Of Dramatic Poesy and Other Essays,* ed. George Watson, 2 vols., London, 1962, I, 199.

63. Rose Zimbardo, *A Mirror to Nature: Transformations in Drama and Aesthetics, 1660-1732,* Lexington: University Press of Kentucky, 1986. Also see Zimbardo, "The Late Seventeenth Century Dilemma in Discourse," *Rhetorics of Order/Ordering Rhetorics,* ed. J.D. Canfield and J.P. Hunter, Cranbury, N.J.: University of Delaware Press, 1989.

64. Cf. particularly, Zimbardo, *Wycherley's Drama: A Link in the Development of English Satire,* New Haven and London: Yale University Press, 1965.

65. Anne Righter, "William Wycherley," *Restoration Theatre,* ed. J.R. Brown and B. Harris, New York: Capricorn Books, 1967, p. 81. James Sutherland, *English Literature of the Late Seventeenth Century,* OHEL, Oxford: Oxford University Press, 1969, p. 119.

66. Bernard Harris, "The Dialect of Those Fanatic Times," *Restoration Theatre,* ed. J.R. Brown and B. Harris, New York: Capricorn Books, 1967, pp. 226, 227.

67. All references are to Wycherley, *The Plain Dealer,* ed. James L. Smith, London: Ernest Benn, Ltd., 1977.

68. I have done close analysis of the conventionality of the figure, and have provided substantial evidence that Manly is a satyr-satirist in *Wycherley's Drama,* which I shall not repeat here.

69. Augustine, *Confessions,* pp. 343-344.

70. Epistle Dedicatory to Mrs. Bennet, p. 190. Cf. chapter 1.

71. Paul de Man, "Pascal's Allegory of Persuasion," *Allegory and Representation,* ed. Stephen Greenblatt, Baltimore: Johns Hopkins University Press, 1986, p. 11.

72. David Vieth, Introduction, *The Works of John Wilmot, Earl of Rochester,* p. xl.

73. Jonathan Culler, *The Pursuit of Signs,* p. 37.

74. George Bentley, Preface, *Phalaris,* 8th ed., London, 1771.

75. Everett Zimmerman, *Swift's Narrative Satire,* p. 60.

76. John Traugott, "A Tale of a Tub," p. 84.

77. Jonathan Swift, *A Tale of a Tub,* ed. A.C. Guthkelch and D.N. Smith, 2nd ed., Oxford: Clarendon Press, 1958, p. 46. All references are to this edition.

78. Ann Cline Kelly, *Swift and the English Language,* p. 83.

79. Augustine, *de Dialecta,* tr. B. Darrel Jackson, Boston: Dordrecht, 1975, p. 5.

80. Montaigne, *Essays of Michael Seigneur de Montaigne,* tr. Charles Cotton, 3 vols., London, 1693, I, 211.

81. Augustine, *Confessions,* p. 164.

82. Zimmerman, *Swift's Narrative Satire,* p. 61.

Chapter 4. Genders, Sexualities, and Discourse at Restoration Zero Point

1. Michel Foucault, *The Order of Things: An Archeology of the Human Sciences,* New York: Random House, 1970, p. 382.

2. John Gonson, *The Second Charge . . . to the Grand Jury of . . . Westminster,* London, 1728, p. 39.

3. Richard Smalbroke, *Reformation Necessary to Prevent our Ruin,* London, 1728, p. 21.

4. Thomas Bury, *For God or Satan,* London, 1709, p. 30.

5. Nahum Tate, *A Proposal for Regulating the Stage and Stage Plays,* 6 February 1698/9. Lambeth Palace MS 933, fol. 57. Quoted by Dudley W.R. Bahlman, *The Moral Revolution of 1689,* New Haven: Yale University Press, 1957, p. 5.

6. John Dennis, *The Stage Defended,* London, 1726, p. 20.

7. Randolph Trumbach, "The Birth of the Queen: Sodomy and the Birth of Gender Equality in Modern Culture 1660-1750," *Hidden from History: Reclaiming the Gay and Lesbian Past,* ed. M. Duberman, M. Vincinus, and G. Chauncy, Jr., New York: New American Library, 1989, p. 131. Inner quotation *The Diary of Samuel Pepys,* 4 vols., ed. R. Latham and W. Matthews, London, 1971, IV, 209-210. As is evident, my argument here is heavily dependent upon that of Mr. Trumbach. This segment of my research was also inspired by his work, and I am most grateful to him for allowing me to read his essay in manuscript.

8. Pepys, p. 210.

9. Rochester, *Letters of John Wilmot, second Earl of Rochester,* ed. Jeremy Treglown, Chicago: University of Chicago Press, 1980, p. 160.

10. Bahlman, *The Moral Revolution of 1688,* p. 5. Inner quotation from *Spectator* no. 8 (March 9, 1711).

11. *Historical Manuscripts Commission, Portland MS.,* London, 1901, 7, 420. Quoted by Bahlman, *Moral Revolution of 1688,* p. 5.

12. Robert Drew, *A Sermon Preached to the Societies for the Reformation of Manners,* London, 1735, p. 11.

13. John Disney, *A View of the Ancient Laws Against Immorality and Profaneness,* Cambridge, 1729, p. 324.

14. George Ash, *A Sermon Preached to the Societies for the Reformation of Manners,* London, 1717, p. 31.

15. Francis Hare, *A Sermon Preached to the Societies for the Reformation of Manners,* London, 1731, p. 4.

16. Norman Sykes, *Edmund Gibson,* London, 1926, p. 188. Quoted by Bahlman, *Moral Revolution of 1688,* p. 9.

17. Rochester, "The Disabled Debauchee," *The Complete Poems,* p. 117.

18. Oldham, "Sardanapalus," Brooks and Selden.

19. *Sodom, The Plays and Poems of Rochester,* Princeton MS AM 1440.

20. Trumbach, "The Birth of the Queen," pp. 133-134.

21. Elizabeth Fox-Genovese, "My Statue, My Self," *Reading Black / Reading Feminist,* ed. H.L. Gates, New York: Meridan, 1990, p. 189.

22. Phyllis Rackin, "Historical Difference/Sexual Difference," a paper delivered at the annual Shakespeare Conference, City University of New York Graduate Center, April 23, 1990. I am very grateful to Professor Rackin for allowing me to see this work in MS.

23. Rackin, "Historical Difference/Sexual Difference," p. 3.

24. Rackin, "Historical Difference/Sexual Difference," p. 6.

25. E.A. Wrigley and R.S. Schofield, *The Population History of England, 1541-1871: A Reconstruction,* Cambridge, Mass.: Harvard University Press, 1981.

26. Henry Abelove, "Toward a History of 'Sexual Intercourse' during the Long Eighteenth Century in England," *Genders* 6 (November, 1989), p. 128.

27. Abelove, "History of 'Sexual Intercourse'," pp. 128-129.

28. Hans Blumenberg, *The Legitimacy of the Modern Age,* p. 220.

29. Blackmore, "Essay on Wit," p. 215. See chapter 1.

30. This position begins with R.S. Crane, "Suggestions toward a Genealogy of

the 'Man of Feeling,'" *Studies in the Literature of the Augustan Age,* ed. R.C. Boys, Ann Arbor: George Wohr Publishing Co., 1952. The genesis is pushed back in time to the 1680s and the hypothesis modified by Donald Greene, "Latitudinarianism and Sensibility: The Genealogy of the 'Man of Feeling' Reconsidered," *Modern Philology* (winter, 1977).

31. William Popple, "Rondeau," quoted by Peter Laslett, "John Locke, the Great Coinage and the Origins of the Board of Trade," p. 154.

32. Charles Davenant, *An Essay upon the Probable Methods of making a People Gainers in the Ballance of Trade,* London, 1699, pp. 24-25.

33. For evidence of mass arrests and trials, cf. Trumbach, "The Birth of the Queen," p. 136.

34. John Dunton, *Atheneanism,* 1707, 2 vols., rev. ed., London, 1710, II, 94. Quoted by Trumbach, "The Birth of the Queen," p. 135.

35. Abelove, "History of Sexual Intercourse," p. 128.

36. Defoe, "Giving Alms no Charity," London, 1704, Introduction, p. 6.

37. Peter Laslett, "John Locke, the Great Recoinage, and the Origins of the Board of Trade, 1695-1698," *John Locke: Problems and Perspectives,* ed. John W. Yolton, Cambridge: Cambridge University Press, 1969, pp. 137-161, see pp. 143-144.

38. Davenant, *Gainers in the Ballance of Trade,* p. 35.

39. Davenant, *Gainers in the Ballance of Trade,* p. 35.

40. Davenant, *Gainers in the Ballance of Trade,* pp. 226-227.

41. Anonymous, "The Virtuous Wife: A Poem in answer to 'The Choice', that would have no Wife," London, 1700. The poem is a reply to John Pomfret, "The Choice," 3rd ed., London, 1700.

42. Teresa De Lauretis, describing the position Eco takes in *Semiology and the Philosophy of Language,* in her *Umberto Eco,* Florence: La Nuova Italia, 1981, p. 3.

43. William Congreve, *The Way of the World, Comedies,* ed. Bonamy Dobree, The World Classics, London: Oxford University Press, reprint, 1966. All references are to this edition.

44. Zimbardo, *A Mirror to Nature,* cf. particularly chapter 7.

45. Samuel Parker, *A Demonstration of the Divine Authority of the Law of Nature,* London, 1681, p. 248.

46. David Lawrence, "Jonathan Edwards, John Locke, and the Canon of Experience," *Early American Literature* 15 (1980).

47. Addison, *Tatler* no. 8 (April 28, 1709), *The Tatler,* ed. George A. Aitkin, 4 vols., London: Duckworth, 1898, I, 75.

48. Pope, "Prologue to Mr. Addison's *Cato,*" *Pope,* ed. H. W. Boynton, The Cambridge Edition of the Poets, Boston: Houghton Mifflin, 1903, p. 100.

49. Addison, *Spectator* no. 446 (August 1, 1712), *The Spectator,* ed. Donald Bond, 5 vols., Oxford: Clarendon Press, 1965.

50. Jeremy Collier, "Of Popularity," *Essays,* London, 1697, p. 69.

51. Aphra Behn, *The Feign'd Courtesans, Works,* ed. Montague Summers, 6 vols., London, 1916, reprint, New York: Phaeton Press, 1967, II.

52. Behn, "Epistle to the Reader," *The Dutch Lover, Works,* I, pp. 222-223.

53. Behn, "Dedication to the Right Honorable *Laurence,* Lord *Hyde,*" *Lucky Chance, Works,* III, p. 183.

54. Hans Blumenberg, Introduction, *The Legitimacy of the Modern Age,* p. 19, note 9.

55. Louise O. Vasvari, "The Geography of Escape and the Topsy-Turvey Literary Genres," *Imagining New Worlds: Essays in Figural Discovery in the Middle Ages,* ed. Scott D. Westrum, New York: Garland Press, in press. I am most grateful to the author for allowing me to read her article in MS.

56. M.M. Bakhtin, "Epic and Novel," *The Dialogic Imagination: Four Essays,* ed. Michael Holquist, trans. M. Holquist and C. Emerson, Austin: University of Texas Press, 1981, p. 6.

57. John Wilmot Earl of Rochester [*sic*], *Sodom, or the Quintessence of Debauchery,* intr. Albert Ellis, North Hollywood, Cal.: Brandon House, 1966. All references are to this text, or, where indicated, to Princeton MS AM1440.

58. J. W. Johnson, "Did Rochester Write *Sodom?*" *The Papers of the Bibliographical Society of America* 81 (June, 1987), 119-153, p. 124. Although I cannot agree with Professor Johnson's conclusions, I am greatly indebted to his work.

59. Umberto Eco, *The Role of the Reader,* p. 8.

60. Robert Howard, *The Indian Queen, Five New Plays,* 2nd ed., London, 1692.

61. Preface to *Valentinian, A Tragedy,* As 'Tis Alter'd by the Laste Earl of Rochester, *Critical Essays of the Seventeenth Century,* ed. J.E. Spingarn, Bloomington: Indiana University Press, 1957, III, 15-289, quoted by J.W. Johnson, "Did Rochester Write *Sodom?*" pp. 123-124.

62. "Theatrical History," *The Conquest of Granada,* Part I, *Dryden, The Dramatic Works,* 6 vols., ed. Montague Summers, Nonesuch Press, 1932, reprint, New York: Ovidian Press, 1968, III, 13.

63. Cf. Bakhtin, "Epic and Novel," p. 6.

64. Johnson, "Did Rochester Write *Sodom?*" p. 127.

65. Zimbardo, *A Mirror to Nature,* p. 37. Inside quotations are from Thomas Stanley, *The History of Philosophy, 1655-1662,* 2nd ed., London, 1687, p. 72; and *A Description of the Academy of the Athenian Virtuosi,* London, 1673, p. 18.

66. Stanley, *The History of Philosophy, 1655-1662,* p. 74.

67. Dryden, Preface to *Tyrannic Love, The Works of John Dryden,* ed. Maximillian E. Novak and George Guffy, Berkeley and Los Angeles: University of California Press, 1970, X, p. 109.

68. Kathleen M. Lynch, *The Social Mode of Restoration Comedy,* Macmillan and Co., 1926, repr. New York: Octagon Books, 1965, p. 43.

69. William Davenant, *The Platonick Lovers, Dramatic Works of Sir William Davenant,* 2 vols., London: Sothern & Co., 1892, II, p. 43. Subsequent references to this edition appear in the text.

70. Cf. my reading of Dryden's *Tyrannic Love* in *A Mirror of Nature,* pp. 40 ff.

71. Eugene M. Waith, *The Herculean Hero,* New York: Columbia University Press, 1962.

72. Bakhtin, "Epic and Novel," p. 19.

Chapter 5. The Discursively Central "I"
and the Telescope of Discourse

1. Cf. Claudio Guillen, *Literature as System,* Princeton: Princeton University Press, 1971, and Richard Rorty, *Philosophy and the Mirror of Nature,* Princeton: Princeton University Press, 1979.

2. Robert Boyle, "The Doctrine of Thinking," p. 184.

3. Locke, *Works,* III, 139.

4. Locke, *Concerning Human Understanding,* p. 104.

5. René Descartes, *The Method, Meditations and Selections from the Principles of Descartes,* tr. and ed. John Vieth, Chicago: The Open Court Publishing Co., 1908, p. 10.

6. Thomas Stanley, Preface, *The History of Philosophy,* p. 74.

7. Samuel Parker, *A Demonstration of the Divine Authority of the Law of Nature,* p. 248.

8. Justinian Isham, *A Sermon,* London, 1700, p. 3.

9. Karlis Racevskis, "Genealogical Critique: Michel Foucault," p. 234.

10. Descartes, *The Method, Meditations and Selected Principles,* p. 19.

11. Timothy J. Reiss, *The Discourse of Modernism,* p. 31.

12. Charles Davenant, *Gainers in the Ballance of Trade,* pp. 5-6.

13. Sprat, *History of the Royal Society,* p. 114.

14. Sprat, *History of the Royal Society,* p. 87.

15. Charles Gildon, "Epistle Dedicatory," *Miscellaneous Letters and Essays on Several Subjects,* London, 1694, Sig. A2v-A3r.

16. Sprat, *History of the Royal Society,* p. 110.

17. George Savile, 1st Marquis of Halifax, *The Lady's New-Year's Gift, or Advice to a Daughter,* 6th ed., London, 1699, p. 16.

18. Author unknown, *The Manuscripts of . . . the Duke of Bucceuch,* London: Historical Manuscripts Commission, 1897-1903, p. 736.

19. William Wollaston, *The Design of Part of the Book of Ecclesiastes . . . Represented in an English Poem,* London, 1691.

20. Raman Selden, *English Verse Satire, 1590-1765,* p. 16.

21. Selden, *English Verse Satire,* p. 15.

22. Wollaston, *The Design of Part of the Book of Ecclesiastes,* p. 9.

23. Thomas, Baron Fairfax, *Advice to a Young Lord written by his Father,* London, 1691, p. 127.

24. Wollaston, *The Design of Part of the Book of Ecclesiastes,* p. 11.

25. Wollaston, *The Design of Part of the Book of Ecclesiastes,* p. 17.

26. Umberto Eco, *The Role of the Reader,* p. 7, 8.

27. Wollaston, *The Design of Part of the Book of Ecclesiastes,* p. 13.

28. Eco, *The Role of the Reader,* p. 8.

29. Wollaston, *The Design of Part of the Book of Ecclesiastes,* p. 13.

30. Dryden, *A Discourse concerning the Original and Progress of Satire, The Works of John Dryden,* Volume 4: *Poems 1693-96,* ed. A.B. Chambers and William Frost, Berkeley, Los Angeles and London; University of California Press, 1974, pp. 74-75.

31. Dryden, *Discourse,* p. 75.

32. Blackmore, "Essay on Wit," p. 199.

33. Sprat, *History of the Royal Society,* p. 418.

34. Sprat, *History of the Royal Society,* p. 418.

35. Addison, *Freeholder* no. 45 (1716), *Augustan Reprint Series One: Essays on Wit,* ed. Richard C. Boys, Ann Arbor: University of Michigan Press, 1946, p. 325.

36. Paul de Man, "The Rhetoric of Temporality," pp. 195-196.

37. de Man, "The Rhetoric of Temporality," p. 197.

38. Raman Selden, *English Verse Satire,* p. 73.

39. Andre Dacier, *Preface sur les satires d'Horace,* tr. Tom Brown as *Essay upon Satyr* in Charles Gildon, *Miscellaneous Poems upon Several Occasions,* London, 1692, Sig. B6r. Also paraphrased by Dryden, *Discourse concerning the Original and Progress of Satire, The Works of John Dryden,* IV, p. 75.

40. Dryden, *Discourse,* p. 66.

41. Dryden, *Discourse,* p. 78.

42. Walter Harte, *An Essay on Satire, particularly on The Dunciad to which is added A Discourse on Satire by Monsieur Boileau,* London, 1730, p. 19.

43. Harte, *An Essay on Satire,* p. 19.

44. Harte, *An Essay on Satire,* p. 21.

45. Harte, *An Essay on Satire,* p. 21.

46. Dryden, *Discourse,* p. 76. Subsequent references to this source will be cited in the text.

47. William Frost, "Commentary," *The Works of John Dryden,* IV, p. 526.

48. William Frost, "Commentary," p. 525.

49. Harte, *An Essay on Satire,* p. 6.

50. Harte, *An Essay on Satire,* p. 7.

51. Harte, *An Essay on Satire,* p. 8.

52. Harte, *An Essay on Satire,* p. 21.

53. Harte, *An Essay on Satire,* p. 6.

54. Harte, *An Essay on Satire,* p. 16.

55. Harte, *An Essay on Satire,* p. 17.

56. Dryden, *Discourse,* p. 79.

57. Although the conception of mimetic narrative discourse as inscribing the transparent "order of nature" is modern, it may well be that a much earlier association of *prose narrative* with orderly monarchic succession, as in the Chronicles, is also at work here. Gabrielle Spiegel argues that medieval English discourse, while it uses verse to heroically elevate monarchy, employs prose to delineate orderly succession. Cf. Gabrielle Spiegel, "History, Historicism, and the Social Logic of the Text in the Middle Ages," *Speculum* 65 (January, 1990), 59-87.

58. Richard Helgerson, *Forms of Nationhood: The Elizabethan Writing of England,* Chicago: University of Chicago Press, 1992, p. 296.

59. Helgerson, *Forms of Nationhood,* p. 295.

60. All references are to Dryden, *Absalom and Achitophel, The Norton Anthology of British Literature,* 5th ed., New York: W. W. Norton and Co., 1986.

61. Charles Davenant, *On Trade,* London, 1699, p. 13.

62. Edward Said, *Orientalism,* London: Peregrine Books, 1985, p. 8.

63. John Eldred, *The First Englishmen in India: Letters and Narratives of Sundry Elizabethans,* ed. J. Courtenay Locke, London: George Routledge and Sons Ltd., 1930, p. 37.

64. Henry Teonge, *The Diary of Henry Teonge, 1675-1678,* transcribed from the original manuscript by G.E. Manwaring, London: George Routledge and Sons Ltd., 1927, p. 144. The city is Aleppo.

65. Teonge, *Diary,* p. 145.

66. Teonge, *Diary,* p. 145.

67. Teonge, *Diary,* p. 146.

68. Thomas Stevens, *The First Englishmen in India,* ed. J. Courtenay Locke, London: George Routledge and Sons Ltd., 1930, p. 30.

69. John Eldred, *The First Englishmen in India,* p. 44.

70. Teonge, *Diary,* p. 142.

71. Daniel Defert, "The Collection of the World: Accounts of Voyages from the Sixteenth to the Eighteenth Centuries," *Dialectical Anthropology* 7 (1982), p. 16.

72. Said, *Orientalism,* p. 1.

73. Said, *Orientalism,* p. 3.

74. M.M. Bakhtin, "Epic and Novel," *The Dialogic Imagination,* pp. 16-17.

75. Paul de Man, "Pascal's Allegory of Persuasion," p. 7.

76. Cf. particularly, *A Mirror to Nature;* "The Seventeenth-Century Dilemma in Discourse," *Rhetorics of Order/Ordering Rhetorics in English Neoclassical Literature,* ed. J.D. Canfield and J.P. Hunter, Newark: University of Delaware Press, 1989; and "The King and the Fool: *King Lear* as Self-Deconstructing Text," *Criticism* 32 (winter, 1990).

77. Richard Flecknoe, Introduction, *A Collection of the Choicest Epigrams and Characters, Printed for the Author,* 2nd ed., London, 1673.

78. Timothy Reiss, *The Discourse of Modernism,* p. 30.

79. Theophilus Gale, *The Court of the Gentiles,* London, 1669, p. 62.

80. See Dryden, "Of Dramatic Poesy," *Of Dramatic Poesy and Other Essays,* 2 vols., ed. G.B. Watson, London: Dent, 1962, I, 666.

81. Thomas Shadwell, Epistle Dedicatory, *The Humorists: A Comedy,* London, 1671, Sig. A5.

82. Anthony Ashley Cooper, 3rd Earl of Shaftesbury, *Characteristics of Men, Manners, Opinions,* 3 vols., 5th ed., London, 1732, I, 143.

83. Bernard Bergonzi, *The Situation of the Novel,* Harmondsworth: Pelican, 1972, p. 42.

84. Bakhtin, "Epic and Novel," p. 20.

85. Earl Miner, "Commentary," in Dryden, *Don Sebastian, The Works of John Dryden,* vol. 15, Berkeley, Los Angeles, London: University of California Press, 1976, p. 388.

86. Dryden, Preface, *Don Sebastian,* p. 70.

87. Dryden, Preface, *Don Sebastian,* p. 65.

88. Dryden, Preface, *Don Sebastian,* p. 66.

89. Dryden, Preface, *Don Sebastian,* p. 66.

90. Miner, "Commentary," p. 389.

91. Miner, "Commentary," p. 389.

92. Teonge, *Diary,* pp. 159–160.

93. Bakhtin, "Epic and Novel," p. 35.

94. Teonge, *Diary,* pp. 115–116.

95. Said, *Orientalism,* p. 3.

96. Leonhart Rauwolff ("A person very Famous for his Skill in Natural Products and in the Practice of Physick, though he travelled as a merchant"), *A Collection of Curious Travels and Voyages,* ed. John Ray, Fell. of Royal Society, London, 1693, pp. 42–43.

97. Rauwolff, *Curious Travels,* p. 81.

98. Teonge, *Diary,* p. 100.

99. Ray, Preface to Rauwolff, *Curious Travels,* p. 2.

100. Henry Maundrell, *A Journey from Aleppo to Jerusalem at Easter AD 1697,* London: J. White & Co., 1810, p. 52–53.

101. Maundrell, *A Journey from Aleppo,* p. 127.

Conclusion

1. Lacan, "The Freudian Thing," *Ecrits: A Selection,* ed. Alan Sheridan, New York and London: Norton, 1977, p. 65.

2. Steven Shapin says that for late seventeenth-century science, "Knowledge is supposed to be the product of a sovereign individual confronting the world." Shapin, *A Social History of Truth,* p. 17.

3. See Judith Butler, *Gender Trouble,* New York and London: Routledge, 1990.

4. Dollimore, *Radical Tragedy,* p. 7.

INDEX